Language Maintenance and Shift

What motivates some linguistic minorities to maintain their language? Why do others shift away from it rather quickly? Are there specific conditions – environmental or personal – influencing these dynamics? What can families and communities do to pass on their 'threatened' language to the next generation? These and related questions are investigated in detail in *Language Maintenance and Shift*. In this fascinating book, Anne Pauwels analyses the patterns of language use exhibited by individuals and groups living in multilingual societies and explores their efforts to maintain their heritage or minority language. She explores the various methods used to analyse language maintenance, from linguistic demography to linguistic biography, and offers guidance on how to research the language patterns and practices of linguistic minorities around the world.

ANNE PAUWELS is Professor of Sociolinguistics at the School of Oriental and African Studies, University of London.

KEY TOPICS IN SOCIOLINGUISTICS
Series editor: Rajend Mesthrie

This series focuses on the main topics of study in sociolinguistics today. It consists of accessible yet challenging accounts of the most important issues to consider when examining the relationship between language and society. Some topics have been the subject of sociolinguistic study for many years and are here re-examined in the light of new developments in the field; others are issues of growing importance that have not so far been given a sustained treatment. Written by leading experts, the books in the series are designed to be used on courses and in seminars, and include useful suggestions for further reading.

Already published in the series:

Politeness by Richard J. Watts
Language Policy by Bernard Spolsky
Discourse by Jan Blommaert
Analyzing Sociolinguistic Variation by Sali A. Tagliamonte
Language and Ethnicity by Carmen Fought
Style by Nikolas Coupland
World Englishes by Rajend Mesthrie and Rakesh Bhatt
Language and Identity by John Edwards
Attitudes to Language by Peter Garrett
Language Attrition by Monika S. Schmid
Writing and Society: An Introduction by Florian Coulmas
Sociolinguistic Fieldwork by Natalie Schilling
Multilingualism by Anat Stavans and Charlotte Hoffman
Languages in Contact by Umberto Ansaldo and Lisa Lim
Language Maintenance and Shift by Anne Pauwels

Language Maintenance and Shift

ANNE PAUWELS
School of Oriental and African Studies, University of London

CAMBRIDGE
UNIVERSITY PRESS

University Printing House, Cambridge CB2 8BS, United Kingdom

Cambridge University Press is part of the University of Cambridge.

It furthers the University's mission by disseminating knowledge in the pursuit of education, learning and research at the highest international levels of excellence.

www.cambridge.org
Information on this title: www.cambridge.org/9781107618923

First published 2016

Printed in the United Kingdom by Clays, St Ives plc

A catalogue record for this publication is available from the British Library

Library of Congress Cataloging-in-Publication Data
Names: Pauwels, Anne, author.
Title: Language maintenance and shift / Anne Pauwels.
Description: New York : Cambridge University Press, 2016. | Series: Key Topics in sociolinguistics
Identifiers: LCCN 2016007902| ISBN 9781107043695 (Hardback) |
ISBN 9781107618923 (Paperback)
Subjects: LCSH: Language maintenance–Research. | Linguistic change–Research. | Linguistic minorities–Research. | Code switching (Linguistics) | Sociolinguistics. | BISAC: LANGUAGE ARTS & DISCIPLINES / Linguistics / General.
Classification: LCC P40.5.L32 P38 2016 | DDC 306.44–dc23 LC record available at
https://lccn.loc.gov/2016007902

ISBN 978-1-107-04369-5 Hardback
ISBN 978-1-107-61892-3 Paperback

For my mother, whose bilingualism was long seen as a hindrance and weakness rather than an asset. Bedankt – vielen Dank! Thank you for your persistence!

Contents

Acknowledgements

This book is the result of many years of professional interactions and personal encounters with questions of bi- and multilingualism and of languages in transition. In professional terms I am most indebted to three 'giants' of the field: Michael Clyne, who was my PhD supervisor and, later, colleague in Australia, and Joshua Fishman and Einar Haugen, with whom I had the privilege and pleasure to meet and converse during their visits to Australia. I would also like to thank many current and past colleagues working in the fields of multilingualism, language contact and language maintenance and shift whose work has been inspirational as well as important in the structure and content of this book. My particular thanks go to Camilla Bettoni, Jan Blommaert, Tove Bull, Francesco Cavallaro, Ng Bee Chin, Guus Extra, Friederike Luepke, Marilyn Martin-Jones, Nina Rubino, Itesh Sachdev, Mandana Seyfeddinipur and Li Wei.

I am also indebted to the generous assistance and understanding of the Cambridge University Press staff, especially Dr Andrew Winnard and Helen Barton.

Introduction

Writing a book on language maintenance and language shift in the second decade of the twenty-first century poses some interesting challenges. The term 'language maintenance' evokes both a sense of 'stability' and a level of abstraction that may seem increasingly at odds with the linguistic realities characterising many communities and societies around the world. These new realities are best described as highly dynamic, with constantly and rapidly changing language constellations. As a result, a range of new terms has surfaced to describe these hyperdynamic language situations, including hyperlingualism (Pauwels 2014), metrolingualism (Otsui and Pennycook 2010) and many more variations along these lines. The term 'language maintenance' has had limited currency in the description of societies where multilingualism was or is the norm for communication among individuals: most African and many Asian communities would be prime examples of such communities. The term 'language maintenance' has been and continues to be used extensively in the context of societies where only specific sectors of the community (e.g., immigrants, indigenous minorities) engage in bi- or multilingual practices, sometimes only for a limited period of time. These sectors of the community were and are the ones facing questions of maintaining their 'home', 'heritage', 'ethnic', 'community' language in light of competition from the language(s) of the new environment and/or of the linguistic majority. It is this second group of communities and societies, i.e., those in which only sectors of the population engage in multilingual practices, that has changed and continues to change quite dramatically in terms of linguistic constellations. Most pronounced are the linguistic changes observed in (large) urban settings: such environments are now characterised by a panoply of languages and a growing number of plurilingual speakers for whom the question of language maintenance would be quite complex or perhaps even futile, as they engage, often daily, in communicative practices that draw upon various languages rather than just two. In some respects these 'new' linguistic realities and

1

new communicative practices found in a growing number of 'western' urban settings or in westernised societies increasingly resemble the multilingualisms found in parts of Africa or Asia. Indeed, the multilingual repertoires typical of a spice merchant in India (Edwards 1994) or of young Africans in sub-Saharan Africa as described, for example, by Lüpke and Storch (2013) are now also increasingly found in many European and American cities: for example, the multiple codes and linguistic varieties used by a family from Nigeria and now living in a suburb of Antwerp, Belgium, have many similarities with those found in African cities (Blommaert 2010). Similarly, my own work, involving a Vietnamese family whose members ended up in different countries in Europe, revealed that their offspring's communicative practices drew upon multiple languages associated with their mobility and family networks (see Chapter 10). What constitutes language maintenance in such contexts is not exactly straightforward. The growing presence of such linguistic realities poses considerable challenges to the examination of the phenomena of language maintenance and language shift. Are these terms still appropriate and relevant to discussing these consequences of language contact? Are the methods for and approaches to studying the phenomena of language maintenance and shift suitable to those changed constellations? These are important questions facing the study of language maintenance and shift in current times. We will elaborate on these in the final part of the book. The main focus of the book remains, however, on how these phenomena have been studied throughout the twentieth century and into the twenty-first century by scholars representative of various disciplines.

Another challenge in writing this book concerns the delineation of the topic: it is impossible to write about language maintenance or language shift without touching upon closely related areas, such as language contact, bilingualism, multilingualism, language and ethnicity, or on related phenomena, such as language endangerment, language death, language revival or language revitalisation. The past six or seven decades have seen the publication of numerous comprehensive volumes on these phenomena (see the section on Suggestions for Further Reading) which often contain a chapter or section devoted to the topic of language maintenance and/or language shift. This inclusion testifies to the close relationship between these phenomena, and it is therefore inevitable that this book will have some areas of overlap with such volumes. However, it is also interesting to note that to date there has not yet been a book entirely dedicated to language maintenance and shift as a field of study. There are of course a growing number of book-length studies that explore the issues of maintenance and shift in particular groups, communities and regions of the world but not one that deals comprehensively with the topic. This book is therefore an attempt to bridge the gap between the many relatively concise over-view chapters in comprehensive volumes and the detailed studies of language maintenance and/or language shift in specific contexts and settings.

In line with its aim to provide a more comprehensive insight into the study of language maintenance and shift, henceforth abbreviated as LM and LS, respectively, the book is organised around the following key issues: concepts and terms used in this field of study, major approaches to the study of the phenomena, the main methods of investigation and the interpretive frameworks developed for understanding the process of LS. Furthermore, particular attention is paid to research into efforts and initiatives (to be) undertaken to maintain languages in minority and migrant settings. Finally, the question of the future of LM studies is addressed.

There are five main parts to this book, each subdivided in a number of chapters. In Part I we cover the history of this field of study, discuss concepts and terms relevant to study of language maintenance and language shift and identify the main contexts within which such studies of LM and LS have taken or continue to take place. In Part II the focus moves to describing and discussing the various methods of researching LM and LS. We cover the methods of investigation and tools of analysis that pertain to different approaches to the study of maintenance and shift: some of these examine the phenomena at a macro-level, i.e., at the level of entire countries, regions or communities, whereas others are linked to the micro-level, for example, in-depth studies of language maintenance in families, groups or small communities. In Part III we move to a documentation of the main findings emerging from research on LM and LS. This will include, where possible and relevant, the identification of common trends and patterns across communities and contexts. This part also provides a discussion of the various models and frameworks (in some cases, theories) that have been developed to account for the observed trends and patterns and to 'predict' the process of LS or its opposite. LM efforts are the theme of Part IV: here we move beyond description and discus-sion of the dynamics of LM and LS to focus on the efforts, actions and initiatives of individuals, families, groups and communities to main-tain their ethnic/community/heritage language(s) and pass it on to future generations. As part of this section we also raise the question about the possibilities of reversing language shift. The final part (Part V) focuses on emerging and future developments of this field of study.

Here, we discuss new challenges and opportunities for the study of LM and LS resulting from the often dramatic changes in language environments and linguistic constellations.

Questions of LM and LS are universal and global. The loss of a language and the pressures of maintaining a threatened language or a minority language have occurred or can occur in any part of the world. It can also affect any language. It is true, however, that some language communities and linguistic regions are more susceptible than others, especially given past and current power relations between nations and the linguistic consequences of globalisation. Despite the ubiquitous nature of the phenomena, research into these phenomena is still very much undertaken by scholars located, associated and/or trained in western institutions. Furthermore, the dominant language of publication for these studies continues to be English. This bias is also reflected in this book: although I have tried, where possible, to comment on studies written in other languages or that cover regions and groups not often mentioned in the study of language maintenance, my own linguistic limitations mean that I have been able to access studies in only a handful of mainly European languages. I hope that some of these limitations can be overcome by readers exploring some of the issues raised and questions posed for settings and languages *not* covered in the text.

POINTS FOR DISCUSSION AND TASKS

1. Can you find other terms that are used to describe the heightened linguistic diversity that is now so often a feature of cities around the world? If you speak another language, do you know how this phenomenon is expressed in that language?
2. What terms are used in your community or country to describe languages that have minority status? What does that say about their value?
3. Are minority languages in your country recognised as minorities and do they have any legal or protected status?

SUGGESTIONS FOR FURTHER READING

Next is a short list of some more recent handbooks that contain chapters on LM or LS as well as language loss and death. It is worthwhile reading these chapters as they give you an opportunity to see how the concepts of LM and LS are dealt in relation to other phenomena such as language death, loss, endangerment and language contact and multilingualism.

Auer, Peter, and Li Wei. Eds. 2009. *Handbook of multilingualism and multilingual communication*. Berlin: Mouton de Gruyter.

Bhatia, Tej K., and William C. Ritchie. Eds. 2013. *The handbook of bilingualism and multilingualism*, second edition. Malden, NJ: Wiley-Blackwell.

Crystal, David. 2000. *Language death*. Cambridge: Cambridge University Press.

Enfield, Nick J., Paul Kockelman and Jack Sydell. Eds. 2014. *The Cambridge handbook of linguistic anthropology*. Cambridge: Cambridge University Press.

Fishman, Joshua, and Ofelia García. Eds. 2010/2011. *Handbook of language and ethnic identity*. Volumes 1 and 2. New York: Oxford University Press.

Hickey, Raymond. Ed. 2010. *The handbook of language contact*. Malden, NJ: Wiley-Blackwell.

Martin-Jones, Marilyn, Adrian Blackledge and Angela Creese. Eds. 2012. *The Routledge handbook of multilingualism*. Abingdon: Routledge.

PART I
History, concepts, contexts and approaches

PART I

1 Pioneers in the study of language maintenance and language shift

1.1 THE ESTABLISHMENT OF LM AND LS AS A SEPARATE FIELD OF ENQUIRY

Although tracing the exact origins of this field of enquiry is no doubt a fascinating enterprise, it is best left to forensic enthusiasts more knowledgeable than me in discovering the relevant historical data. The task of identifying the origins and pioneers is further complicated by the fact that this area of study is intricately intertwined with other areas such as the study of language contact, bi- and multilingualism, language death and language change. Trying to disentangle the origins of each of these is probably futile. However, these complexities and complications should not be an excuse for ignoring the contexts and phenomena that encouraged scholars to establish LM and LS as a significant field of enquiry linked to the overarching fields of language contact and multilingualism.

There is a considerable degree of consensus that LM and LS emerged as a field of enquiry in the mid-twentieth century and that it was initially linked to contexts of language contact arising from migration, especially from the 'old' world, Europe, to the 'new' world, North America and, later, predominantly Australia and New Zealand.

A key text in its establishment is undoubtedly the paper entitled 'Language maintenance and language shift as a field of enquiry. A definition of the field and suggestions for its future development', written by Joshua Fishman in 1964. In this article he states:

> The study of language maintenance and language shift is concerned with the relationship between change (or stability) in habitual language use, on the one hand, and ongoing psychological, social or cultural processes, on the other hand, when populations differing in language use are in contact with each other. That languages (or language variants) SOMETIMES replace each other, among SOME speakers, particularly in CERTAIN types or domains of language behavior, under SOME conditions of intergroup contact, has long

aroused curiosity and comment. However, it is only in quite recent
years that this topic has been recognized as a field of systematic
inquiry among professional students of language behavior. (Fishman
1964: 35)

1.2 SPRACHINSELFORSCHUNG – *STUDY OF LINGUISTIC ENCLAVES* – *AS A FORERUNNER OF THE FIELD*

In Fishman's (1964) seminal text he identifies scholars such as Uriel
Weinreich, Einar Haugen, Heinz Kloss and Charles Ferguson as key
contributors to the establishment of the field, at least in the Anglophone world. In turn, each of these scholars has been influenced by
traditions and developments in related fields concerned with the investigation of language contact including anthropology, ethnology,
dialectology and its rather German-specific sub-branch known as *Sprachinselforschung* (the study of linguistic enclaves). *Sprachinselforschung*
may have been a precursor, at least partially, to the modern study of
LM. In 1928 Victor Schirmunski investigated the transformations and
changes in Swabian dialects (southern German dialects) spoken by
German farmers who had migrated to parts of Russia (Transcaucasus
and Southern Ukraine) between 1764 and 1830. They often belonged to
the religious movement known as 'Pietists' who sought more religious
freedom by migrating. They settled in closed German-speaking enclaves
in which their main language continued to be (forms of) German
(Schirmunski 1928a, 1928b). As German dialectology, of which *Sprachinselforschung* is a subfield, was a particularly strong field of study in the
late nineteenth and early twentieth century, it wielded considerable
influence on the international linguistic and philological scene. It is
therefore likely that scholars such as Einar Haugen and Uriel Weinreich
would have been familiar with and possibly influenced by studies such
as Schirmunski's and other scholars (see, e.g., Kuhn 1934 for more
references). Although the main focus of these studies was on linguistic
features, they also included comments and observations about changes
and shifts in the use of various languages in these settlements.

1.3 THE WORK OF HEINZ KLOSS

An early pioneer or possibly forerunner in this field is Heinz Kloss. In
1927 he published an article entitled '*Spracherhaltung*' (language maintenance) in which he talked about language issues for linguistic

minorities (Kloss 1927). Clyne (2004: 803) in fact names Heinz Kloss as the initiator of the systematic study of LM. Unfortunately, his early work was published in journals dedicated to political science and history, that linguists were largely unaware of it. Clyne (2004: 803) further mentions that Kloss' work on linguistic minorities 'became increasingly susceptible to abuse by National Socialism and its ideology of "*Volk*" so that it became "tainted" and ignored or even avoided by other scholars'. It was only after the Second World War that Kloss' later work (e.g., Kloss 1966) became more influential when it was included in the seminal volume edited by Fishman and colleagues (1966) entitled *Language loyalty in the United States*. In his contribution entitled 'German-American language maintenance efforts', Kloss identified a series of individual and group factors – clear-cut and ambivalent – that play a role in the process of LM or LS in migrant contexts. This paper continues to be a key text in the discussion of factors that influence LM or LS (see Chapter 7).

1.4   THE WORK OF EINAR HAUGEN AND URIEL WEINREICH

Besides Joshua Fishman, Einar Haugen and Uriel Weinreich are probably the other key figures who shaped the field. Both scholars started working on issues related to language contact, bilingualism and immigrant languages in the United States in the 1930s and 1940s. In 1938 the journal *Language* published a paper by Haugen on phonological shifting in American Norwegian (Haugen 1938b) and in the same year Haugen also wrote a paper in which he addressed the wider issue of language and migration (Haugen 1938a). The year 1939 saw the publication of his comprehensive study on the Norwegian language in America. The initial version (Haugen 1939), published in Norwegian, was entitled *Norsk i Amerika* (*Norwegian in America*). The English version of the book (considerably expanded and revised), *The Norwegian language in America: A study in bilingual behavior*, appeared in 1953, followed by *Bilingualism in the Americas* in 1956 (Haugen 1956). These works continue to be canonical reference points for contemporary studies on LM and LS.

Uriel Weinreich's work did not appear until the early 1950s, although his father, Max Weinreich, had started to write in the 1930s on issues of bilingualism and immigrant languages in Yiddish (e.g., Weinreich 1931, 1932). Uriel followed in his father's footsteps and in 1949 he wrote his Master's thesis at Columbia University on the topic of 'Present-day approaches to the study of bilingualism', followed by a doctoral thesis on Swiss bilingualism. These works then led to the seminal text *Languages in contact* that appeared in 1953 (Weinreich 1953).

Both Haugen and Weinreich were trained as linguists and their initial main focus was on describing (and explaining) the linguistic phenomena found in immigrant language contact situations. This is particularly the case for Weinreich, whose 'typology' of linguistic interference phenomena continues to be a major reference point for linguistic contact studies (Weinreich 1953). However, both scholars increasingly engaged also with the sociocultural aspects of language contact touching upon the questions of LM and LS. Weinreich (1953) devoted a quarter of his book to the sociocultural setting of language contact, in which he discussed concepts and phenomena such as language shift and language loyalty. Haugen's branching out into socio-cultural aspects of language contact and language use probably went further than Weinreich's. Volume 1, entitled *The bilingual community,* of his two-volume book *The Norwegian language in America* is entirely devoted to social aspects of language contact. He examined the institutions that influence the maintenance or shift of Norwegian in America and he described the struggle of (parts of) the community to keep Norwegian alive. Later Haugen (1972) also coined the term 'ecology of language' (which has become a major approach to the study of language in society).

1.5 CHARLES FERGUSON

The influence of Charles Ferguson on the establishment of LM and LS as a field of study is mainly through his article 'Diglossia', published in 1959. Spolsky (2010) writes that Ferguson is probably seen as one of the founding 'fathers' of sociolinguistics, whereas Fishman, a sociologist or a 'refurbished social psychologist', as he referred to himself, is regarded as the founder of the sociology of language. Because he was trained as a linguist, Ferguson's work focused on the linguistic analysis of types and varieties of language rather than on examining the functions, roles and the status of languages. However, his article 'Diglossia' did influence the field of LM and LS, especially when Fishman drew upon the concept of diglossia to develop his matrix of speech communities whose linguistic constellations would be more or less prone to LS. In his later work, Ferguson (e.g., Ferguson 1968) also focused on issues of language planning and management, bringing him closer to the field of LM and LS.

1.6 JOSHUA FISHMAN

The scholar who has, however, done most to elevate the investigation of LM and LS to a genuine and legitimate field of enquiry is undoubtedly Joshua Fishman. In his key text (Fishman 1964), revised and expanded in later versions (e.g., Fishman 1970, 1972), Fishman approached the topic from the perspective of social science, in particular, sociology and social psychology, whose primary interest concerns the social and societal aspects of language. The main focus in such an approach is on the users and uses of language rather than on the language itself, i.e., the linguistic features of languages. While he strongly advocated for a multidisciplinary approach to the study of LM and LS he foregrounded the sociological aspect in defining the field. Three major areas of focus were distinguished: (1) the definition and examination of 'habitual language use', (2) the identification and examination of extralinguistic factors that impact on language maintenance and/or language shift and (3) the role of language attitudes and language policy/planning in influencing language maintenance or shift. These three areas, especially the second and third, continue to define and shape the field, as we shall see throughout this book. Aside from his agenda-setting 1964 paper, early publications by Fishman and students as well as colleagues, such as *Language loyalty in the United States* (Fishman et al. 1966), *Readings in the sociology of language* (Fishman 1968), *Advances in the sociology of language* (Fishman 1971) and *Bilingualism in the Barrio* (Fishman et al. 1971), further shaped the study of LM and LS. For example, many of the contributions to Fishman et al. (1966) and Fishman (1968) continue to be quoted as canonical texts in investigations of LM or LS around the world. To this day, Fishman's work continues to exert significant influence on the field, either directly through his own work or through that of his many students around the world. My own earlier work in this field is also heavily indebted to Fishman (e.g. Pauwels 1986, 1988) and this influence is also reflected in this book.

1.7 PIONEERS OF LM AND LS IN INDIGENOUS MINORITY SETTINGS

At the beginning of this chapter we mentioned that the 'origins' of LM and LS as a field of enquiry were linked primarily to immigrant contact settings. The other key setting to which questions of LM and LS are pertinent is that of the so-called indigenous linguistic minorities. These are speech communities whose continued use of their language in their own territory may be under 'threat' or even 'endangered'. The reasons for this threat are diverse, ranging from being 'invaded' by another linguistic group, being annexed to another polity or experiencing an exodus of speakers for economic and other reasons. In this setting the focus has long been more on shift, loss and even death than on maintenance. Tsunoda (2005: 31) credits Morris Harry Swadesh with possibly being the first scholar to point out 'the value of research into language endangerment', although Leonard Bloomfield, according to Hall (1987), may be seen as one of the first scholars to raise issues about changes occurring in endangered languages. Other early contributors include Miller (1971) working on the Shoshoni of Utah and Nevada, Dressler examining Breton (Dressler 1972), Dorian (1973) investigating East Sutherland Gaelic and Denison (1977) working on the German spoken in the linguistic enclave of Sauris in Northern Italy (for more examples, see Tsunoda 2005). Many regard Nancy Dorian's work on the death of a Scottish Gaelic dialect (Dorian 1973, 1981) as the first 'truly holistic and detailed work' (Tsunoda 2005: 32). However, these works focus mainly on the linguistic features of endangered languages with only limited attention to factors or forces that lead to LS. It is Susan Gal's study of language shift in Oberwart, Austria (Gal 1978, 1979), that has been most influential, especially in Anglophone academia, in raising awareness of the fate of many indigenous linguistic minorities and in stimulating studies exploring LS and LM in such communities. Her work on German–Hungarian bilingualism and language shift in Oberwart not only has become a key text in the study of LS affecting indigenous linguistic minorities but also has triggered many similar studies, especially in Europe (e.g., Gorter et al. 1990). We shall come back to her work in relation to methodology as well when discussing trends and patterns in language maintenance.

Finally, it is important to keep in mind the linguistic and cultural limitations identified in the Introduction. Undoubtedly, there may have been scholars working in other disciplines and/or examining language issues in communities in Europe and Asia around the time of these pioneers whom we have not covered in this book. It is hoped that readers could identify some of these so that they can be included in a next version.

POINTS FOR DISCUSSION AND TASKS

1. Dialectology has been identified as a possible forerunner of LM and LS studies. Which aspects, elements or topics in dialect studies have been carried over into studies of LM or LS?

2. Linguistic enclaves – *Sprachinseln* – play an important role in the development of the field of LM and LS. Can you provide some examples of linguistic enclaves in South America, Canada, East Asia and Russia? What is their history? Have they survived to this day?

3. Most pioneers discussed in this book have worked on questions of LM or LS in migrant Anglophone settings. Why would this be the case?

4. Choose a linguistic minority anywhere in the world and examine what sort of linguistic research has been done on it and when.

SUGGESTIONS FOR FURTHER READING

The three texts below focus on the emergence of fields of study relevant to that of LM and LS. They also touch upon the main pioneers and explore how they have shaped the respective fields of study.

Clyne, Michael. 2004. History of research on language contact. In U. Ammon, N. Dittmar, K. J. Mattheier and P. Trudgill (eds.), *Sociolinguistic. An international handbook of the science of language and society/ Soziolinguistik. Ein internationales Handbuch zur Wissenschaft von Sprache und Gesellschaft*. Volume 1. Berlin: De Gruyter-Mouton, 799–805.

Spolsky, Bernard. 2010. Ferguson and Fishman: sociolinguistics and the sociology of language. In R. Wodak, B. Johnstone and P. Kerswill (eds.), *The Sage handbook of sociolinguistics*. London: Sage, 11–23.

Tsunoda, Tasaku. 2005. *Language endangerment and language revitalization: an introduction*. Berlin: Mouton de Gruyter.

The following are key texts written by the pioneers in the field of LM and LS and therefore very worthwhile reading to understand the development of the field and its main foci.

Ferguson, Charles A. 1959. Diglossia. *Word* 15: 325–340.

Fishman, Joshua. 1970. *Sociolinguistics: a brief introduction*. Rowley, MA: Newbury House.

1972. *The sociology of language: an interdisciplinary social science approach to language in society*. Rowley, MA: Newbury House.

Ed. 1968. *Readings in the sociology of language*. The Hague: Mouton.

Fishman, Joshua A., Robert L. Cooper and R. Ma. 1971. *Bilingualism in the barrio*. Bloomington: Research Center for the Language Sciences, Indiana University.

Fishman, Joshua A. Ed. 1971. *Advances in the sociology of language*. Volume 1. The Hague: Mouton.

2 Concepts, contexts and approaches to the study of language maintenance and shift

2.1 THE STUDY OF LM AND LS AS A SUBFIELD OF LANGUAGE CONTACT STUDIES

In the introduction of this book we already hinted that the study of LM and LS is heavily intertwined with that of related phenomena such as multilingualism, language loss, language death, language endangerment and language revival and revitalisation. All these phenomena are, in one way or another, the outcome or the consequence of a plethora of language contact situations. Contact between languages and language varieties is not only omnipresent but also the norm rather than the exception in linguistic constellations around the globe.

Mobility of people – of individuals, families, groups and entire communities – is at the source of most language contact. Reasons for mobility are multiple, ranging from individual adventurous exploring and a desire or need for trade, education or employment beyond one's own territory to the results of expulsion or invasion. All these forms of mobility, voluntary or forced, short or long term, are most likely to involve contact between speakers of different languages or language varieties. Short-term language contact between individuals or groups is not likely to induce (major) changes in linguistic constellations or the language practices of the speakers. For example, many people now holiday in places where other languages are spoken. While some holidaymakers may be motivated to learn the local language, this is not likely to reshape or affect their linguistic practices drastically, once they return from their holiday. Conversely, long-term contact between people is much more likely to have a linguistic effect. Migration – voluntary as well as forced – colonisation and invasion are the types of mobility that have had the most impact on changes in linguistic constellations and language practices. In most cases, speakers of one language move (long term or permanently) into the territory of another speech community. Where colonisation or other types of 'invasion' are the trigger for the contact, the language or languages of the 'intruders' often not only upset the existing linguistic hierarchies and dynamics but may also lead to the extinction of some of the indigenous languages.

Changes in nation-states are also possible triggers for language contact. Some of these are in fact outcomes of invasions, so they are ultimately linked to mobility.

These forms of contact, amongst many others, have led to or have the potential to result in one of many language contact phenomena. These include the development of individual bi- or multilingualism, various forms of societal bi- or multilingualism, diglossic or polyglossic situations (we define these later in this chapter) and the emergence of pidgin languages with some later developing into creole languages, the rise of a lingua franca, the maintenance of a language without status in a polity or, conversely, the abandoning of a first/native language in favour of another, language loss and ultimately language death.

This volume focuses on the phenomena of LM and LS and the two main contexts with which they are mostly associated and in which they are most frequently studied. Next we will therefore provide some definitions of the two main concepts, LM and LS, and outline the two settings in which these phenomena have been studied most. In the final section of this chapter we will introduce the main approaches to the study of LM and LS.

2.2   KEY CONCEPTS IN THE STUDY OF LM AND LS

2.2.1   Language shift

We start by defining LS rather than LM because LS has affinity with a number of other terms such as language loss, language attrition, language obsolescence and language death, so that some delineation is desirable, where possible. If a language contact situation results in one or more languages being abandoned by speakers, the terms 'language shift', 'language loss', 'language obsolescence' and 'language death' can be applied. The term 'language shift' is used when the abandonment of one language for another language results not in the complete disappearance or death of the former but merely the disappearance of it from the specific speech community (or part thereof) that finds itself in the contact situation. In sociolinguistic terms, LS involves the gradual replacement of one's main language or languages, often labelled L1, by another language, usually referred to as L2, in all spheres of usage. Important in this definition are the phrases 'gradual' and 'spheres of usage': LS is both a process and an outcome. It is a process because the move away from one language to another occurs gradually: this implies that it may take one or more generations of speakers before the language is entirely abandoned. It also implies that the shifting away from the L1 does not occur simultaneously across all its uses or functions; rather, it gradually recedes across an increasing number of uses, functions and settings. LS is also an outcome when the language in question is no longer used by members of the community in any sphere of usage. The rate and speed of the shift process will vary from community to community. In some cases the process is relatively swift, within one or two generations, and in other contexts it will take much longer. An example of the former is the Dutch migrant community in Australia where over 95 percent of second-generation Dutch Australians (i.e., the first generation to be born in Australia) no longer use and, in many instances, can no longer speak Dutch. This means that the shift from Dutch to English has occurred in one generation. A much slower process of LS is one that spreads over many generations and/or centuries. Such a process is less likely to occur in migrant settings, although it can be witnessed among a number of communities that have maintained a life style that sets them apart from that of the new society (e.g., Mennonite and Amish groups in North America). Slower rates of LS are more likely to be found in settings that we will label territorial minority settings, especially if they have resulted from changed political boundaries or political developments.

The terms 'language loss', 'language death', 'linguistic/language extinction' and 'linguistic/language obsolescence' are used for the more dramatic outcomes of a language being abandoned by an entire speech community so that it is no longer used or spoken anywhere in the world. The process leading to language death or language extinction may also vary considerably in terms of speed and intensity. This will depend on the specific circumstances of the community and the triggers for change. Yet in comparison to the process of LS, language death is less likely to occur within one generation. However, there are circumstances where language death may occur relatively quickly after language contact: for example, if a speech community is fully eradicated, through illness, aggression or natural causes, then their language dies with them and this can of course happen swiftly. The violent eradication of Australian Aborigines living in Tasmania illustrates this scenario (e.g., Reynolds 1995). 'Linguicide' is the term that is sometimes used for the more violent and radical examples of language death (Phillipson and Skutnabb-Kangas 1999). Indeed, use of the term 'abandonment' should not imply that this is mainly a voluntary process undertaken by the community in question. In most cases various forces and pressures external to the speech community are the triggers leading to language death as already exemplified previously.

The term 'language attrition', sometimes also labelled 'language loss', is mostly used to refer to reduced or diminishing linguistic competence of an individual speaker. Schmid (2011), author of a book on language attrition in this series, Key Topics in Sociolinguistics, stresses that the term mainly applies to the loss or changes in grammatical and other linguistic features of a language as a result of its declining use by speakers who have changed their linguistic environment and language habits. While the process of LS may go more naturally hand in hand with language attrition for certain speakers, the same can also be said for a relationship between LM and language attrition. For example, a speaker of language A continues to maintain language A for certain functions and in some contexts, but, because he or she has little contact with the source community for that language, this speaker's language may start exhibiting linguistic features typical of attrition, for instance, simplification of grammatical structures. Language attrition is also found in speakers of 'dying' languages: Dorian's (1981) study of a dying Scottish dialect clearly illustrates this point.

Neither the topic of language death nor that of language attrition will be pursued further in this book. Both topics have, of course, links to the study of LS, but they have also become significant fields of study in their own right, generating numerous scholarly works that describe and document the process leading up to the (possible) extinction and death of a language (e.g., Austin and Sallabank 2011; Dorian 1992; Grenoble and Whaley 1998; Janse and Tol 2003).

2.2.2 Language maintenance

If LS is defined as the process in which a language is gradually replaced by another language, often labelled L2, dominant language or majority language, in all spheres of usage, then LM is best described as the continued use or retention of an L1, a minority or heritage language in one or more spheres of language use. Definitions of LM rarely if ever address the issue of the *degree* of usage that needs to be in place by either a speaker or a community to speak about LM. More extreme cases of LM are those where a community or language group moves from one linguistic territory into another but does not adopt the other language (L2) and continues to use its own language for all functions and in all contexts. Only a few members of the community develop bilingualism involving the majority language so that essential communication with the wider community can take place. This scenario of LM can occur only in settings where the 'migrated' community or group is self-sufficient and needs only minimal contact with the wider community for its survival. Linguistic enclaves or *Sprachinseln* are examples of these more extreme versions of LM. In fact, in the previous chapter we pointed to *Sprachinselforschung* as a precursor of LM and LS studies. Today, there are still some communities that exhibit features of the original linguistic enclaves, e.g., the Amish communities in parts of the United States and Canada, but they are unlikely to be able to maintain the same degree of linguistic isolation that former linguistic enclaves could maintain. The dominant or majority language that 'surrounds' them tends to infiltrate the community either for certain functions or in certain contexts. The term LM is, however, also applied to situations where an L1 continues to be used in some but not all contexts by various generations of speakers. Key elements in identifying a situation of LM are, therefore, (1) the period of continued use since the initial language contact, (2) the extent to which it is the exclusive language in any given context and (3) the number of contexts (usually called 'domains' or spheres of usage) in which the L1 continues to be used either exclusively or in conjunction with another language. Later in this book we shall explore these elements further. Here it suffices to say that situations that exhibit some continuation of L1, however minimal, over an extended period of time attract the label LM.

2.2.3 Language revival and revitalisation

Where a language is in some state of endangerment or decline ranging from (near) extinction in terms of usage to low levels of usage by the speech community, attempts may be made to increase its usage again. In some cases the term LM is also applied to these situations. However, in more recent literature terms such as 'language revival' and 'language revitalisation' are being used rather than LM. While there are some similarities between LM and language revitalisation, especially in sociolinguistic terms, the challenges, both linguistic and sociolinguistic, involved in the process of revitalisation are much more immense than those in an LM process. For example, depending on the state of endangerment, revitalisation may involve significant linguistic 'repair' work relating to vocabulary, grammar and even the sound system to make the language suitable for communication in the targeted community (see also Chapter 9). Sociolinguistically speaking, both processes involve maintaining and, where possible, growing the speech community. In the case of languages with only a handful of 'active' speakers, these speakers will become the pivot around whom the entire revitalisation or reversal process will need to take place. Their responsibilities and tasks are immense: they need to become teachers of the language and pass on the language to others, turning the latter into speakers who feel competent to engage in intergenerational transmission. While these responsibilities are also found in LM settings, there are usually more human and material resources available to aid the process of maintenance. Another comparable and important element in the LM and revitalisation process concerns the expansion of the domains and contexts within which the language can or should be used. Again the tasks facing endangered language communities are more demanding than those of communities facing LS. In this book we will not expand further on describing situations that involve language revival or revitalisation. However, we will include some relevant works on revitalisation in the suggested readings for this chapter.

2.3   KEY SETTINGS FOR THE STUDY OF LM AND LS

The two most prominent settings that have been subjected to scholarly investigations of LM and LS are those linked to various forms of migration and to 'indigenous' linguistic minorities in nation-states. The discussion around the pioneers of LM and LS pointed towards the migration context being the key setting for such investigations. Another important setting for research into maintenance and shift concerns the so-called minority languages and language communities that are indigenous to a specific territory or region within nation-states, and sometimes across nation-states. Examples of the former are Welsh in the United Kingdom, Breton in France and Catalan in Spain. Examples of the latter include Sami, a language that is used in the northern parts of several Scandinavian countries – Norway, Sweden and Finland – or Basque in France and Spain. These languages also attract the label 'territorial' or 'regional' as they are seen as 'inherently' linked to the area in which they are or were used. Other descriptive labels for these languages and their communities include 'indigenous', a term most widely used in the context of the 'aboriginal' languages in the Americas, Australia and New Zealand, and 'autochthonous', the term used mainly in Europe for its minority languages. In this book we shall use the label 'minority language' for those languages that are associated with linguistic minorities that are considered to be 'indigenous' to a particular territory. We will use the term 'territorial minority setting' to refer to the territory with which the language and speech community are associated. There are many terms in circulation to denote the languages linked to migrant or diasporic settings: migrant language, immigrant language, community language, heritage language, ethnic language, language other than [fill in the name of the majority language] or home language. At the time of writing, the term 'heritage language' is probably the most widely used one, at least in the Northern Hemisphere. Community language is more widely used in places such as Australia and New Zealand. Here we shall use the term 'heritage language' rather than 'community language' as the latter term is used to denote the national languages of countries in the European Union.

2.3.1 Migrant settings

The most researched setting for the investigation of LM and LS is that of *migration*. Migration refers to the movement – voluntary or forced – of families, groups and large sections of communities across national and linguistic borders. The term also implies settlement in a new environment. Until recently, this settlement was seen as long term, if not permanent. A large number of studies, especially those undertaken between the 1960s and 1980s, have focused and continue to focus on the linguistic consequences of mass migrations, mainly following the Second World War from the 'old' world (Europe) to the Anglophone 'new world', i.e., North America, Australia, New Zealand, but also to South America and South Africa. The first major studies in the United States concerned northern European, German and Dutch migrants (e.g., Daan 1987; Dejong 1975; Hasselmo 1961, 1974; Haugen 1953; Kloss 1966, 1985). Later the focus shifted away from these groups to other European groups such as Italians, Greeks and Poles but also to Asian migrants (Chinese, Japanese and Korean) and, of course, to the many Spanish-speaking groups that have come to the United States (for an overview, see Ferguson and Heath 1981). A similar trajectory developed in other Anglophone new world countries (for Australia, e.g., Clyne 1982 and Romaine 1990; for Canada, e.g., Edwards 1998). Europe also became increasingly the locus for the study of LM in migrant populations. In fact, in the second half of the twentieth century Europe had started to change from a continent sending migrants to one receiving them. Initially this involved the arrival and settlement of (former) colonised 'subjects' in the European 'base' of the former colonial powers. This was particularly the case for France, Great Britain and the Netherlands (e.g., Alladina and Edwards 1991 and the

Linguistic Minorities Project 1985 for the United Kingdom, and Extra and Verhoeven 1993 for the Netherlands). The European economic boom of the 1960s also saw the arrival of another category of migrants, often labelled 'guest workers' because they were 'meant' to return to their country after a period of employment in (parts) of Europe. At first they came from European countries around the Mediterranean, mainly Greece, Italy and the former Yugoslavia. Later, they were joined by people from Turkey and the Magreb countries (e.g., Extra and Verhoeven 1993). More recently, the migration setting is being reconceptualised into one that highlights constant transitions and movements experienced by a group living outside its 'home' territory rather than the long-term settlement of such a group into a new territory (e.g., Urry 2007). We shall take this up in the final chapter of the book.

2.3.2 Territorial minority settings

The other main setting in which questions of LM and LS are being explored involves linguistic minorities who have occupied a specific territory within a nation-state for a long period of time. A rather simplistic but nevertheless helpful distinction between the migration setting and the territorial setting is that in the former, the focus is on the linguistic consequences of individuals, a group or community *arriving into* another linguistic territory. In case of the latter, the focus is on the linguistic consequences for a linguistic group with a long-term association or history in a given territory when another group, indigenous or exogenous, takes up a dominant role in that territory. There are a number of variations for the latter scenario. For example, there are communities whose association with a particular territory is very old (e.g., Native Americans in the Americas, Aboriginal peoples in Australia, Maoris in New Zealand) and who have become linguistic minorities in this territory through the subsequent arrival (invasion) of other groups whose language(s) came to dominate. Other scenarios include territorial annexations or losses following wars and other conflicts as well as political restructuring. As a result of these changes a specific linguistic group may become a minority in their own territory. For example, a section of speech community X living in a specific territory of nation-state X may find itself embedded or annexed to nation-state Y dominated by language Y. Whether or not speech community X can keep its language will now be in the hands of nation-state Y, leading not only to a situation of language contact but possibly also to one of LS. Other changes that may result in groups becoming linguistic minorities in their own territory can be the result of state internal rearrangements or reorganisations: the break-up of the former Yugoslavia has led to languages such as Croatian and Serbian becoming minority languages in some of the new states. Territorial minority settings do indeed experience LS but the ultimate outcome for many is language death rather than simply LS. Here we will focus mainly on those territorial minorities whose language is unlikely to be lost completely because it is spoken in another territory (often adjacent) where it could be treated as a minority language (possibly with more rights) or where it is the majority language. An example of the former is Basque in France and Spain, and of the latter the German-speaking community in Belgium. We will, however, also include some other minority languages and territorial minority settings (mainly in Europe) that have enjoyed or enjoy some 'protection' so that they are unlikely to face extinction in the near future. An example is Catalan in Spain.

Given the overwhelming focus on migrant settings in the study of LM and LS, this setting will also make up the central locus for the investigation and discussion of LM and LS issues in this book.

2.4 DIGLOSSIA AND MULTILINGUALISM IN THE STUDY OF LM AND LS

Two other terms or concepts require some further clarification in the context of LM and LS research. They are multilingualism (or bilingualism) and diglossia.

2.4.1 Multilingualism and bilingualism

We have stated that LM and LS are possible consequences of language contact. If the outcome of language contact is some degree of LM, then we have a situation of bilingualism or multilingualism. The term 'bilingualism' rather than 'multilingualism' was preferred in earlier work on LM and LS. This was probably due to the fact that the overwhelming majority of studies were concerned with language situations involving or seen to involve two languages. Only a minority of studies dealt with situations involving three or more languages. In migrant settings, this meant that the focus was on the heritage language and its competition with the dominant or majority language of the new environment. In the case of territorial minority settings, the bilingualism under investigation involved an individual's or group's use of the minority and majority languages. More recently, the term 'bilingualism' has given way to 'multilingualism', especially in relation to groups and communities rather than individuals. An example of this is the renaming of the *Handbook of Bilingualism* (Bhatia and Ritchie 2004) to the *Handbook of Multilingualism* in the 2013 revised edition (Bhatia and Ritchie 2013).

The original preference for the term 'bilingualism' was most likely linked to the prevalence of descriptive and analytic frameworks based on structuralism and operating with the (abstracted) notion of language rather than with the notion of language repertoires that is made up of several languages and language varieties (e.g., Weber and Horner 2012). The greater prominence of the term 'multilingualism' can also be seen as a reaction to a heightened visibility and presence of linguistic diversity in communities, societies and countries around the world. It is also triggered in part by a reconceptualisation of language use as a set of linguistic practices and repertoires on which an individual draws to communicate (see also Chapter 10). Within current LM and LS research these two terms tend to be used interchangeably when describing the two, three or multiple languages or language varieties used by individuals or groups in a contact situation.

The definitions of bilingualism that have most currency in LM and LS research do not generally include a measure of proficiency, or, if they do, it is not seen as a central feature. For example, Haugen (1953) included people with a smattering of another language and those who have a high degree of competence in two languages. In Pauwels (1986: 7) bilingualism or bilinguals were defined as 'those people who make use of more than one language and who recognize themselves, and are recognized by others as using more than one language, regardless of their degree of competence in those languages'.

There are numerous typologies of bi- and multilingualism (e.g., Baetens-Beardsmore 1982; Grosjean 1982; Hamers and Blanc 1983) but many of these have no direct relevance to LM research as they pay considerable attention to degrees of fluency or 'mastery' in the languages. A distinction that is pertinent for the study of LM and LS is that between 'stable' bilingualism and 'transitional' bilingualism. Although the term 'stable' is somewhat clumsy, given that dynamism and fluidity are prominent features of any kind of bi- or multilingualism, it is meant to refer to situations where the result of language contact is one of continuing multilingualism (albeit with some changes over time). 'Transitional' multilingualism, on the other hand, is a more straightforward term indicating that the multilingual state of play in a group or community is a passing phase, most likely resulting in a reduced number of languages used, or even monolingualism. The outcome of this process is then indeed referred to as either LS or language death, as discussed before. Our dominant setting for analysis – the migrant setting – is best described as one of transitional multilingualism.

2.4.2 Diglossia

In Chapter 1 we mentioned that Ferguson's impact on the study of LM and LS was particularly linked to his concept of diglossia, especially when Fishman combined this concept with that of bilingualism (or multilingualism) to create a matrix of four types of language scenarios that combine societal and individual forms of bi- or multilingualism.

In his pioneering work on diglossia, Ferguson (1959) used the term to describe the relationship between two language varieties that were differentiated in terms of domains of use, context, style and function. He exemplified and discussed this relationship by describing the language situations in Greece, German-speaking Switzerland, Haiti and 'the Arab-speaking' world. In each of these speech communities, Ferguson identified two distinct varieties – a H(igh) variety and a L(ow) variety: Katharevousa and Dhimotiki for Greece, Standard German and Swiss-German for Switzerland, French and Haitian Creole for Haiti, and Classical and Colloquial Arabic for the Arab-speaking world. Crudely speaking, the L-variety is used for informal and familiar interactions and is usually the variety acquired in the home, whereas the H-variety is usually learnt through schooling and is associated with more formal situations and registers and is the language used for writing. Ferguson considered diglossic situations to be relatively stable. Although later investigations of Ferguson's language situations have questioned some aspects of Ferguson's analyses (e.g., Fasold 1984), the term itself not only became very popular in sociolinguistics but was also broadened to apply to situations of functional differentiation between two distinct languages rather than varieties of the same language. Fishman (1970: 74) acknowledged that John Gumperz' work (e.g., Gumperz 1962) was instrumental in extending the concept beyond the situations described by Ferguson: 'diglossia not only exists in multilingual societies which officially recognize several "languages", and not only in societies that utilize vernacular and classical varieties, but also in societies which employ separate dialects, registers, or *functionally differentiated language varieties of whatever kind'* (Fishman 1970: 74). Fishman built upon this extension of the concept to any type of functional differentiation of language forms (within a given community or society) to develop a matrix that examines the relationship between bilingualism and diglossia. In this context, bilingualism refers to the ability of a speaker to use two or more languages. The matrix contains four possible scenarios:

(1) Diglossia and bilingualism
(2) Bilingualism without diglossia
(3) Diglossia without bilingualism
(4) Neither diglossia nor bilingualism

Scenario (1) implies that almost the entire speech community is able to use the languages or language varieties of the community and that these varieties are functionally differentiated. Fishman cites Paraguay as a typical example of this scenario with Guarani being the L-variety (using Ferguson's terms) and Spanish the H-variety. Luxembourg could also be seen as an example of (1), albeit involving three languages: 'Letzebuergesch' as the L-variety and German and French as H-varieties, each with specific functions (e.g., Fehlen 2002; Hoffmann 1981). This situation represents a 'stable' form of bilingualism.

Scenario (2) is the one that is most commonly linked to the study of LM and LS, especially in migrant settings. Some members of the society (usually the immigrants and their offspring) continue to use their language together with the language of the new society but without clear functional differentiation. As a result this situation is rather unstable and transitional, often ultimately leading to LS.

Scenario (3) involves the presence of at least two groups in a polity or society: one group, normally the one with the power, uses only the H-language or variety, and the other group, usually 'the masses' or those with no or limited power, exclusively use an L-language or variety. Fasold (1984) gives czarist Russia as an example: the nobility spoke French whereas the masses used Russian.

Scenario (4) is perhaps the least realistic and, in fact, possibly fictional. Finding a community where only one variety is used and where there is no need or evidence of functional differentiation even at stylistic level is very unlikely.

Applying these concepts to our main settings for the study of LM and LS, it can be said that the migrant setting is characterised by transitional bilingualism without diglossia. In the case of the indigenous territorial minority setting, the bilingualism may also be transitional although the diglossic nature of the situation may linger longer.

2.5 APPROACHES TO THE STUDY OF LM AND LS

Studies whose foci involve the relationship between language, the individual and society are bound to attract the interest of different disciplines. The study of LM and LS is no exception. In the chapter dealing with the pioneers of the field, the multidisciplinary character of the field was already evident: linguists, sociologists, social psychologists and anthropologists all contributed to the emergence of this field. Meanwhile, other disciplines have been added, each focusing on specific aspects of the field. For example, applied linguistics, especially its sub-field of language policy and planning, has come to play an important role in examining the influence that sociopolitical factors and institutions can exert on LM or LS in a given group. Interestingly, the field of language policy and planning is also multidisciplinary with contributions from such disciplines as applied linguistics, political science and economics. The discipline of education is another major contributor to LM and LS studies, specifically focusing on the language learning and the educational provisions and models for the teaching of minority and heritage languages. Other contributing approaches include ethnography, sociolinguistics, philosophy and demography, some of which have influenced methodologies and others explanations of observed phenomena. The three main approaches, however, that have defined the field and shaped the study of LM and LS are the sociology of language, the social psychology of language and the anthropology of language (sometimes referred to as anthropological linguistics). The sociology of language approach is most clearly associated with the scholar Joshua Fishman. Although Fishman's (1971) definition of this approach encompasses all aspects of the relationship between language and society, as exemplified in this quote,

> focuses on the entire gamut of topics related to the social organization of language behavior, including not only language usage per se but also language attitudes and overt behaviors towards language and language users (Fishman 1971: 271),

he specifies two major foci: the first relates to identifying 'who speaks what language to whom and when', and the second focus concerns the exploration of the differential rates of change in language use across groups. This approach is often described as one that is primarily concerned with the macro-level: it examines language use patterns in (larger) groups and communities and makes comparisons across such groups.

The social psychological approach is another major contributor to researching LM and LS. Giles et al. (1980: 2) defined social psychology 'as the study of the ways in which the thoughts, feelings, and behaviours of others are influenced by the actual, imagined and implied presence of others and by the sociostructural forces operating in society.' When it comes to the social psychology of language, the authors state: 'Hence, language behaviour, in addition to being a product of people who are influenced by others, is also one of the means by which we can exert influence' (Giles et al. 1980: 2). In the context of LM and LS studies, this approach has been particularly helpful in highlighting how beliefs and attitudes that individuals and groups hold may influence their behaviour. It has also foregrounded issues of language and identity and how they are shaped in intergroup relations. A third major approach in the study of LM and LS is linked to anthropology and ethnography. Here, the focus is more on undertaking detailed studies of language use and behaviour in (smallish) communities or groups. Susan Gal's (1979) work on language use in the village of Oberwart, Austria, was one of the pioneering studies that illustrated that approach. Although such studies are also guided by exploring who speaks what language to whom, when and why, the methods to obtain insights into these questions are quite different from those employed in the sociology of language approach: the former focuses primarily on qualitative data and the latter on quantitative data. In the next chapter we discuss how these different approaches have provided the field of LM and LS with a rich array of data collection and analysis methods. In Chapter 7 we shall discuss how some of these approaches have dealt with explaining differential rates of LM and LS across groups and communities.

POINTS FOR DISCUSSION AND TASKS

1. Fishman created a matrix with two parameters, diglossia and bilingualism. Can you find specific examples of language situations around the world that represent the three main scenarios?
2. If you were to do a search of research that has been done on immigrant languages in the North America, Australia and New Zealand, which five ethnolinguistic groups have been examined most across these continents? Why do you think there has been so much work done on them?
3. If you were to do a search of studies on the language situation of indigenous territorial minorities, which territorial minorities

(whose language is *not* close to extinction) have received most attention, and why?

4. *Ethnologue* keeps data on the status of languages in terms of their vitality. It distinguishes five levels: (1) threatened, (2) shifting, (3) and (4) refer to dying languages and (5) extinct languages. Here we are interested in level (1): identify where most of the languages whose vitality is threatened are found and examine for five languages how much and what sort of work is being done on them.

5. There are three 'dominant' approaches to the study of LM and LS. Examine whether there are studies reflecting these three approaches for the following languages or language communities in migrant or territorial minority settings: Korean, Italian, Polish, Gujarati, Yiddish, Welsh, Frisian and Sami.

6. Do you believe that, in the study of LM and LS, definitions of bi- or multilingualism should include an element of competence or fluency? Why or why not?

SUGGESTIONS FOR FURTHER READING

There is a very large collection of handbooks, textbooks and edited volumes that cover key concepts in general as well as in the settings identified in this chapter. A set of more recent handbooks was already mentioned in the Introduction, and further key texts and handbooks were mentioned in the list of readings in Chapter 1.

Below we list some country- or region-based volumes that survey language questions in relation to our two main settings: migrant and territorial minority settings.

Australia

Clyne, Michael. 1991. *Community languages in Australia*. Cambridge: Cambridge University Press.

Romaine, Suzanne. Ed. 1991. *Language in Australia*. Cambridge: Cambridge University Press.

North America

Edwards, John. Ed. 1998. *Language in Canada*. Cambridge: Cambridge University Press.

Ferguson, Charles, and Shirley Brice Heath. Eds. 1981. *Language in the USA*. Cambridge: Cambridge University Press.

Finnegan, Edward, and John R. Rickford. 2004. Eds. *Language in the USA: Themes for the 21st Century*. Cambridge: Cambridge University Press.

British Isles

Trudgill, Peter. Ed. 1984. *Language in the British Isles*. Cambridge: Cambridge University Press.

Europe

Extra, Guus, and Durk Gorter. Eds. 2001. *The other languages of Europe*. Clevedon: Multilingual Matters.

Gorter, Durk, and Guus Extra. Eds. 2008. *Multilingual Europe: facts and policies*. Berlin: Mouton de Gruyter.

PART II
Investigating language maintenance and shift

Collecting and analysing data

3 Linguistic demography

Census surveys

3.1 LINGUISTIC DEMOGRAPHY AND THE STUDY OF LM

In this first chapter dealing with data collection, we focus on linguistic demography. Linguistic demography is concerned with the study of numerical or statistical aspects of languages and their distribution across the world. Major sources of information include Census and large-scale surveys. A number of countries collect information on language use and language proficiency through their periodic Census surveys, usually done every five to ten years. The language data collected in this way have been of assistance to language scholars interested in the linguistic make-up of a country, state or region and in the dynamics of these linguistic landscapes, including major and minor shifts in the usage of particular languages and language varieties. In line with a purpose of Census surveys, they have also been used in the shaping or changing of language policies and planning initiatives. In this chapter we will look at some issues that surround the use of language data drawn from Census surveys in the study of LM and LS.

3.2 LANGUAGE DATA FROM CENSUS SURVEYS

Census surveys are periodical population surveys that collect information from individuals (typically over the age of five years) about a large set of variables, factors and behaviours. These surveys facilitate planning in a variety of fields such as transport, education, social services, health, housing, trade, business, the economy and even political representation. Countries with a linguistically diverse population increasingly include questions around language use and language proficiency. Reasons for such inclusion can range from a desire to document and monitor trends in the linguistic diversity of the national population to a need for the planning of language services (interpreting, translation and language learning) to formulating policies on language use and language rights. These questions, albeit that their formulation is often problematic, are regularly used by a variety of scholars, including those working on LM and LS, to assess the state and vitality of territorial minority, immigrant or heritage languages within a country or large polity. In some cases where the Census does not include language questions researchers may draw upon other variables (e.g., ethnic origin, birthplace) to gain some insight into language matters. Of course the latter way of gaining information on language matters is very fraught as neither ethnicity nor birthplace is an appropriate substitute or reliable indicator of linguistic background. Obvious examples are people of Jewish origin: they are not all likely to be Yiddish speakers or speakers of Hebrew, for instance. Even if one could cross-tabulate ethnicity with birthplace, e.g., a Jew from Russia, or a Jew born in the United States, assigning a 'mother tongue' to them is highly speculative.

Using language data from large-scale population surveys is of course a powerful tool in revealing macro-level trends in the language dynamics of a country, state or polity. It allows for comparisons across groups, across generations and possibly across states and countries. The latter is possible if the formulation of the language question(s) is relatively similar. Yet most scholars of LM or LS working with such data are well aware of their limitations and will take care not to over-rely on Census-based language data in understanding trends and patterns of language behaviour. In the following sections, we will review some of these limitations but also point out some of the strengths of Census-based language data in LM and LS research.

3.2.1 Language questions in Census surveys: formulation and processing

Formulation of questions and responses. If the decision has been made to include questions around language (knowledge, use, proficiency), then the drafting of the question(s) is very important. Unlike surveys entirely dedicated to language matters (e.g., the periodical *Eurobarometer* language surveys that the European Commission undertakes), the number of language-specific questions in a Census will be limited, making their formulation indeed quite critical. On average, no more than two to four questions are dedicated to language issues in a typical Census. Although linguists occasionally get consulted in drafting the questions, the demands and complexities of Census questions and their processing often lead to compromises that affect the quality of the linguistic information that scholars can use. After all, the purpose and use of Census data for government and related agencies may be quite different from those of the language researcher. For the latter, the information gathered through the Census should assist in documenting not only the linguistic diversity of a country, but also the vitality of the languages, i.e., to what extent a language is passed on to the next generation(s) as well as people's (self-assessed) proficiency in a set of languages relevant to the country. Furthermore, scholars would also hope to gain insight into a range of factors and variables (usually through cross-tabulation) that could account for differential language-use patterns and differences in linguistic vitality. Amongst the more typical variables of interest to LM scholars are age, gender/sex, race/ethnicity, country of birth, income, education and occupation. Other variables that have attracted the interest of researchers are period of residence (mainly in migrant settings), family size, place of residence (e.g., small village, large city, border area, region or province), political association and religious affiliation.

The formulation of language questions has attracted significant comments and indeed criticism from language scholars around the world. Clyne (1982, 1991), De Vries (1985, 1990), Extra (2010), Lieberson (1966), Mackey and Cartwright (1979), Nicholas (1988) and Sillitoe (1987), among many others, have commented in detail on the complexities of formulating language questions for Census and other large-scale surveys. Here, we discuss briefly the main complexities in the formulation of a question around *use*. We draw upon existing questions found in the Australian, Canadian, US and English (UK) Censuses.

(a) Which language does the person use regularly? (Australian Census 1976)
(b) Does the person speak a language other than English at home? If so, which language? (Australian Census 1986, also in the US Census since 1960)
(c) What language does this person speak most often at home? (Canadian Census 1996)
(d) Does this person speak any other languages on a regular basis at home? (Canadian Census 2001)
(e) What is your main language? (Census 2011 for England and Wales)

The most problematic of these question formulations for LM research is (e), the question used in the English Census (2011). Such a question forces a respondent to name only one language. If respondents are bi- or multilingual, they can name only the language that they believe to be the one they use 'mainly'. 'Mainly' is generally interpreted as 'most frequently used'. Such a question is unlikely to capture actual linguistic diversity and is of little value in trying to understand the vitality of a language and its speech community. For example, the multilingualism of the following speaker would be invisible or go unrecorded: a woman born in India who speaks fluent Tamil, fluent English and some Hindi, and now permanently resides in the United Kingdom where she uses English as her main – most frequently used – language. However, she continues to use Tamil regularly with family and friends, in some shops and other settings. Similarly, such a question is unlikely to expose any use of languages other than English by members of the second or subsequent generations, as they almost always use English as their main language.

With regard to the other question formulations ((a) to (d)), the problematic elements relate to expressions of 'frequency' and the (non-) identification of locale or interlocutor. With regard to 'frequency', expressions such as 'regularly', 'on a regular basis', and 'most often' may be interpreted very differently by the respondents. This is especially the case in the formulation found in question (a) – Which language does the person use regularly? – as no context is given. In many modern households the time spent away from home for employment and leisure purposes is much longer than time spent in the home. Yet the language of public life is in most circumstances the dominant or majority language: this may lead to a respondent whose home life is nevertheless entirely conducted in the minority or heritage language to give a reply stating that the majority language is most regularly used. Even more challenging is the issue of locale, or context (sometimes referred to as domain). As we shall see in future chapters, the location of heritage language use varies from generation to generation. For those born overseas or outside the country of residence, the home continues to be the heartland for such language use. However, for those born in the new environment (second and subsequent generations), it may be their parents' rather than their own home that is the prime location for such language use. This question is therefore likely to lead to an underestimation of heritage or minority language use, especially in the case of second- and third-generation speakers in migrant settings. Some Census surveys (e.g., Canada) include questions about language use outside the home, notably the workplace. The inclusion of more than one context is of course very helpful in understanding language use patterns in bi- and multilingual environments.

Sometimes, Census questions about language also contain an element of proficiency or skill measurement. In countries with indigenous territorial minorities this question relates mainly to the minority language. For example, in the 2011 Census for England and Wales, Welsh residents were given a question to rate their skills in Welsh as follows: 'Can you understand, speak, read or write Welsh?' or its Welsh equivalent '*A allwch ddeall, siarad, darllen neu ysgrifennu Cymraeg?*' and could respond with:

- Understand spoken Welsh
- Speak Welsh
- Read Welsh
- Write Welsh
- None of the above

However, in a migrant setting such a question seldom targets the heritage language but almost always the official, dominant or majority language in the country. For example, the Australian Census asks the question 'How well does the person speak English?' with response possibilities around a four-point scale:

□ very well,   □ well,   □ not well,   □ not at all.

Similar questions are also asked in the Census surveys of the United States and New Zealand. Canada, with its official bilingualism, asks the question 'Can this person speak English or French well enough to conduct a conversation?' Although a self-assessment of language skills is never a reliable instrument to accurately measure linguistic proficiency, its value is improved by including some elements that can aid in benchmarking the competence.

More recently, some Census surveys have started including a question that targets a self-assessment of proficiency in the heritage language. For example, the 2013 New Zealand Census had the following question: 'In which language(s) could you have a conversation about a lot of everyday things?'

Although the information about proficiency is still minimal, it does provide some insight into skills in the heritage language. An interesting observation in relation to these questions about minority or heritage languages is the move away from using labels such as 'mother tongue', 'native language', 'first language' and 'home language'. This is in response to the increasing mobility among many language users and the resulting complexity of defining such speakers. The nomenclature that would need to be used to describe language varieties in countries with a long history of multilingualism (e.g., most countries in Africa or the Indian subcontinent) is even more complex: many speakers use multiple languages in the same domain or context so that questions (a), (b) and (c) listed previously would not capture their linguistic reality

(Webb 2002). However, some multilingual states such as India continue to use the term 'mother tongue' in their Census surveys.

A potentially problematic issue that affects both question formulation and responses to the questions is the name of the language(s). Census surveys usually opt for a multiple-choice approach with only a limited amount of open-ended responses. This not only assists respondents in managing the multitude of questions but also facilitates the processing of data. Either approach – multiple choice or open-ended – has its complexities for language research. Where the respondent can fill in the name of the language him- or herself, this may lead to a discrepancy between the 'official' name of the language and the name by which its speakers know the language. Examples of this phenomenon are numerous: some speakers of the language 'officially' known as Dutch will refer to it as Flemish, Dutch or Hollands (Hollandic). In countries where regional dialects are strong, its speakers may mention the dialect rather than the language of the country, e.g., Sicilian instead of Italian. Then there are examples where political or national feelings may influence how the respondent names the language: some Cypriots are likely to indicate that they speak Cypriot rather than, e.g., Greek, Cypriot-Greek or Greek-Cypriot. In other cases respondents may use terms like *patois, pidgin* or *dialect* to describe their language (use). While this approach gives the respondent control over the naming of the language, this poses problems for the processing, which is almost always done by those without significant linguistic expertise or expert training. For example, the 'named' language may be attributed to the wrong official language category, or it may simply be ignored. An example of the former may have occurred in Australia with regard to English: many Australians use the term 'Australian' to refer to the variety of English they speak. Indigenous languages spoken by Aboriginal Australians are referred to in the Census as Australian languages. This gave rise to confusion about the attribution of speakers of Australian (English) to the category of Australian languages. If the approach is one where the languages are named in the response, the most obvious problem is linked to the number of languages that will be named on a Census form. Usually the list is restricted to the ten or twenty most widely used languages (often based on the results of a previous survey) followed by an option: *Other language: which ...* ? Of course, some problems that arise in the open-ended approach may also be found in the multiple-choice approach: a speaker of Swiss German may decide not to choose the option *German* but state *Swiss* (or *Swiss German*) in the 'Other language' box.

Another stumbling block for researchers keen on establishing trends of language use over an extended period of time is the changing of the question between Census surveys. This happened in Australia between 1976 and 1986: in 1976, the first Census to dedicate a question to language use, the formulation was: 'Which language does the person use regularly?' but this formulation was changed in 1986 to 'Does the person speak a language other than English at home? If so, which language?' Responses to these two questions are likely to be affected by the different formulation, although it is not known to what extent. Although researchers will continue to draw comparisons across Census surveys, these changes do have an adverse effect on the establishment of trends.

Processing language data. Two further limitations that linguists need to be aware of when working with Census-generated data concern the processing of language data. Both involve the extent to which all languages mentioned in responses are processed. In question (d) previously, the respondent has the possibility to name more than one language. If the respondent names four languages, it may very well be that only two of these will be processed by the statistician, skewing the linguistic information relating to this respondent. Similarly, the extent of linguistic diversity of a country may be restricted because only a certain number of languages will be processed. The statistical presentation of linguistic diversity may thus be at odds with the linguistic reality. Although statistical services have become more aware of these matters, financial considerations usually do constrain the extent to which such data can be fully processed.

3.3 USING CENSUS DATA IN LM AND LS RESEARCH

Identifying factors (forces, variables) that influence the vitality of a language and its speaker base is a central pursuit in LM research. In Part III of this book we will examine in more detail the types of factors that can play a role in influencing whether a language is maintained and how well it is maintained. Here we look at how Census data – linguistic and sociodemographic data – can help in identifying some such factors. This is done primarily by cross-tabulating information about language use with sociodemographic data found in the Census. Typical examples of such data include sex/gender, age, birthplace, marital status, level of education, income, occupation, religious affiliation, ethnicity/race and period of residence in the country and place of residence (state/territory/province). For example, a simple cross-tabulation between language use and gender could identify whether women (claim to) use the minority or heritage language more than men or vice versa. A cross-tabulation between language use, gender and ethnicity/race could reveal if the greater use of the minority/heritage language by women applies across various ethnic or racial groups or not. For example, are Greek, Italian, Chinese, Indian, Burmese, Moroccan and Basque women all likely to use the minority language more than their male counterparts, or are there ethnospecific differences? A further cross-tabulation between language, gender, ethnicity and birthplace could reveal if gender differences apply to both those born outside the country and those born in the country of residence. In a migrant setting this reveals potential differences between the migrants (first generation) and their locally born offspring. In the territorial minority settings this may refer to those living or having lived outside the minority territory. In other words, cross-tabulations of Census data can aid researchers in gaining some insight into the kind of factors or variables that affect language use and choice.

The most extensive use of Census-based language data has been by researchers working on questions of LM and LS in migrant settings (e.g., Barni and Extra 2008; De Vries 1980; Extra and Yağmur 2004; Lieberson 1963, 1965; Mackey and Ornstein 1979; Stevens 1986; Wiley 2005). One of the most detailed analyses of Census data for the study of language ecology and vitality is that undertaken by Michael Clyne and colleagues in Australia. This Australian scholar has systematically examined language data from numerous Australian Census surveys between 1976 and 2006 (e.g., Clyne 1982, 1991; Clyne and Kipp 1997, 2002; Clyne et al. 2008; Kipp and Clyne 2003; Kipp et al. 1995). The detailed analysis of Census data over a period of thirty years has given researchers interested in language issues in Australia not only a rich database on linguistic ecology but also insights into the dynamics of multilingualism in Australia. Besides collecting information on the number of languages used in the Australian community, these analyses have also delivered data on the number of speakers per language, their geographical distribution in Australia and rates of across different types of communities. Numerous cross-tabulations between the language questions (one of home language use and one of English proficiency) and various sociodemographic and other variables have allowed for the construction of detailed sociodemographic profiles of speakers of these languages, as well as of their respective speech communities. Among the more prominent cross-tabulations were the following:

- Language use (other than English) by age
- Language use (other than English) by gender
- Language use (other than English) by birthplace and parents' birthplace
- Language use (other than English) by years of residence
- Language use (other than English) by type of marriage (endogamy/exogamy)
- Percentage of persons using community/heritage languages by state and by capital city

The cross-tabulation between country of birth or parental country of birth, and the language use response – English only – provides a general measure of LS. This can then be traced, for instance, across generations and ethnolinguistic groups, thus establishing similarities and differences in the process of LS. A further strength of this Australian work is the ability to compare language use data and the degree of LS across thirty years of Census material. These comparisons are critical in understanding the dynamics of LM and LS and in charting the language ecology of a region or a country. For example, a comparison of the 1991, 1996 and 2001 Australian Census data regarding heritage language use shows that Italian continues to be the most widely spoken language other than English in this period but that the number of speakers have dropped by more than 15 percent. Conversely, Vietnamese, which ranked sixth in 1991, was in fifth place in 2001 but saw a 58 percent increase in speaker base. Mandarin, a language that ranked only twelfth in 1991, has experienced a stellar rise to being placed sixth in 2011 and with a 156 percent increase in speaker base, i.e., from 54,573 to 139,288. When it comes to documenting LS, the Australian analyses show that there is significant variation among ethnolinguistic groups in the rate of LS. For example, in the 1996 Census only 5.5 percent of immigrants from Greece claimed to only use English at home (hence 94.5% claimed to continue using Greek at home), whereas 62.2 percent of people born in the Netherlands claimed to only speak English at home (with a mere 37.8% still using Dutch at home). Other analyses and cross-tabulations have revealed that age, gender, marital patterns (endogamy vs exogamy) are influential in understanding individual language use patterns and that location (urban vs rural) and the size of the community (i.e., its numerical strength) are important group level factors affecting LM or LS. For scholars working on a specific ethnolinguistic group or a migrant community across a range of diasporic locations (countries), the existence of Census-based language data from different countries allows for a comparative study of LM and LS patterns. Such comparisons make it possible to shed light on the primacy of certain factors over others in shaping the dynamics of LM and LS. For example, a cross-national analysis could show that urban environments are generally more conducive to LM than rural or remote regions or vice versa. Such analyses could also reveal that some ethnolinguistic migrant groups have a strong record of LM irrespective of the country in which they settle. Of course, if the formulation of the language question(s) across countries is very different, sensible comparisons may be rather limited.

Although the previous discussion of Census-based language data has been primarily focused on migrant settings, the observations and comments also apply to Census data relating to territorial minority settings. In the case of such linguistic minorities, Census surveys may be undertaken by the country within which the minority is located and by the region or territory of the linguistic minority. For example, the Netherlands does not have a language question in its national Census, but the province of Friesland, the home territory of Frisian, does undertake regular surveys of Frisian language use (e.g., Gorter 1994). Spain, on the other hand, does include questions on the languages of the autonomous regions of the Basque country, Catalonia and Galicia. In addition, the Basque region itself has been running some language surveys since 1990 (Extra 2007). For some territorial linguistic minorities Census data may go back a very long time, allowing for a longitudinal analysis of the state and vitality of a language and its speech community. For example, there are more than 100 years of Census data available on Welsh. These show not only the steady decline in the use of Welsh between the nineteenth and twentieth century (with a first increase recorded in the 2001 Census and then again a small drop in 2011), but also where the Welsh heartland is. Further, it provides some information on the sociodemographic profile of the speakers, showing that the main users of Welsh are elderly.

This section has given an insight of how Census surveys that include language questions can be used in the exploration of patterns in LM and LS. A major strength of Census (and other large-scale language) surveys for LM and LS is their sheer scope; i.e., they capture almost an entire population of a specific polity. They give the researcher the ability to gain some insight into how (mainly) sociodemographic personal and group factors interact with language use. Of particular benefit to the LM/LS researcher is the longitudinal perspective that language data from subsequent Census surveys can bring to investigating and understanding language dynamics and linguistic vitality. There are, however, a series of weaknesses and pitfalls associated with using Census data for such investigations. Besides the ones mentioned here – question formulations and processing limitations – there are other ones with the most obvious one being that Census surveys rely entirely on self-reports. Of course, this is also the case with smaller-scale surveys but the impact may be more severe in the case of the former. Both migrant and minority group members may be apprehensive to record their real language use patterns in nation-wide, 'official' surveys for fear of retaliation, if a society is perceived as anti-multilingual (e.g., Hunnicutt and Castro 2005). In that case they may be underreporting the use of the minority or heritage language. Alternatively, such group members could use the Census to seek more recognition and services for their community by overreporting minority language use. In fact some communities will actively encourage its members to record their minority language use in Census surveys: more recently this activity is increased due widespread use of social media. Another element that is especially problematic in the context of migrant settings is the way in which the variable 'race' or 'ethnicity' is presented or operationalised. In some cases there is a detailed list of possibilities. For example, in the English Census (2011) the following categories and sub-categories are mentioned;

> **White:** □ British □ Irish □ Any Other White background (to be specified)
> **Mixed:** □ White and Black Caribbean □ White and Black African
> □ White and Asian □ White and any other Mixed Background
> **Asian or Asian British:** □ Indian □ Pakistani □ Bangladeshi □ Any other Asian Background
> **Black or Black British:** □ Caribbean □ African □ Any other Black Background
> **Chinese or other ethnic group:** □ Chinese □ Any ethnic group

In the 2011 Australian Census, on the other hand, there is only a question about ancestry with the following options:

□ English, □ Irish, □ Scottish, □ Italian,

□ German, □ Chinese, □ Australian □ other (please specify)

In other cases, the Census may contain a question not about race/ethnicity or ancestry but only about birthplace. The latter is a poor substitute for information about a person's ethnicity or race and will affect the reliability of any cross-tabulations with language(s) used.

In conclusion, language data extracted from Census surveys can be a rich source of information for studies in linguistic diversity and vitality and to gain insights into macro-level trends of LM and LS provided that there is a strong awareness of the weaknesses and limitations of such data. This has been successfully demonstrated by studies undertaken by scholars such as Michael Clyne for Australia (references given previously), John De Vries (De Vries 1994; De Vries and Vallee 1980) for Canada and Terence Wiley (Wiley 2005a, 2005b) for the United States to name but a very few.

POINTS FOR DISCUSSION AND TASKS

1. A growing number of countries include a question or questions pertaining to language and language use. Compare the formulation of language questions in the Census surveys of three or four countries (excluding those discussed in this chapter) and comment on their usefulness in terms of investigating issues of LM and LS.
2. Choose a country that has a language question in its Census pertaining to minority, heritage or other nondominant languages and explore what sort of cross-tabulations can be undertaken that shed light on LM and LS.
3. If you would like to find out whether a third-generation 'immigrant' continues to use the heritage language, what kind of data would you need to have access to (in a Census) to explore this question?
4. We have identified a range of weaknesses of using census-based information on language use. Can you think of some others? Why are they weaknesses and how could they be overcome or minimised?
5. The naming of languages is a sensitive issue: if the majority allocates the name to the minority or heritage language and this name does not coincide with the name minority members use to designate the language, what kind of consequences could this have for the information provided? Can you give some practical examples?
6. If you were consulted to formulate two questions on language for a nation-wide survey in your country, how would you formulate them and why?

SUGGESTIONS FOR FURTHER READING

The following texts provide detailed information on the various aspects of linguistic demography and the use of language data extracted from census surveys.

Arel, Dominique. 2002. Language use in censuses: backward- or forward-looking? In D. Kertzer and D. Arel (eds.), *Census and identity: the politics of race, ethnicity, and language in national censuses.* Cambridge: Cambridge University Press, 92–120.

This is a critical look at language issues in census surveys.

Clyne, Michael. 1982. *Multilingual Australia.* Melbourne: River Seine.
Clyne, Michael. 1991. *Community languages: the Australian experience.* Cambridge: Cambridge University Press.

These two books not only contain a discussion of the strengths and weaknesses of linguistic data and language questions in Australian Census surveys but also provide detailed analyses of language data in these surveys.

De Vries, John, 1990. On coming to our census: a layman's guide to demolinguistics. *Journal of Multilingual and Multicultural Development* 11.1–2: 57–76.

This article is an accessible guide to understanding linguistic demography and its use in the study of LM and multilingualism.

Extra, Guus and Kutlay Yağmur. 2004. Demographic Perspectives. In G. Extra and Y. Kutlay (eds.), *Urban multilingualism in Europe: immigrant minority languages at home and in school.* Clevedon: Multilingual Matters, 25–72.

This is an extensive chapter in which the authors look critically at the language and ethnicity questions in a number of national census surveys including Australia, Canada, the Netherlands, South Africa and the United States.

Ryan, Camille. 2013. Language use in the United States. www.census.gov/prod/2013pubs/acs-22.pdf (accessed 17 June 2015).

This is a brief paper providing an analysis of the 2011 US Census data on language use.

4 Reporting language use and exploring language attitudes

Questionnaires

4.1 CHALLENGES OF USING QUESTIONNAIRES IN MULTILINGUAL RESEARCH

Questionnaires are widely used to examine various forms of social behaviour and practices. They are the preferred data-gathering tool for macro-scale projects and surveys. Census surveys, discussed in the previous chapter, are a prime example. Questionnaires are also widely used in macro-scale research focusing primarily on language issues: usage patterns and linguistic practices. Typically, scholars investigating questions of LM or LS try to gather data from a representative sample of the group or community in question to make assessments on the state of play. However, questionnaires are also a useful tool in small(er)-scale research, for example, when you want to identify what languages primary-aged school children use at home and with their friends. In such types of research, the questionnaire is seldom the only data-collection tool but is complemented by other modes of data collection, including case studies, ethnography, participant observation, testing and experiments. The use of questionnaires in research on linguistic diversity shares many elements with its use in other types of social research: sampling issues, the distribution and administration of the questionnaire, the formulation of questions. Some of these, however, are more challenging because of the linguistic diversity of the respondents. For example, the standard sampling techniques may not be very efficient for locating participants when the focus is on their bi- or multilingualism. Similarly, a decision needs to be made in which language the questionnaire should be presented. If the questionnaire is to be administered by an interviewer, should this interviewer be bilingual, should he or she be a member of the same ethnolinguistic group or not? These are some issues and questions facing researchers who rely on the use of questionnaires in exploring language use and language attitudes in a multilingual context. In the next sections we will discuss some of the challenges particularly pertinent to research into LM or LS. They include the sampling of participants and the language(s) used in the questionnaire. The rest of the chapter will be devoted to a discussion of the types of questions used to probe both (reported) language use and language attitudes. Finally, we will mention some aspects of data processing.

4.1.1 Sampling participants for research on LM and LS

Research into LM and LS typically involves gathering data from people who are almost always considered to be linguistic minorities within a polity. These minorities can be indigenous to the region or country or may have migrated into the polity from other linguistic environments. The sampling of 'special' populations or subgroups is often more complex because standard reference points such as electoral registers, telephone and other contact directories or 'door knocking' are mostly too broad to access relevant informants and are therefore inefficient to find a sample of the desired group. Sometimes, the sampling of indigenous linguistic minorities may be easier than that for immigrant minorities if the former are concentrated in a specific territory or neighbourhood; for example, this may be the case for Sami people living in some rural areas in northern Scandinavia, for Welsh people living in specific regions of Wales or for Sioux in South Dakota. In some cases this could also apply to immigrant minorities if there is information, for instance, through Census data, on their geographical distribution. For example, Australian Census data revealed that the Vietnamese immigrant community in Melbourne is heavily concentrated in a few surburbs (Richmond, Footscray, Sunshine and Springvale) (Bao and Cahill 2001). The 2010 US Census revealed that the highest concentration of Puerto Ricans in New York City is found in the Bronx (nearly 22%).

Trying to build in some degree of randomness into the participant sampling technique is a very difficult proposition for this type of research. For example, the researchers involved in the large-scale Linguistic Minorities Project (LMP) undertaken in England in the early 1980s faced these problems when they tried to find representative samples of ten immigrant linguistic groups – Bengali, Gujarati, Panjabi, 'Chinese' (incorporating various Chinese dialects), Italian, Portuguese, Greek, Turkish, Polish and Ukrainian – in several parts of England. Initially they drew upon three main sources to establish a sampling frame for their work: electoral registers, telephone directories and community lists. Interestingly, they scanned the first two sources for 'distinctive ethnic names' to find members of the language groups. They were fully aware that the use of ethnic names was 'a blunt instrument' (LMP 1985: 164), commenting,

> Firstly there are certain names which are common across different ethnic minorities. For example, we found that the name Mahers could belong to people of either Sikh or Irish ancestry with almost equal probability. And the name Mann could belong to Panjabi, English, German or even Chinese mother tongue speakers (LMP 1985: 164).

Furthermore, there is of course no certainty that someone with an ethnic name is also a speaker of that language, as the team found out:

> For example, in Coventry we came across a person with a Polish name who was in fact a Canadian citizen and spoke no Polish, and in Haringey we discovered several families with Chinese names, whose families had lived for several generations in the Caribbean, who spoke only English and who described themselves as West Indians (LMP 1985: 164).

In reaction to these sampling challenges, a common practice has been, and continues to be, to establish contact with ethnolinguistic and immigrant associations to obtain a base sample of contacts. If the association is willing to give access to its membership list, researchers may then select a random sample from it to select the participants. It should be obvious that a certain bias has already been introduced by focusing on members belonging to agencies and organisations that focus on, foster and promote a particular view about language and cultural issues. The 'friend of a friend' approach that works quite well when looking at linguistic variation and language practices within a 'monolingual' community does not work well for examining such matters in a multilingual community. The sampling technique known as 'snowballing' is similar to the 'friend of a friend' approach and is equally problematic. Yet in many instances there is no suitable alternative so that researchers do resort to these, even in the case of larger surveys. Most LM researchers learn to 'live' with the hazard of sampling and become quite creative in trying to overcome the main obstacles. They, however, do fully realise that the statistical reliability and representativeness of their samples are adversely affected, reducing the generalisability of any findings. The sampling difficulties described here particularly affect research on the adult population. Researching the language-use patterns of school-age children presents fewer barriers in terms of sampling if the students can be contacted through the school system *and* the majority of children undertake schooling. A large project on the use of minority languages by school-aged children in six European countries, known as the Multilingual Cities Project (Extra and Yağmur 2004) gathered data on 160,000 students. This project did not encounter such major sampling challenges because the sampling frame was relatively straightforward: all students in the primary schools of six cities were included and permission to distribute questionnaires to them was obtained through the school authorities. As a result the overall response rate was above average for this type of research.

If the questionnaire is used to gather language-use data of a well-defined or relatively small group or community, then sampling is also far less problematic. For example, undertaking a study of LM and LS of the Amish in Lancaster County, Pennsylvania, or of the members of the Dutch Reformed Church in Victoria, Australia, would not pose the same challenges to participant sampling as one that aims to examine the language-use patterns of Turkish speakers in Germany.

4.1.2 The language(s) of the questionnaire

The primary target for language-use questionnaires is a population that is characterised by linguistic diversity and by bi- or multilingualism. Questionnaire respondents are therefore likely to have varying degrees of fluency and skills in one or more of the languages under investigation. Hence the choice of language in which the questionnaire is to be presented is a crucial consideration. This choice is affected not only by matters of linguistic competence but also by sociopolitical or sociocultural factors. It is further influenced by the mode in which the questionnaire is administered: written or oral. If it is a written questionnaire that is left with the respondents to fill in, then linguistic competence is not limited to which language(s) are used in the questionnaire but also needs to take account of the respondent's degree of literacy in that language. If an interviewer or a researcher reads the questions, then the lack of literacy in the respondent may have minimal influence on the responses, although other language-related matters linked to the linguistic competence of the interviewer may come into play. We shall discuss those in the next chapter. Here, our attention is on language issues linked to a written questionnaire. Normally, researchers of LM and LS choose to present the questionnaire in the language or languages with which the respondent is most comfortable or which he or she prefers. In the case of respondents who are literate in one or more of the languages under investigation, this is a straightforward matter in linguistic terms – they mostly choose the language in which they have the best literacy. This is likely to be the minority language for older or newly arrived immigrants, whereas younger immigrants or children born and raised in the new environment tend to have better literacy in the majority or dominant language. For territorial linguistic minorities whose language has not been available in education (for many years), the language in which they are literate tends to be the dominant or majority language. If the language of the indigenous minority exists only in oral form, then a written questionnaire would make sense only if respondents were literate in another language (probably the dominant or majority language). There are of course a range of people who are bi- or even multiliterate and whose choice of language may be based more on personal preference or influenced by other factors, often of a sociopolitical or ideological nature. For example, an individual may choose to respond in the minority language to show loyalty or to showcase his or her competency in that language. Alternatively, choosing to respond in the national or dominant language may be triggered by a desire to distance oneself from the minority language and culture or to demonstrate one's competence in the dominant language. The sociopolitical treatment of linguistic minorities, their status in a polity and the attitudes of the dominant group to such minorities are undoubtedly also factors that can play a role in a respondent's choice of language. For example, if the Latin alphabet rather than the Cyrillic alphabet was used in a language questionnaire aimed at Serbs who had migrated from the former Yugoslavia, or if the label Serbo-Croatian would be used to describe their language, this would most likely spark controversy amongst some Serbian informants. A similar challenge faces researchers whose questionnaire respondents may be seen as belonging to the same linguistic minority in relation to their spoken language but who do not share the same language of literacy. The LMP encountered such a situation with immigrants to Britain who came from the Panjab region that stretches across two countries, India and Pakistan:

> most families in England with origins in the Panjab, whether in India or Pakistan, and whether Muslim, Sikh or Hindu by religion, will use spoken varieties which are likely to be mutually intelligible ...
> However, Muslims, Sikhs and Hindus would normally expect tuition in their distinct languages of literacy, e.g., Panjabi in the Gurmukhi script for the Sikhs, Panjabi in the Gurmukhi script or Hindi for Hindus originating from the present Indian state of Panjab, and Urdu for Muslims for the Pakustani part of the Panjab. (LMP 1985: 47)

If researchers are fully familiar with the sociolinguistic situation of their respondents and have the means (linguistic and financial) to provide questionnaires in a variety of languages of literacy, then that is possibly the best way to deal with this complexity. If not, then the researcher may wish to opt for an oral version.

4.2 TYPES OF QUESTIONS PROBING LANGUAGE USE

Questionnaires have been the preferred tool to obtain detailed information about language use and to probe issues of LM and LS in projects and studies undertaken within the framework of the sociology of language. Joshua Fishman (1965), one of the earliest and main proponents of this approach to the study of LM and LS, introduced the question 'Who speaks what language to whom and when?' as the guiding beacon for exploring language use and LM or LS issues in bi- and multilingual settings. This question continues to guide the design of questionnaires exploring these issues. Over the years this basic question has been expanded to suit specific situations or to obtain a more comprehensive view of the factors and forces that shape language use and language behaviour in linguistically diverse settings. Prominent extensions or additions (marked by italics) to this question include: Who speaks (*uses*) what language (*language variety/code*) to whom, when, *where and to what end/for which purpose*? This question – in its original or amended version – in turn triggers a range of detailed questions exploring each element of the base question. Questionnaires usually have a section that seeks sociodemographic information on the respondent – the *who* of the question – and their language repertoire (*what* language(s)) followed by sections that probe the interlocutors (*whom*), the locations/locales (*where*) and the situations or contexts (*when*) in relation to the respondent's choice of language from their repertoire. Frequently, researchers are also interested in assessing the respondent's competency in the declared languages/varieties or codes. This is usually restricted to self-assessment, especially in the case of written questionnaires. Questions about 'for what purpose or to what end' may be tackled in different ways. Often researchers probe respondents' views, opinions and/or *attitudes* under this heading. In the following sections we will exemplify how the base question has been operationalised in questionnaires.

4.2.1 Seeking sociodemographic information

In order to examine which factors pertaining to an individual may shape or influence language behaviour, questionnaires seek information about a person's key sociodemographic characteristics including sex/gender, age, education and occupation. Depending on the specific focus of the research, other personal information may also be sought such as nationality, country of birth, length of residence in the 'new' country, marital status, ethnicity/race and religious affiliation. In written questionnaires these questions are usually constructed as closed-ended ones where a respondent chooses from a number of predetermined options. Options around sex/gender and age and marital status are or were generally considered relatively straightforward, although it should be noted that the binary nature of the gender category – female/male – is increasingly questioned and that the increased diversity in forms and types of cohabitation poses some challenges for the operationalisation of the variable 'marital status' in questionnaires. Response options relating to occupation are more complex, especially in the context of migrant settings. For example, a respondent's occupational status may have changed quite dramatically as a consequence of migration so that it may be necessary to probe occupational status in more than one location. Furthermore, the classificatory systems of occupations can also be quite different across cultures so that respondents may not be familiar with certain descriptors. If the identification of suitably clear response options is not possible, then it may be better to seek the information in an open-ended way, e.g., 'What is your occupation?' Most researchers tend to position these questions at the start of a questionnaire although there may be reasons for moving them to the end. For example, some individuals or groups may be reluctant to reveal certain types of personal information (e.g., country of birth, marital status, occupation, ethnicity, religious affiliation) because of cultural taboos, fear of persecution or other reasons. Placing these questions upfront may lead to an individual's decision not to fill in the questionnaire at all, whereas their positioning at the end may limit the number of questions left unanswered.

4.2.2 Constructing a linguistic history

Researchers often aim to obtain a linguistic history of the respondent, as this helps to contextualise and to understand the language-use patterns that they are investigating. If this information is sought through the questionnaire approach, then this is mostly done through closed-ended questions (see also Chapter 5). They usually cover such elements as languages known by parents or grandparents, linguistic environments in which the respondent has grown up, languages learned in educational contexts and a self-assessment of linguistic proficiency in the individual's languages. Self-evaluation of competence in a range of languages is usually sought through questions that ask respondents to rate their proficiency in the four skills (speaking, understanding/listening, reading and writing) against a three- to four-point scale (generally known as a Likert scale). For example:

Do you speak *language X*?
☐ well   ☐ not well   ☐ not at all
☐ very well   ☐ well   ☐ not well   ☐ not at all

Can you read *language X*?
☐ very well   ☐ well   ☐ not well   ☐ not at all

In some cases, the scaling is expressed more elaborately by providing *can do* statements about particular language activities. These *can do* statements may be formulated by the researcher with or without reference to benchmarks or frameworks used for self-assessment of language skills and proficiency, e.g., Common European Framework of Reference for Languages (2001). Examples include:

Please indicate which of these statements best reflects your speaking skills in *language X*
☐ I can hold a simple conversation about familiar topics.
☐ I can talk about complex matters.
☐ I can use simple greetings and other set phrases.

4.2.3   Exploring language use

The main aim of the questionnaire is to obtain detailed information on how individuals use their languages in various contexts and situations. As stated before, Fishman's question 'Who speaks what language to whom and when?' combined with the construct 'domain of language use' has formed the basis for the formulation of language language-use questions. Fishman saw 'domain' as a useful tool to structure the data about language language-use behaviour. He states that domains 'are defined, regardless of their number, in terms of institutional contexts and their congruent behavioral co-occurrences. They attempt to summate the major clusters of interaction that occur in clusters of multilingual settings and involving clusters of interlocutors' (Fishman 1972: 441). Later in this book we come back to the domain concept in the context of understanding the process of LS. Here our focus is on its role in structuring questions around language use. A domain is seen as a construct built around three key elements: interlocutors, topics and locales, with the latter comprising both time and place. Examinations of language use in New York's ethnolinguistically diverse neighbourhoods (e.g., Fishman et al. 1971) gave rise to the identification of five domains: the family, friendship, religion, education and employment.

These domains were seen as central to understanding both language behaviour and the dynamics of LM or LS in bi- or multilingual settings. Of course, depending on the specific context in which issues of LM and LS are studied, additional domains may feature in the questionnaire. For example, the transactional domain (e.g., shops, service encounters) and secular social settings (e.g., clubs, societies) are often included in research on migrant settings because of their possible relevance in LM/LS. For each of these domains, a set of questions is then formulated that takes account of the various interlocutors that are linked to a particular domain. For example, the family domain, also known as the home domain, will typically cover as interlocutors spouse/partner/wife/husband (a variety of nomenclature is used to describe these interlocutors), children, grandparents, grandchildren, siblings and members of the extended family, especially if they live in the same household or nearby. In other domains the range of interlocutors may be more limited. For example, for the workplace interlocutors may be restricted to work mates, colleagues, clients or customers and one's boss or manager. Similarly, the domain of religion or spiritual worship may distinguish only between fellow worshippers and the spiritual leader (priest, imam, rabbi etc.). Although the majority of language-use questions focuses primarily on the respondent's interaction with other speakers, generally labelled 'interlocutors', the influence of topic and locale is sometimes also examined. For example, in my own investigation of the language-use patterns of Dutch and German migrants in Australia (Pauwels 1986), I wanted to find out if the topic of conversation or the place where the conversation was held triggered a language switch between the same interlocutors. To explore this I formulated three questions for a range of interlocutors, mainly associated with the family and friendship domains, to probe the influence of topic and locale on their language choice:

- At home you are talking to your spouse about a phone call you received from a close Dutch/German friend of the family. What language or dialect do you use to talk about this to your spouse?

This question presented a *congruent* situation in terms of interlocutor, topic and locale; i.e., all elements are clearly associated with the domain of family or home.

- At home you are talking about a documentary or a film you have just seen on television. What language/dialect do you use to talk about this to your spouse?

This question represented a situation where the topic of conversation may trigger a language switch as it is related to a TV film/documentary presented in English.

- In the waiting room of a surgery where other people are waiting, you are talking about some everyday matters to your spouse. What language/dialect do you use with your spouse?

In this case the locale – a doctor's surgery and the presence of other people – may impact on language choice and cause a switch to the majority language, in this case English.

Although most questionnaires mainly focus on investigating spoken forms of language use, sometimes questions are introduced to examine a respondent's language choice for reading and writing purposes. This can cover language use by type of reading materials (e.g., personal correspondence, news media, books) and writing genres (e.g., shopping lists and personal notes, letters or, more recently, emails, tweets and blogs). Some researchers also cover 'private' or 'internal' speech, which refers to such language forms as silent prayers, dreaming and mental arithmetic.

The formulation of language-use questions tends to be both closed-ended and open-ended although with a predominance of the former, especially in written questionnaires. Respondents are usually given a range of precoded language options (scaled or not). For example, in response to the question 'What do you speak to the shopkeeper?' the following options could be given:

☐ Language X
☐ Language Y

or

☐ Language X only
☐ Language Y only
☐ Sometimes language X and sometimes language Y
☐ Mostly language X

Mostly language Y

or

☐ Language X only
☐ Language Y only
☐ A mixture of Language X and Language Y

Open-ended questions are usually kept to a minimum as there is often a reluctance to respond in an open-ended way. However, respondents are more willing to provide some additional information to some closed-ended questions. For example, if a question such as 'Are there any other people not mentioned in these questions with whom you are likely to speak X?' is included, then those who respond affirmatively to the question are usually happy to provide more detailed information.

4.3   QUESTIONS EXPLORING LANGUAGE ATTITUDES AND BELIEFS

4.3.1   The link between language attitude and language behaviour

It remains a contentious issue as to what extent beliefs about or attitudes towards language influence or shape actual linguistic behaviour (e.g., Ajzen and Fishbein 2005 for a review on the link between attitudes and behaviour). Yet many scholars working on endangered languages as well as those studying LM/LS in a variety of settings agree not only that the relationship between the two is worth exploring but also that attitudes may explain differential rates of LM and LS. In the context of language endangerment Bradley (2002: 1) writes, 'Why is it that one minority group assimilates and its language dies, while another one maintains its linguistic and cultural identity? Perhaps the crucial factor in language maintenance is the attitudes of the speech community concerning their language'. This is echoed by Wurm (2002: 11) when he states that

> one of the most important factors for the maintenance and reinvigoration of a threatened language is the attitude of the speakers towards their own language and the importance which they attach to it as a major symbol of their identity.

Many LM researchers working within the sociology of language approach also adopt this position and usually build attitudinal questions into questionnaires. When it comes to those working within a social psychological framework, the investigation of language attitudes and beliefs is central. These researchers see language attitudes as the key to understanding language behaviour, as we shall see in Chapters 5 and 7.

A mental rather than a behaviourist view of attitudes prevails in language attitudinal research focused on multilingualism. This entails seeing attitudes as 'an internal state aroused by stimulation of some type and which may mediate the organism's subsequent response' (Williams 1974: 21). Such a view poses a methodological challenge because it is an internal state rather than an observable fact or event that needs to be investigated. This has led to the development of a variety of methods and tools for measuring and exploring language attitudes, especially by social psychologists of language (see Chapter 5). Within the context of LM research two methods have prevailed: the inclusion of a range of attitudinal questions or statements in a questionnaire and the matched-guise technique. Here we shall explore the questionnaire approach; the matched-guise technique will be dealt with in the next chapter.

4.3.2 Types of attitudinal questions in questionnaires

In LM/LS research attitudinal questions target respondents' views, beliefs and attitudes towards their language(s) or language varieties or language practices, towards the maintenance of their 'first' language – the immigrant/heritage or minority language – and towards the learning of the heritage/minority and majority languages. Questions or statements around their language(s) may cover such issues as the importance of the heritage or minority language for expressing or maintaining identity (ethnic, cultural, symbolic) and its perceived functionality and status in the minority/migrant setting. Further questions may probe the respondent's view on how the minority or heritage language is perceived by members of the majority group and by other minority groups within the polity, and who should take responsibility for the maintenance of minority languages. Although open-ended questions have been used to probe language attitudes within a written questionnaire, this type of questioning approach is more useful in interviews or interviewer-administered questionnaires. The format preferred in written questionnaires is that of a set of statements expressing specific views or opinions to which the respondent is asked to reply via Likert-scale response options. Next are some examples of both (semi-) open-ended questions and closed-ended questions around language attitudes.

Open-ended questions

Example 1
Should the public schools in your region provide education in (*name of the minority/heritage language*) to children who have it as home language?
☐ yes, why ? . . . ☐ no, why not ? . . .

In this example a respondent's view towards responsibility for minority/heritage language education is probed.

Example 2

> Do you think it is important for your children to know (*name of the minority/heritage language*) to understand their heritage?
> ☐ yes, why ? ... ☐ no, why not ? ...

In this example a respondent's attitude towards the role of language in maintaining the minority culture is explored.

Example 3

> When you go to the market to sell a chicken, if two people offer the same price at the same time, one speaks Bai, another speaks Chinese, to whom would you sell the chicken?
> a. Bai speaker
> b. Chinese speaker
> c. either one
> d. neither one
>
> Why?

In this example the researcher Duan (2004) explores the respondent's view towards minority speakers and dominant language speakers.

Closed-ended questions and statements

Example 4

> Should the public schools in your region provide education in (*minority/heritage language*) to children who have it as home language?
> ☐ strongly agree   ☐ agree   ☐ neither agree nor disagree   ☐ disagree
> ☐ strongly disagree

This question seeks the same information as that mentioned in Example 1 but does so via Likert-scale responses.

Example 5

> It has been said that it is more important for children to be fluent in (*name of the dominant/majority*) than maintain (*name of the minority/heritage language*).
> ☐ strongly agree   ☐ agree   ☐ neither agree nor disagree   ☐ disagree
> ☐ strongly disagree

In this case an opinion is expressed via a statement attributed to a third party and the respondent is asked to express his or her (strong) agreement or (strong) disagreement with the statement.

> **Example 6**
> Which of the following statements reflects your opinion about (*name of minority/heritage language*) best?
> ☐ Giving up my language is like giving up an important part of my identity.
> ☐ I feel I can express myself best in (*name of language*) but I also like it that I can speak (*name of language*).
> ☐ I see myself as a bilingual, able to use two languages well in the relevant settings.
> ☐ Which language I speak has never mattered that much to me.
> ☐ I will continue speaking (*name of language*) but do not see value in making my children learn it.

In this example the respondent is asked to make a choice response out of a set of responses to an attitudinal question. Sometimes the respondent is asked to rank them in order of agreement or importance.

4.4 PROCESSING QUESTIONNAIRE DATA

As stated earlier, a questionnaire approach is best suited for macro-level studies of LM and LS. It generally allows for detailed data collection about language use and attitudes on (relatively) large samples (between 100 and well over 1000) within a reasonable amount of time. The inclusion of (sometimes detailed) sociodemographic information allows for the investigation of how certain personal characteristics influence language behaviour and how they shape attitudes towards language and LM. The closed-ended and multiple-choice questions lend themselves well to statistical processing and analyses. The existence of numerous statistical packages specifically developed for the social sciences (e.g., SPSS and SAS) has made it relatively easy for LM/LS researchers to submit their questionnaire data to both basic and more sophisticated statistical tests (e.g., t-test, chi-square, analysis of variation, regression analysis). Furthermore, the less-statistically trained language researcher has access to a wide range of guides to assist with processing, analysis and interpretation (e.g., Rietveld and Van Hout 1993; Sirkin 2006).

4.5   A FINAL NOTE ON QUESTIONNAIRES IN LM RESEARCH

In this chapter we have shown the value of using questionnaires in LM research. Although we alerted to the complexities and challenges surrounding the use of questionnaires in LM and LS research, we should stress again its main limitation: it gives us insight *not* into *actual* behaviour but only into *reported* behaviour. Although researchers have become quite sophisticated in question formulations and in building in questions that could expose contradictions or shed doubt on the veracity of some replies (e.g., commitment questions in language attitudinal questionnaires), there is no fail-safe solution to closing the gap between reported and actual behaviour. The latter needs to be established through other modes of data collection, including experiments or tests and observation (participant and otherwise), some of which we discuss in Chapter 5.

POINTS FOR DISCUSSION AND TASKS

1. Questionnaires are able to probe reported language use rather than actual language use. If you are not in a position to observe people's language behaviour and rely entirely on questionnaire data, what kind of strategies can you employ to reduce the potential gap between reported and actual language use?
2. Finding and selecting informants or participants for LM research has its challenges. How would you go about identifying and selecting participants for the following project: studying the language practices of Somali refugees in Stockholm.
3. Find three questionnaire-based studies dealing with the language practices of Korean migrants (and their offspring) in a European country, the United States and New Zealand, respectively. Compare the questionnaires in terms of type of questions and question formulation in relation to the research topic and discuss whether you would have opted for similar or different questions, and why.
4. The opinions of majority group members towards a linguistic minority are known to influence the language attitudes and even practices of minority group members. Devise a set of questions that probe how minority group members perceive the attitudes of the majority towards their language and its maintenance.
5. Your questionnaire is targeted at recent emigrants from rural Senegal into Marseille, France. These emigrants are in their

thirties and have had some education in their country. Discuss which language(s) you would use in the questionnaire, and why.

SUGGESTIONS FOR FURTHER READING

Dollinger, Stefan. 2012. The written questionnaire as a sociolinguistic data gathering tool. *Journal of English Linguistics* 40.1: 74–110.

This paper has some useful information on question formulation.

Fasold, Ralph. 1984. *The sociolinguistics of society*. Oxford: Basil Blackwell.

Chapter 4 of this sociolinguistic textbook is devoted to basic statistics that can be used in the analysis of questionnaire data.

Lieberson, Stanley. 1980. Procedures for improving sociolinguistic surveys on language maintenance and language shift. *International Journal of the Sociology of Language* 25: 11–28.

This is an early paper looking critically at the weaknesses of using surveys/ questionnaires in the study of LM and LS. It is also relevant reading for Chapters 3 and 4.

The Language Attrition website at the University of Groningen, the Netherlands, makes available a sample of sociolinguistic questionnaires that are used in the study of language attrition, loss and shift. It also provides information on coding and processing data from such question- naires: www.let.rug.nl/languageattrition/SQ.

Li Wei, and Melissa Moyer. Eds. 2008. *The Blackwell guide to research methods in bilingualism and multilingualism*. Oxford: Blackwell Publishing.

This handbook includes contributions that specifically cover question- naires (Codò) and the selection of informants (Lanza).

Holmes, Janet, and Kirk Hazen. Eds. 2014. *Research methods in sociolinguistics*. Oxford: Wiley Blackwell.

This edited collection includes contributions on questionnaires (Schleef) and one on statistical analysis (Guy).

5 Beyond surveys

Interviews, participant observation and experiments

5.1 BEYOND SURVEYS AND QUESTIONNAIRES

Talking with people about their language use (interviews) and observing how people use languages in a range of settings (participant observation) are probably the two most frequently used methods, besides questionnaires, in the exploration of LM and LS. Experiments and tests are another tool, although these are used primarily for investigating attitudes and linguistic proficiency.

Even when the research is more quantitatively focused, such as in large-scale language surveys, it is sometimes complemented with a small sample of interviews in which a more detailed discussion about language use and language choice takes place. Where the focus of the research is on the language behaviour and language choice of a specific community or group, such as Maori adults in Wellington, New Zealand; Bangladeshi children in London; Puerto Rican youngsters in New York or Turkish immigrant women in Hamburg, Germany, interviewing members of these groups and communities is the standard way of exploring relevant language issues. Participant observation is also a common way of investigating language behaviour as it allows researchers to observe actual linguistic behaviour and practices in various settings or locations rather than having to rely on self-reports.

In the following sections we will discuss these main 'other' tools for researching language practices in the context of LM and LS. Section 5.2 deals with the interview, followed by Section 5.3 on participant observation. In Section 5.4, we discuss the use of experiments in exploring attitudes towards language use. In Section 5.5, we touch upon some other 'methods' that are used in exploring questions of LM and LS. These could be collectively described as biographic and/or autobiographic narratives.

5.2 INTERVIEWS

We have repeatedly noted that the question 'Who speaks what language to whom, when, where and to what end/for which purpose?' has become the guiding beacon for the exploration of language-use patterns in multilingual settings, through either written questionnaires or interviews. In fact, if an interview is used to pursue this question in the context of macro-oriented research, then such an interview is best described as an interviewer-administered questionnaire. In such an interview, the content of questions will be very similar to that discussed in relation to written questionnaires. However, more attention may need to be paid to the formulation of questions. For example, using more open-ended questions may be more suitable in such situations. These give the interviewee greater opportunity to elaborate and/or refine answers. If the interview is recorded, it also gives the interviewer more material to work with. Furthermore, in interviews even more attention needs to be paid to the cultural appropriateness or sensitivity of questions, their formulation and the order in which they are asked (see Section 5.2.3). The most common type of interview in the context of LM and LS research, at least to date, is one where a researcher or interviewer is in the physical presence of the interviewee(s). In some instances interviews have been conducted by telephone. This channel of communication, however, does not offer the same opportunities that a face-to-face interview provides. It therefore tends to be used only when a concise set of questions needs to be answered. More recently, advances in information technology have opened up new ways of conducting language interviews using various video-conferencing tools. Where internet access is reliable video interviews may very well be an excellent alternative to the traditional face-to-face interview: visual contact is established with the interviewee; the recording of the interview (provided permission is obtained) may be less susceptible to failing equipment (the bane of any researcher/ interviewer!) and privacy and/or safety for both interviewee and interviewer may also be enhanced. We may very well see more of this type of interview being used in language research, but for now the face-to-face interview with an interviewer physically present is the most widespread tool.

Where interviews are used to complement rather than to undertake macro-oriented research on LM, the interviewees tend to be chosen from those who participated in the macro-survey. In most cases they are people expressing a willingness to participate in a follow-up interview rather than a carefully selected group (see our comments about sampling in Chapter 4). Open-ended questions tend to dominate in these interviews, allowing participants to freely report their language patterns and practices, to provide a personal narrative about their language experiences and history and to express attitudes and opinion about language matters without being constrained by interviewer-imposed formulations (see also Section 5.5 for language memoirs and narratives).

An added bonus of interviews is that they can constitute a valuable resource for exploring linguistic competence. Phenomena such as code-switching, code-mixing, transfers and other contact features may be observed within the conduct of the interview. Although participant observation is the preferred method to make an assessment of actual language use and of language practices in action, interviews also provide, albeit in a more limited fashion, an opportunity to observe and assess linguistic practices and skills. These actual competencies can then be compared, formally or informally, with the participants' self-assessments of linguistic skills. A typical example is where an interviewee claims to 'always' speak the minority or heritage language with their spouse and yet, when the spouse drops in on the interview, the opposite is demonstrated. Views expressed by interviewees about their code-switching and code-mixing practices also often differ from observed practices. A poignant example of that occurred in one of my interviews with a Dutch-born man in Australia. He responded to my question '*Is het moeilijk om de twee talen gescheiden te houden?*' (Is it difficult to keep the two languages separate?), with '*Nee hoor,* we mixen *onze talen niet echt,* but our children do' (Not really, we don't really mix our languages, but our children do'). His answer contained a morpho-logically integrated lexical transfer, *mixen,* and an instance of code-switching, 'but our children do'. Interviews can also incorporate actual tests of specific linguistic features. Here we can see the influence of the sociolinguistic interview as developed by William Labov (e.g., Labov 1971) on the structure of interviews linked to language use. For example, interviewees can be asked to describe a scene or a picture in their languages to ascertain syntactic influences, lexical transfers or grammatical features. In Clyne's (1967) pioneering research on German-English bilinguals in Australia, the interviewees were asked to describe in German a number of scenes. Some of these scenes could be said to trigger associations with the 'home' country, others with the new country and yet others could have an ambiguous association. One of the photographs used by Clyne (1967) was of people sitting on a beach. Many interviewees used the lexical transfer 'beach' in their German language description. As German has grammatical gender and lexical transfers need to be grammatically integrated, the interviewee had to assign a gender to the word, e.g., *der* Beach (masculine), *die* Beach (feminine) or *das* Beach (neuter). This allowed the researcher to explore the integration of certain lexical transfers in a systematic way. In other cases interviewees are asked to talk about a major event or experience in their lives or about their experience with LM or LS; these conversations often produce quite lengthy narratives that, in turn, can be subjected to a linguistic and discursive analysis (see Section 5.4 on linguistic autobiographies). Both of these analyses assist in shedding light on the linguistic history or biography of the interviewee and in better understanding their language choices and practices.

A key contributor to a successful interview is, of course, the interviewer. For interviews that involve multiple languages and focus on language practices, the (ethno)linguistic profile and linguistic competencies of the interviewer are critical elements in conducting the interview. Other key factors are the choice of language(s) for the interview and the formulation of questions. Each of these elements warrants some discussion.

5.2.1 The interviewer

Here we start from the assumption that the topic of the interview and the research project dictate that the interviewer has knowledge of the language(s) under investigation and needs to be able to use these languages in the interview. For interviews that concern language use, attitudes and competence, the interviewer's (perceived) group membership in terms of language is particularly relevant. Of course the in- or out-group status of an interviewer is an important element in all forms of social research. For language research, though, there is the added issue of linguistic features that characterise someone as an in- or out-group member. Scholars working in multilingual situations are well aware of the sensitivities around this, especially in dynamic language situations where there is evidence of language loss or shift. Being considered as an in-group interviewer in such situations is often a complex matter; it is a case of being able not only to speak the language(s) of the interviewee but also to meet the often contradictory linguistic expectations of interviewees. For example, in my research on the language dynamics in first- and second-generation Greek Australians, I employed a graduate student who was a second-generation Greek Australian. Her linguistic experiences and trajectory were very much in line with that of her peers. Her linguistic competences in English and Greek were accepted by her interviewees as 'typical' of her status as a young, second-generation Greek Australian woman. She knew when to speak Greek and when to speak English, when code-switching was appropriate and when not. In brief, she displayed the appropriate linguistic profile and behaviour for a genuine in-group member and thus met their expectations. In another project involving Dutch Australians, I had opted similarly for a female graduate student who was a second-generation Dutch Australian. Although fully accepted by her interviewees as a member of the Dutch Australian community, her linguistic profile was considered at odds with those of many of her peers: she was still able to converse relatively well in Dutch, especially when speaking to members of the first generation. She told me that her interviewees often commented about her proficiency in Dutch: they were surprised that she could still converse well in Dutch, as their own children had lost this capacity. Some praised her (and her parents) for keeping up the language, but others reacted in a more jealous way, suspicious of how she had managed to maintain her Dutch. Another linguistic scenario concerns an interviewer who belongs to the wider (ethno) linguistic community and is a fluent speaker of the interviewee's language(s) but is not a member of the local community under investigation. This often occurs in language research in migrant settings: for example, a Turkish-speaking researcher from Turkey conducts interviews with immigrant Turks living in Germany. While this type of interviewer may not have an impact on the language used by interviewees belonging to the first generation, younger (second-generation) German Turks may find the linguistic competence of Turkish displayed by such an interviewer intimidating and may therefore avoid using Turkish altogether. Another pattern is represented by an interviewer who is ethnically, culturally and linguistically a member of an out-group (sometimes belonging to the linguistic majority in the region), but who has acquired proficiency in the language(s) under examination. These different (ethno)linguistic profiles will impact on how the interviewers are perceived by their interviewees and, consequently, how they talk about their language experiences and patterns. In some cases, the ethnolinguistic and cultural affinity between interviewer and interviewee creates a greater sense of mutual trust so that the interviewee may be more willing to disclose information that would not be shared with out-group interviewers. In other cases, such affinity may create suspicion about the purpose of the research, raising questions like 'Why investigate the language behaviour of your own group as you should be familiar with it!' Being interviewed by an out-group member may create similar ambivalent reactions: pride or surprise because their language behaviour is of interest to outsiders, or suspicion and distrust because the interviewer may be 'policing' their linguistic behaviour. Of course these are only a few examples of how the in-group and out-group membership status of the interviewer can influence the interview.

5.2.2 The language(s) of the interview

Students planning to undertake research interviews in multilingual settings often ask which language to use when interviewing informants. If the interview is part of ethnographic fieldwork involving living in the community and undertaking participant observation, then it may be more transparent which language or language variety to use when conducting interviews. After all, if a researcher/interviewer has spent considerable time in the group or community, he or she will have acquired some communicative competence in the language(s) of the community thus aiding the choice of language or language practice for interviews. Where interviews are not part of such in-depth fieldwork, it is more difficult to decide which language or language practice to opt for. Often the interviewer will not have met the interviewee beforehand and the interview may well be the one and only encounter with him or her. Of course most researchers will have gathered some preliminary sociolinguistic information about the group or community to assist them in this choice. Furthermore, one's (perceived) status as a linguistic in-group or out-group member may also influence the language choice for the interviews. For example, if the interviewer is perceived as an out-group member belonging to the majority group, bilingual interviewees may sometimes prefer to speak in the majority language to demonstrate their skills, whereas others may opt for the minority language to 'check' how competent the interviewer is in that language. Another issue that has the potential to affect the interviewer's linguistic behaviour is whether or not to accommodate to the interviewee's code-switching or mixing behaviour. If the interviewer is a member of the same ethnolinguistic group and shares the linguistic practices of the interviewee, it would be most natural to engage in switching and mixing practices. Where code-switching is not a practice of the interviewer, for whatever reason, then its introduction in the interview situation would probably make sense only if it serves a particular purpose; for example, it may help in building trust or expressing solidarity with the interviewee or may be a ploy to examine the interviewee's code-switching patterns.

5.2.3　Formulation of questions for the interview

In Chapter 4 we discussed various aspects of question formulation, including the order of questions, to take account of cultural sensitivities or practices. The importance of phrasing questions in a culturally appropriate manner is even more relevant in an interview situation. Although asking questions about language use may be seen as less confrontational or intrusive than those about one's religion, political allegiances, financial state, health regimes or sexual practices, interviewers do need to be alert to question formulation. In some cultures, direct questions about age, earning capacity or marital status are perfectly acceptable: How old are you? How much do you earn? Are you married? or even, 'Why are you not married?' In other communities a more indirect approach to questions is needed. In some cases, it is preferable not to seek information through questions but through statements and comments or for the interviewer to share some 'personal' information in order to obtain a response. Although the context of research undertaken by Eades (2013) is not oriented towards LM and LS, her discussion of how to ask questions when speaking with Australian Aboriginal people using English is a poignant example of the importance of appropriate question formulation in linguistically and culturally diverse settings.

5.2.4　Analysing interview data

In the case of interviewer-administered questionnaires, data analysis will be treated most likely in the same way as that associated with written questionnaires, i.e., by statistical analysis. Although such interviews may be recorded, the recording is used more often as an *aide-memoire* rather than to complement information (however, see Section 5.2). For other types of interviews, a (video-)taped record is essential as its analysis will rely on the transcribed report. There are various types and protocols for transcribing interviews. Which one to choose will depend on the kind of analysis to be undertaken. The most common type of analysis used in LM research is a content analysis: the transcribed text is searched for themes, topics, phrases and terms that aid and organise the documentation of reported language use. Increasingly, interviews are also subjected to various forms of discourse analysis, especially if they focus on questions of language use, multilingualism and identity (e.g., Gardner and Martin-Jones 2012).

5.3　PARTICIPANT OBSERVATION

Participant observation is a research technique intrinsically associated with anthropology but also widely used in sociolinguistic and linguistic documentation work (e.g., Bernard 2006; Johnstone 2000; Wei and Moyer 2008). Participant observation is a component of an ethnographic approach that requires 'the intensive involvement of the researcher in a given social setting in order to describe and identify, through the use of a variety of complementary research techniques, the cultural patterns and regularities that structure and perpetuate a society' (Poplack 1979: 60). Its use within sociolinguistics is associated with the study of variation in language and with the examination of language choices in multilingual settings. In the latter case, participant observation has taken several forms. These variations are linked to the type of setting in which the research takes place. For example, if the target community is a (small) rural community that is relatively isolated, then the researcher may in fact live in the community for a period of time, participating in daily activities, rituals and events to which he or she has been granted access. Susan Gal's detailed study of bilinguals in Oberwart, Austria (Gal 1979), is a well-known example. She lived in the village for some months where she observed the villagers going about their daily business. She also accompanied some of them when they went to neighbouring towns and observed how contact with outsiders influenced their language practices. If the research locale is urban, then the researcher may decide to regularly participate in a range of events, meetings and activities that involve the group and/or individuals in the research but may not 'live' in the community. The majority of in-depth studies on immigrant communities have opted for this approach. Zentella's work (1997) with Puerto Rican children in New York is a good illustration of this urban approach. Either way, the researcher establishes close and regular contact with the community over an extended period of time.

Using participant observation to examine language behaviour and language practices in multilingual settings is not significantly different from its use to examine other social and cultural phenomena. It therefore shares with those the benefits and weaknesses associated with observing people's behaviour (see, e.g., De Walt and De Walt 2011 for more information on participant observation as a method in general). The main benefit of participant observation in LM and LS research is the opportunity for direct observation of the language practices associated with the question 'Who speaks what language to whom and when?' The scale and scope of the study will determine which domains, events and activities will be subjected to observation. If the focus is on language choice and language use in multilingual families, then participant observation mainly takes place in the home and related familial settings. Typical activities included in this setting are family meal times, family visits and outings, children playing and adults-only interaction. Rubino's (1993, 2014) studies on trilingual Sicilian Australian families in Sydney are a clear demonstration of the use of participant observation in studying language patterns in families. If the aim is to document the language practices of a small group of individuals who may or may not be related, then the researcher may wish to observe the individuals in a variety of settings undertaking a range of activities. Sometimes the focus could be on a specific domain or setting rather than on a particular group or individuals. For example, Goldstein (1997) is a study of bilingual patterns on the shop floor in a Canadian workplace that relies heavily on participant observation. My own work on Dutch Australians who speak a Dutch dialect – Limburgs – included regular participant observation of some participants' social activities surrounding the event of Carnival. This regional Dutch group has a strong cultural tradition associated with this pre-Lent (Catholic) celebration that involves various rituals, parades and the selection of a Prince Carnival (Pauwels 1986; see also Chapter 8).

In addition, participant observation allows for the recording of actual language use and an assessment of linguistic competencies. Although the primary focus in LM and LS research is on discovering and describing language practices that may be indicative of LS rather than on assessing the proficiency speakers have of their languages, the latter may shed light on the process of LS. For example, if a person has very limited skills in one of the languages, the chances are that he or she will rely more heavily on the other language. This in turn may affect the language choice in an encounter. Similarly, observation over a prolonged period of time may reveal the increased use of code-switching, which could be a sign of LS. Furthermore, if participant observation forms part of a multimethod approach to examining language use, then the researcher can contrast actual language behaviour with reported language behaviour.

Most forms of participant observation go beyond simple observation by a silent or unengaged researcher/fieldworker. This leads to the famous observer's paradox: according to Labov (1972: 209) 'the aim of linguistic research in the community must be to find out how people talk when they are not being systematically observed; yet we can only obtain these data by systematic observation'. In addition the field-worker's own language use can influence that of the 'observed' participants. Although the plight of the fieldworker engaged in participant observation is similar to that of the interviewer in multilingual settings, the impact may be more drastic because the fieldworker participates in a variety of contexts, all of which may have their own linguistic characteristics. How researchers deal with this is influenced by the research paradigm within which they place their research. Those working within a positivistic paradigm tend to focus on minimising the fieldworker's impact, whereas acceptance of the impact of a researcher is the more likely stance of those working within a social constructivist paradigm or adopting a participatory approach.

Another element linked to the observer's paradox in linguistic research is the need to go beyond note-taking (for more details on how to write and analyse field notes, see De Walt and De Walt 2011) and to audio-record or, where possible, to video-record the various interactions. The impact of recording devices on the participants' behaviour is well acknowledged by researchers (e.g., Clemente 2008; Erickson 1982; Milroy 1987); when working in environments where such technology is scarce or even unknown, the impact will be greater than in communities or groups with extensive use of various communication technologies. Indeed the ever-expanding use of mobile communication devices such as smartphones, handheld video-recorders and lapel microphones have meant that most communities not only are familiar with them but also make multiple use of them. Hence their use by a researcher is less likely to drastically alter the nature of the interaction.

The data obtained through participant observation include extensive field notes about language practices and choices and audio and audio-visual recordings of the observed events. The processing and analysis of these data can be done in various ways; indeed, researchers now have access to an arsenal of software to analyse qualitative data on language. For example, the Language Archive at the Max Planck Institute in Nijmegen lists numerous tools to transcribe, annotate and analyse audio and video language data (https://tla.mpi.nl/tools/). In terms of analysis, De Walt and De Walt (2011) provide detailed information on not only how to write but also how to analyse one's field notes. As to language recordings, these can be submitted to various forms of textual analysis (see Section 5.2.4).

5.4 EXPERIMENTS – MATCHED-GUISE TECHNIQUE

In language-oriented research, testing and experiments are methodological tools typically associated with the investigation of linguistic proficiency and linguistic phenomena rather than with language use. However, the matched-guise technique (MGT) is one type of experiment that is commonly used in social psychological studies of multilingualism and of LM and LS, with specific reference to language attitudes. Developed by Wallace Lambert and colleagues in the 1960s (Lambert 1967; Lambert et al. 1960) in the context of Canadian bilingualism, the original version of MGT aimed at testing attitudes towards specific languages by asking respondents to listen to recordings made by competent bilingual speakers. In the MGT informants are unaware that some passages are read by the same speakers using different languages, hence their responses reveal attitudes towards the language or language variety rather than towards differences in speakers. The respondents are asked to rate these speakers according to certain features (e.g., friendliness, competence, intelligence, likeability), using sets of semantic differential scales typically around the notions of status or solidarity. For example, Bettoni and Gibbons (1988: 32) used the following adjectives in rating scales to examine Italian migrants' attitudes towards Italian (dialect, standard and mixed) varieties and English found in the Italo-Australian speech community:

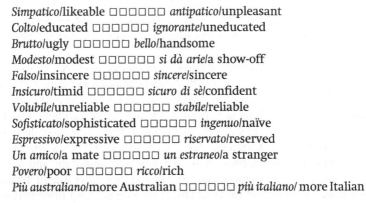

Simpatico/likeable □□□□□□ *antipatico*/unpleasant
Colto/educated □□□□□□ *ignorante*/uneducated
Brutto/ugly □□□□□□ *bello*/handsome
Modesto/modest □□□□□□ *si dà aria*/a show-off
Falso/insincere □□□□□□ *sincere*/sincere
Insicuro/timid □□□□□□ *sicuro di sè*/confident
Volubile/unreliable □□□□□□ *stabile*/reliable
Sofisticato/sophisticated □□□□□□ *ingenuo*/naïve
Espressivo/expressive □□□□□□ *riservato*/reserved
Un amico/a mate □□□□□□ *un estraneo*/a stranger
Povero/poor □□□□□□ *ricco*/rich
Più australiano/more Australian □□□□□□ *più italiano*/ more Italian

The original MGT was felt to be rather artificial and as a result a number of modifications were made to overcome this impression. For example, Bourhis and Giles (1976: 14) left the 'lab' setting behind and tested attitudes towards Welsh and English amongst theatregoers in Wales. Instead of being exposed to language passages read in an experimental setting, participants were actual theatregoers attending a performance and the language 'passages' in Welsh and English were real announcements during the interval. Here is the English version:

> Good evening ladies and gentlemen, may we have your attention for a moment. We are conducting a short audience survey to help plan future programs. You will find questionnaire forms in the foyer. We would be most grateful if you could complete the questionnaire forms and return them to the box office this evening. Thank you for your cooperation.

Another problem of the MGT concerns finding speakers who 'sound' competent and natural in all the languages or varieties to be tested. This is particularly the case in immigrant language settings where different generations of speakers vary significantly in their linguistic competencies. Typically, members of the first generation could produce speech samples that sound 'native-like' in their first language and (some of) its varieties such as regional dialects and the standard language. They are unlikely to be able to produce the same range of varieties for the majority language of their new environment, with most able to produce only a (heavily) accented version of the language. Conversely, the second generation is likely to be able to produce speech samples of majority language varieties that sound native-like but could not do so for the heritage or home language. For example, in Callan and Gallois (1982: 349) no details were given of the speakers who produced the voices other than stating that they were 'several young people who spoke both Italian and English with native accents'. If these voices were to represent the linguistic situation of Italo-Australian young people, then the sociolinguistic reality of most young second-generation Italo-Australians was ignored. In the sociolinguistic make-up of the Italian community in Australia (e.g., Cavallaro 2010; Rubino 2014) only young Italo-Australians who are well educated (probably university students who have undertaken some formal study of Italian at university) are likely to produce native-like sounding samples of both standard English and standard Italian. In fact the majority of second-generation Italo-Australians who still use the home language speak an Italian dialect and have limited proficiency in standard Italian, making this experiment rather unreliable. Bettoni and Gibbons (1988), both linguists, were more attuned to this issue and in their matched-guise study they resorted to a compromise to deal with the complex sociolinguistic reality:

> Even in Italy, where professional actors are available, it has proven impossible to find one single person to be able to speak both Venetian and Sicilian with a plausible native accent. In Australia, there was the added difficulty of using the same person for both English and the ethnic varieties. Between one and several speakers, a compromise was reached in choosing first two young men of the second generation whose respective dialects and English were equally native, and whose Regional Italian had been improved by several years of school and university study. (Bettoni and Gibbons 1988: 19)

Despite these 'shortcomings' the MGT has been widely used to probe attitudes towards minority languages in indigenous and immigrant settings. The analysis of MGT is statistically oriented, usually involving a principal components analysis (e.g., Drager 2014; Giles and Powesland 1975). In Chapter 7, the value of attitudinal research in understanding the dynamics of LM and LS will be explored.

5.5 BIOGRAPHIC AND AUTOBIOGRAPHIC NARRATIVES

Some studies of LM and LS that are primarily qualitative in orientation draw upon data that are less commonly used in this type of social science research. They include various forms of narratives mainly produced by speakers themselves (though not exclusively), such as diaries or journals, autobiographies, language memoirs and correspondence. These data have the capacity to 'offer insights into people's private worlds' (Pavlenko 2007: 164) and provide another perspective on language choices and practices in bi- and multilingual settings. Although their analysis has value on their own, these data are probably most powerful when they are used in complementarity with some of the data sources described earlier.

5.5.1 Diaries or journals

Keeping notes and diaries on developments in language acquisition, and recording feelings, experiences and activities relating to language learning, are tools frequently used in the study of child bilingualism and in research on second- and foreign-language learning. Studies of child bilingualism usually involve a parent or caregiver and, sometimes, an external researcher, engaging in a detailed case study of the child or children. Besides regular recordings and testing the child, the parent/researcher usually keeps detailed notes or a diary on the linguistic development and practices of the bilingual child. Although most of these studies focus primarily on language acquisition, the notes recorded in such diaries may very well provide insights into language choices and language preferences over a given time. This is indeed very likely as the authors of these types of diaries are often linguistic experts attuned to keeping field notes (e.g., Leopold 1939–1949; Ronjat 1913; Saunders 1988; Taeschner 1983).

In the context of second and foreign language learning the diaries are usually written by the learners themselves, either prompted by the teacher and/or researcher or out of personal interest. If prompted by a researcher, diary entries tend to be guided by a set of parameters or questions that the learner should comment on. Studies that focus on language learning experiences of minority or heritage language speakers are those most relevant for the field of LM and LS. For example, Hinton's (2001) study examines language attitudes, practices and views of Asian American university students in relation to the heritage language and English based on excerpts from the students' diaries. Students comment on their experiences of learning English, the often alienating or hostile reactions of other students at school, on trying to maintain or being forced to maintain the heritage language at home, on gradually losing the ability to speak the home language and on attempts to revitalise its use. Drawing upon diary data to discover patterns of language use is becoming more widespread in the study of multilingualism, LM and LS. An early example is Romaine (1983), who reviews the use of language diaries in the study of minorities. Although diary data have increasingly been added to studies dealing with minority and heritage language speakers (e.g., Lawson and Sachdev 2000, 2004; Li and Tse 2002; Rubino 2006), Starks and Lee (2010: 242) comment that 'the use of language diaries as a methodological tool for the study of language use is typically relegated to secondary status'. Their own study dealing with Korean-English bilingual families in New Zealand places data drawn from language diaries centre stage. They conclude that 'the study shows how language diaries can be an important tool for the study of community language use. Language diaries have the potential to provide detailed analyses of when and what language is used in a wide range of contexts' (Starks and Lee 2010: 243). Furthermore, they observed that self-reports about language use and language practices noted in the diaries were very similar to those reported through questionnaire-based findings in other studies on Korean in New Zealand (Johri 1998; Park 2001; Starks and Youn 1998). Yet the diary data had the advantage that 'they provide a more sophisticated assessment of language use because respondents do not restrict their comments to predefined categories' (Starks and Lee 2010: 248).

5.5.2 Autobiographies and language memoirs

To date, the autobiographies used in bilingualism and LM research are mainly oral narratives collected by researcher/interviewers, sometimes over an extended period of time. Although these interviews are not identical to the ones described previously, they do pose similar challenges for the interviewer, especially in terms of language choice. The written autobiographies that exist are mainly those of researchers themselves. Furthermore, autobiographies and language memoirs tend to focus on the writer's experiences of learning the new language rather than on using or maintaining the first, minority or heritage language. For example, Dykman's (1999) doctoral dissertation on second-language acquisition collected language memoirs from a range of students about their language learning experiences (for autobiographies, see, e.g., Ogulnick 1999; Santana 1999). An engagement with the writers' two or more languages is found in Besemeres' work on language memoirs including some literary ones (e.g., Besemeres 2002, 2004; Besemeres and Wierzbicka 2007; see also Ryang 2008). Kramsch (2005) is an analysis of literary works by authors such as Elias Canetti, Eva Hoffmann, Alice Kaplan and Yoko Tawada, who wrote about their bilingual learning experiences, about living in and with multiple languages in their 'new' or 'adopted' language. Although her analysis is geared towards enriching foreign-language pedagogy, such literary narratives may also be of value in LM research. Finally, in a paper that reviews the value of autobiographic narratives in applied linguistic research, Pavlenko (2007: 180) urges researchers to move beyond content analysis and to include discursive analyses. She also expresses a note of caution about their use in research linked to language learning and multilingualism. Autobiographic narratives allow insights into a person's private world, making them both unique and appealing. However, their appealing nature does make them also

> dangerous data sources as their immediacy may force researchers to disregard the line between life and text reality and to forget that narratives constitute, rather than reflect, reality. Pavlenko (2007: 180)

5.5.3 Correspondence

Writing letters to family and friends was for many migrants the main, if not the only way of keeping in touch and communicating with relatives in the 'homeland(s)'. Such material is another potentially interesting source of data for LM and LS research. Like language memoirs, diaries or autobiographies they may contain narratives about language experiences and language choices that aid a better understanding of the process of LM or LS. This is especially the case if the correspondence spans a considerable number of years. For example, the letters may display increasing evidence of interference and transference phenomena from the majority language into the heritage language. There may be passages that demonstrate code-switching between the languages, leading ultimately, in some cases, to the sole or dominant use of the majority language in the correspondence. In her study of some Dutch migrant families in New Zealand, Folmer (1991, 1992) was given access to correspondence between them and their families. Although her main focus was on analysing them to examine linguistic features of attrition, she did observe that increased attrition of grammatical elements went hand in hand with a reduced use of the heritage language, eventually leading to LS.

POINTS FOR DISCUSSION AND TASKS

1. In this chapter we reviewed some data collection methods that are mainly associated with qualitatively oriented research. Can you think of any other data methods that would enhance the study of LM or LS?
2. Hymes (1962) developed a model to analyse speech events. It contained sixteen components and is known by the acronym S.P.E.A.K.I.N.G. Familiarise yourself with this model and explore how it could be used in LM research.
3. Design a matched-guise experiment for the following scenario: Compare the attitudes of adolescent Turkish second-generation men (in any country) towards the Turkish spoken in Turkey versus the Turkish used in their (immigrant) community. You can change the language (e.g., Italian, Hindi, Polish instead of Turkish) and focus on women instead of men, or adults instead of adolescents.
4. You have been invited to attend a Greek wedding that is taking place in an immigrant country. You have been told that this is an excellent event to witness language-use patterns among Greek immigrants and their offspring. How would you go about researching this event to document language practices and shed light on LM or LS?
5. If you were to write your own language memoirs involving multi-lingualism, what criteria, issues or questions would guide your writing? In which language(s) would you write, and why? If you do not have a second language, then set this up as an interview with a multilingual person.

SUGGESTED FURTHER READING

De Walt, Kathleen, and Billie R. De Walt. 2011. *Participant observation: a guide for fieldworkers*. Plymouth: AltaMira Press.

This guide covers all aspects of undertaking participant observation in the field.

Holmes, Janet and Kirk Hazen. Eds. 2014. *Research methods in sociolinguistics*. Oxford: Wiley Blackwell.

This edited collection includes contributions on sociolinguistic interviews (Hoffman), experimental methods including MGT (Drager) and discourse analysis (Holmes).

Li Wei, and Melissa Moyer. Eds. 2008. *The Blackwell guide to research methods in bilingualism and multilingualism*. Oxford: Blackwell Publishing.

This handbook includes contributions that specifically cover interviews (Codò), audio- and videorecording (Clementi), transcription (Turell and Moyer) and types of discourse and narrative analyses (Cashman, Blackledge and Pavlenko).

Other books and papers that cover relevant material on interviews, participant observation, the MGT and linguistic (auto)biographies include the following.

Gardner, Sheena, and Marilyn Martin-Jones. Eds. 2012. *Multilingualism, discourse and ethnography*. New York: Routledge.

Milroy, Lesley and Matthew Gordon. 2003. *Sociolinguistics: methods and interpretation*. Oxford: Blackwell.

Milroy, Lesley, Li Wei and Suzanne Moffatt. 1991. Discourse patterns and fieldwork strategies in urban settings: some methodological problems for researchers of bilingual communities. *Journal of Multilingual and Multicultural Development* 12.4: 287–300.

PART III
Identifying and understanding trends and patterns in the dynamics of language maintenance and shift

6 Trends and patterns in language maintenance and shift

In Part II we described various data collection methods and tools that have been used or developed to investigate language practices and patterns associated with our two main settings: migrant communities and territorial linguistic minorities. In Part III we move to a discussion of findings emanating from the wealth of studies that made use of these various methods to examine questions of LM and LS. Indeed there have been hundreds, if not thousands of studies around the world examining LM and LS in our two main settings. Given this wealth, it is not surprising that a multitude of factors and forces influencing the process of LM or LS has been unearthed. Here we will focus on those factors that have been studied most widely and on discussing common trends or patterns that have been observed across this wide variety of studies. Some factors influencing LM and LS concern individual characteristics (variables) such as age, gender, educational background, social class, race/ethnicity, religious affiliation or marital status. Other factors apply mainly to groups. These include but are not limited to, the numerical strength of a group, its settlement patterns and its linguistic or cultural similarity to the dominant or majority group. Further factors that influence LM and LS relate to the majority group and/or the polity within which the minority finds itself. They include, for example, the majority's attitude towards the minority, its language and culture and the existence of laws and policies that support or oppose linguistic diversity, bi- and multilingualism. In this chapter, our discussion of common trends and patterns centres around two focal points: in Section 6.1 our focus is on variables and characteristics of the speaker or language user; i.e., this concerns the 'who' in the central question of 'Who speaks what language to whom and when?' The other focal point relates to other elements of the key question – to whom and when – that refer to contexts of use or domains. These will be taken up in Section 6.2. In both sections we will try to establish whether a specific speaker characteristic or context can be clear-cut, i.e., clearly enhancing LM or clearly leading to LS.

In Chapter 7 we will review some typologies, models and theories that have been developed in an attempt to account for intergroup differences. Before embarking on describing these trends and patterns it is worthwhile noting that studies investigating factors have often foregrounded the ones that stimulate or promote LS rather than LM. This may well be linked to a rather dominant view in this field that LS is in fact the societal norm. Indeed, in a paper on reversing LS, Fishman (2013: 466) posited that LS is the societal norm. Although he was commenting on the fate of immigrant languages in the United States, the same could be said for the fate of the majority of immigrant languages and many territorial linguistic minorities elsewhere in the world.

6.1 WHO *SPEAKS WHAT LANGUAGE TO WHOM, WHEN:* SPEAKER CHARACTERISTICS

In addressing the question 'Who speaks what language to whom, when and to what end?', the 'who' has received most attention. Macro-level studies that draw upon large population samples focus mainly on the speaker or user and on speaker-related variables such as age, gender, race/ethnicity, education, generation and marital situation or type. The variable 'generation' is particularly relevant for immigrant settings as it distinguishes between those speakers who migrated from the 'home' territory and those who were born and raised in the new (migrant) territory. The variable 'marital situation' tries to establish whether a person is in a marriage or similar relationship with someone from the same ethnolinguistic group or from another group, either another ethnolinguistic minority or the majority group. The former is referred to as an endogamous relationship and the latter as exogamous. There are of course more person-specific variables (e.g., religious affiliation, income, social class) that can have an impact on language use, but here we cover the more widely studied ones: generation, age, gender and marital situation. Given the centrality of ethnicity (race) in understanding the differences in LM and LS patterns, this variable will be treated in Chapter 7.

6.1.1   Generation

The generation a speaker belongs to is one of the most clear-cut factors in the process of LS. This is especially the case for migrant communities where there is almost universal evidence that the second generation maintains the heritage language less than the first generation and that its use in subsequent generations further declines. The generation that migrated to the new territory is generally more reliant on the heritage language and will take longer to acquire the dominant or majority language than the generation born in the new environment. Although members of the second generation may very well spend their preschool years in a largely heritage language-speaking environment, they soon encounter the majority language through education or through inter-action with older siblings. In a majority of cases it becomes their dominant language, in terms of both usage and proficiency. In territor-ial minority groups, the notion of generation is more tied to the variable of age: except in situations where the minority language has undergone considerable revival in recent times, it is older speakers who use the language (much) more than younger speakers.

6.1.2 Age

How much and how often the heritage or minority language is used has been found to vary, sometimes considerably, across age categories. For migrant settings, for example, Clyne's (1991) analysis of LS in first- and second-generation migrants in Australia, revealed that the oldest age groups (fifty years and above) within the first generation displayed the lowest levels of LS. Within the second generation the pattern is reversed: the older the speaker, the more likely they are to have undergone LS. These results are not unexpected or unusual: older first-generation speakers rely more heavily on their first language than younger ones, partly because of their more limited proficiency in the majority language and/or because of more limited exposure to that language. The latter is especially the case when first-generation migrants retire from the workforce and their social networks are located mainly within their own group. In the case of the second generation, younger speakers are more likely to use the heritage lan-guage than older ones, because its use is primarily for interaction with older (first-generation) speakers: grandparents and older relatives, friends and acquaintances.

When we look at language use in the lifespan of a first-generation speaker, a not unusual pattern is one where the heritage language is dominant in the initial stages of the settlement process, followed by an increased use of the dominant/majority language, especially during one's working years and then a possible return to a greater use of the heritage language upon retreat from the work force. The pattern for a second-generation speaker is in some ways similar, albeit for different reasons: if the second-generation speaker grows up in a family environ-ment that has the heritage language as its dominant code, then his or her early years may immerse him or her in the heritage language. However, the use of the heritage language tends to recede quite a bit during adolescence and early adulthood when social and institutional networks require or desire more use of the dominant language. This may be followed by a period of increased use of the heritage language when there is greater need to care for elderly parents or relatives. However, with the passing of that generation the use of the majority language tends to take over again.

6.1.3 Gender

Studies across migrant and territorial minority settings have frequently discovered gender differences in language use and choice. Whereas the impact of generation and age on LS is more consistent across groups and thus more 'predictable', this cannot be said for the gender/sex variable. It is not possible to claim that women maintain the heritage or minority language better or longer than men or vice versa. Nevertheless, studies focusing on gender and LM/LS have unearthed some regularly recurring patterns worth discussing. Evidence from large-scale surveys (e.g., Census surveys) often points towards women's greater use of the heritage language in migrant settings. Although there are significant interethnic differences, Table 6.1 illustrates this pattern for first-generation women and men across four Census periods – 1976 to 1996 – in Australia.

The table demonstrates that despite significant interethnic variation, the women belonging to these birthplace groups shift (somewhat) less than the men. Similar differences have been observed in other countries, including the United States (Stevens 1986), Canada (De Vries 1994) and the United Kingdom (LMP 1985). While this trend is not universal, even within migrant communities (see e.g., Meddegama

Table 6.1 *Rate of LS across four Census periods in Australia (%)*

Birthplace	1976 Census		1986 Census		1991 Census		1996 Census	
	Women	Men	Women	Men	Women	Men	Women	Men
Germany	26.6	30.0	36.8	44.7	36.9	44.8	44.6	52.0
Greece	3.1	3.6	3.3	5.5	3.1	5.6	4.7	8.0
Italy	5.1	6.6	7.2	13.3	7.7	14.1	10.5	18.4
Netherlands	39.8	46.8	42.9	53.1	51.5	60.5	57.0	66.4
Poland	14.6	21.4	11.7	19.8	12.9	21.2	16.3	23.1

Source: Clyne and Kipp (1997: 466).

2013, on Malayali women in England, or Clyne 2005, for Philippine, Korean and Japanese women in Australia), its regular occurrence cannot be ignored. Frequently, this pattern has been explained by referring to the differences that (may) exist between women's and men's (perceived) role and status in the minority and the 'host' community. In many societies women are (still) seen as the primary home-makers and caregivers for (young) children and men as the salary providers. Employment outside the home and outside one's own eth-nolinguistic community required men to acquire the L2 earlier and use it more often than the women. The home, seen as a woman's primary domain, is for many minority and immigrant communities the primary locus for the use of the heritage or minority language and for fostering the minority's cultural and other traditions. Furthermore, in many cultures women also have or take on the responsibility for elderly care, adding to the need for the heritage or minority language to be maintained. These roles not only lead to women's greater use of heritage or minority language but may also result in such women having less exposure to the majority or dominant language or less access to its acquisition, further restricting their interaction with the world outside their community. The gender differences observed in the first generation usually decrease in the second generation, although the degree of interethnic difference continues to be in proportion to that of the first generation. For example, in 1986 LS among second-generation Greek Australians was 7.2 percent for men and 5.1 percent for women, and among second-generation Dutch Australians it was 62.4 percent for men and 55.3 percent for women. The reduced difference is linked to locally born women and men having, generally speaking, similar access to the majority language, especially through schooling. It is also linked to the dominant or majority language being the primary vehicle for peer-group interaction, as we shall see later in this chapter.

There is, however, also evidence from both immigrant and regional minority settings that women may lead the change towards the language of the majority. This has been observed in places as different as Austria (Gal 1979), New Mexico, United States (Solé 1978), northern Finland (Aikio 1992), northern Italy (Cavanaugh 2006) and northern Spain (Holmquist 1985). Explanations for women's vanguard role in LS have included a desire to break out of a more restrictive gender role associated with the minority culture. In a social psychological study of attitudes towards the heritage language and its maintenance among second-generation Italo-Australians and Greek Australians, Callan et al. (1983: 423) noted that

Women in upwardly mobile minority groups so far, appear to threaten the maintenance of their minority language by downgrading it, and to lead their children into adopting the majority speech style.

They furthermore remark that 'this tendency is greater in communities where the status of women is lower in the minority group than in the majority group'. Another explanation proffered has echoes of that applied to gender variation within a single language (e.g., Labov 1990; Trudgill 1972) where it is claimed that women's 'preference' or greater use of the standard language is prestige based: unlike men, who have access to a range of status and prestige markers such as income and occupation, women have to revert to language to mark prestige. Judging on the basis of a large number of studies to date, we can conclude that the exact impact of gender on LS or LM is unlikely to be the same across diverse groups and communities, although the patterns described here may continue to exist. Indeed gender is likely to continue shaping linguistic behaviour in line with gender-based role assignments operating in our diverse communities (e.g., Cameron 2003; Pauwels 1995, 1997, 2011; Pavlenko et al. 2001).

6.1.4 Endogamy and exogamy

Census and other large-scale surveys often allow for some cross-tabulations that shed light on the effect that endogamous and exogamous marital practices may have on LM or LS. In LM research, two fundamental subgroups of exogamy are usually identified: exogamy involving a partner belonging to the majority (ethno)linguistic group and exogamy involving a partner who belongs to another ethnolinguistic minority group. The latter occurs more in migrant settings, although it is not exclusive to that setting. Exogamy of the first type has been found to be a clear-cut factor in the promotion of LS. This is not surprising, because it brings the majority or dominant language into the home and family domain. This domain is key to chances for the heritage or minority language to be maintained and passed on to the next generation. In such an exogamous situation, the majority language often becomes the main language in the family. It is used for interactions between the spouses, for parental communication with children and for communication between children. My own work on such marriage situations in the Dutch Australian community confirmed this (e.g., Pauwels 1980, 1985). An in-depth study of thirty couples was undertaken. Ten couples represented an endogamous situation (both Dutch-born) – G1. The second group – G2 – also comprised ten couples where one partner belonged to the majority group (Anglo-

Table 6.2 *Dutch language use by Dutch-born partner in endogamous and exogamous marriage situations (%)*

Marriage type	With spouse	With children
G1	62.4	29.0
G2	35.7	0.0
G3	35.6	10.0

Source: Adapted from Pauwels (1985: 46).

Australian). The third group – G3 – included ten couples in which one partner was Dutch-born and the other belonged to another ethnolinguistic minority group within Australia.

Table 6.2 summarises the use that the Dutch-born partner makes of Dutch when conversing with his or her spouse and children, mainly in the home domain. The table reveals that marrying outside the Dutch group has a significant effect on the amount of Dutch used by the Dutch-born partner and his or her children. The Dutch partner uses almost 50 percent less Dutch in exogamous marriages (G2 and G3) than in endogamous marriages (G1). In the endogamous situation Dutch continues to be an important language of communication between spouses. The type of exogamy (G2 or G3) does not seem to affect the amount of Dutch for interspousal communication; however, in both cases the non-Dutch partner seldom replies in Dutch but mainly in English. The impact of type of marriage on the children's use of Dutch is quite dramatic. While there is still some evidence of language use by the children (29%) in an endogamous situation, this is reduced to 10 percent in the G3 scenario and is completely absent in the G2 scenario. Although Dutch Australians are known to have a high rate of LS compared with some other groups, the studies and reports on linguistic intermarriages in other groups and settings confirm the general trend: that the use of the heritage or minority language is negatively affected by exogamy (e.g., Castonguay 1982; Robinson 1989; Stevens 1985; Yamamoto 2005). Yet despite the observation that exogamy generally promotes LS, we shall see in Chapter 8 that such a situation sometimes presents an ideal setting for the bilingual upbringing of children that follows the practice known as the 'one parent, one language' model. In such situations exogamy may have a positive effect on LM. However, to date this practice seems limited to a small number of families, so that exogamy is still much more associated with LS than LM.

6.2 CONTEXTS OF USE

6.2.1 The domains of language use

Investigating where, when and with whom which language is used has been done mainly through the domain concept (see Chapter 4). The main domains that have been subjected to scrutiny are (1) the family or home domain, (2) the friendship domain, (3) the domain of worship (frequently referred to as the religious domain), (4) the domain of secular societies and clubs, (5) the work domain and (6) the educational domain. The transactional domain, referring to shops and other service agencies involving encounters between clients/customers and service providers, is another domain that has received some attention. In Chapter 4 we also mentioned that questions about language use in these domains usually sought details about interlocutors and locales associated with the domain. For example, the locales associated with the domain of friendship may range from the participant's own home or a friend's home to a public place not linked to the minority group to social and cultural spaces specifically associated with the minority group. Further refinements included specifying a set of topics that could be seen as typical (congruent) or atypical (incongruent) of the domain and thus influence language choice. For example, if a child talks about her school day with her parents at home, she may very well switch to the majority language, as school is associated with that language. The specification of these elements also enables establishing which of these is given precedence in incongruent contexts: the interlocutor, the topic or the locale.

The sheer wealth of descriptions of the language patterns that have been observed in these domains across minorities around the world makes it impossible to do more than scratch the surface in documenting the multitude of practices. Hence, our main purpose here is to identify the domains, the interlocutors and, where relevant, the locales or topics that tend to be key to the use of the heritage or minority language based on the wealth of studies into LM and LS. In Chapter 8 where we discuss LM efforts, we provide more details about some language practices found in various domains and contexts.

6.2.2 Family or home domain

It should come as no surprise that the family domain is the stronghold for the use of the minority or heritage language. Although the usual cautionary note about (over)generalisation needs to be expressed, there is sufficient evidence for this statement. The home or family is the domain in which members are most likely to belong to the same ethnolinguistic group. It is also the domain that is the least subjected to scrutiny and regulatory frameworks or institutional policies operating in any society. Therefore, the family or home domain with its associated interlocutors is the most crucial in terms of LM. If the family is no longer able to provide exposure of this language to the next generation, then its chances of survival are drastically reduced. In fact, if the learning of the heritage and minority languages takes place only via some form of schooling, then the situation is more one of language revival and revitalisation than of language maintenance (see Chapter 9). For families living in immigrant settings, a distinction needs to be made between those families in which the parents belong to the first generation and those that belong to the second generation. Although we have already noted the substantial interethnic variation when it comes to heritage language use, it can nevertheless be observed that first-generation parents are likely to communicate (mainly) through the heritage language with each other and with same-age or older relatives. When it comes to parent–child interactions in such families, it is best to describe the language-use patterns in terms of a continuum ranging from reciprocal use to nonreciprocal use of the heritage language (i.e., the parent uses the heritage language but the children do not) and then to the prominent use of the majority language by both parties. Interactions between children tend to be conducted mainly through the majority or dominant language, especially if the latter were born and raised in the new setting. In families where some children were born outside the country of residence, they may continue to address their younger, locally born siblings in the heritage language. However, this is a rather exceptional pattern to continue long term.

The main interlocutors for heritage language use by children in migrant families are grandparents and those belonging to that generation. Many younger and older children tend to make an effort to use the heritage language to this older generation, especially when the latter's knowledge of the majority language is limited and/or because of their respected status in the family. When it comes to incongruent situations that involve children and parents communicating in a public setting, children tend to prefer or opt for the use of the majority language, although there are some factors that could lead to a continuing use of heritage language in such settings. For example, if the presence of different and multiple languages is a common feature in public spaces and/or the wider community's attitude and reaction to multilingualism in public are not disapproving, then children may be less inhibited to use their 'home' language in such a setting. Conversely, if public opinion leans towards the view that 'home languages should remain in the home', bilingual children and adolescents may refrain from their use to avoid conflict, embarrassment or confrontation.

When it comes to second-generation families, i.e., those where the parents were born and raised in the new environment and their offspring belong to the third generation, the presence of an older generation seems to be an even more critical element in ensuring some continued use of heritage language. In the case of nuclear family units, the locus of heritage language use may no longer be the family's home but that of the grandparents. Second-generation parents may continue to use the heritage language with their ageing parents, and they in turn use it not only with their children but also with their grandchildren. Where the family unit is an extended one, the presence of grandparents or other older relatives in the home or nearby may provide a more constant exposure to the heritage language for both parents and their children. In Chapter 8 we shall comment further on the role of grandparents in LM efforts. Generally, in second-generation families the majority language tends to be the more prominent language of familial communication between spouses, between parents and children and among the children. If such families are not part of a more close-knit (social) network in which the heritage language is used regularly, then its use is severely restricted. If the family or the community does not engage in active LM efforts, then the general prediction expressed by Fishman (2013) and many other scholars applies: LS will occur within three generations.

Many families in territorial minority settings face challenges similar to those in migration settings. This is especially the case where the minority language receives little or no recognition from the majority at present or until recently: examples include Catalan and Basque in France, Kurdish in Turkey or Sunawar in Nepal. Such minority language speakers often have no access to schooling in their language or cannot use it in interactions with public services and authorities. The minority language is therefore largely confined to the informal domains of family and friends. Furthermore, the use of the minority language is primarily associated with older members of the minority. Older generations are both the main users of and the primary interlocutors for the language. Transmission of the minority language to younger generations is not only limited but sometimes discouraged by the families themselves, who perceive it as a barrier to the socioeconomic success of their offspring (e.g., Bull 2002, for Sami). In territorial minority settings where there is more active recognition of or support for the language, the situation of minority language use in the family may be associated somewhat less with aged speakers. This could be said, for example, of some communities in Wales (e.g., Jones and Morris 2007) and of families living in the Gaeltacht (e.g., Antonini 1999). Antonini (1999) surveyed language use in family dyads in two Gaeltacht areas (South Connemara and Donegal) and found that Irish continued to be the main language of interaction between children (89% for South Connemara and 71% for Donegal). Note, however, that this strong use of Irish among the younger generations applies only to the Gaeltacht and is not observed outside these areas in Ireland, despite the fact that Irish has official status and is taught in schools.

6.2.3 The domain of friendship

The friendship domain is another domain that is commonly associated with regular use of the minority and heritage language. It is, however, more difficult to discern 'common' patterns for this domain. Heritage and minority language use in this context is very much a function of the type of friendship network that minority members maintain or have access to. If the minority group members are 'concentrated' in a specific area (e.g., a neighbourhood, a region in a country) the chances are that their friendship networks are also found in this neighbourhood or area and that they can continue to use the language with friends. In migrant contexts, ethnocultural traditions and practices may further influence whether friendship networks mainly involve people from the same ethnocultural background or not. Despite these variations, a common observation for immigrant groups is that the use of the heritage language in this domain is mainly a feature of first-generation and older members of the group. In that respect, there is a clear similarity between language use patterns found in the family and in friendship networks. The variables of age and generation are the main determinants for language use and choice: older speakers and first-generation members make greater use of the heritage language than younger and second-generation speakers, who generally prefer the majority language for their friendship interactions. An interesting observation concerns the language practices of second-generation members in same ethnicity and mixed ethnicity groups. In same ethnicity friendship networks of some migrant and minority groups, there is a considerable amount of conscious code-switching or code-mixing, often to denote solidarity or to enforce loyalty to the group. This has been observed, for example, among Greek Australian male friendship groups (Winter and Pauwels 2006) and Greek Australian female friends

(Tsokalidou 1994). Another interesting practice has been observed in mixed ethnicity groups where minority members of different ethnicities make occasional use of each other's heritage language, as do members of the majority group. Rampton (1995) observed this pattern amongst mixed ethnicity groups of adolescents in Britain and labelled this phenomenon 'crossing'. Similar observations have been made by researchers in other areas (e.g., Auer 2003, for Turkish in Germany; Kamwangamalu 2001, for South Africa and Vermeij 2004, for the Netherlands). Whether this practice assists in the maintenance of the heritage or minority language for the minority member has not yet been widely explored.

6.2.4 Domains of worship, education and employment

The domains of worship, schooling and work have also been the subject of detailed examinations in the context of LM and LS. Whereas the family and friendship domains can be considered to belong to the private realm of activities, the former domains tend to cut across both private and public spheres. Most worship or religious ceremonies involve people beyond one's own family or friendship group and take place in a (semi-)public place. Other than private or home schooling, the same applies to the domain of education. The domain of work is probably the one most exposed to the public sphere. The extent to which these domains act as agents of LM or LS varies enormously not only in terms of our two main settings, but also across groups and polities. It is therefore difficult to discern any 'common' trends or features. For example, in the case of the immigrant setting these domains (especially education and employment) will most likely involve significant exposure to the dominant language and interaction with members of the majority group. In the case of territorial minorities, these domains may be similarly exposed to the majority language and group. However, where the linguistic minority has obtained some territorial linguistic rights, usually in relation to schooling and public services, these domains may in fact be locales where the minority language could dominate or be mandated. In the next section we discuss the variable impact of the domains of worship, education and work on LM and LS.

The domain of worship

The domain of worship, more frequently known as the 'religious' domain, comprises both private events and activities as well as public and formalised ones. The former may include private prayers, incantations and meditations. Where these involve some forms of internal speech or recitations (silent or aloud), there is evidence, based on questionnaire and interview data, that many people continue to do those in the heritage language. For example, despite Dutch Australians recording very high rates of LS even in the first generation, data about their language use in relation to private prayer revealed that most continued to say prayers in Dutch (Pauwels 1980, 1983). This was also observed by Woods (2004) in relation to Indonesian Christians living in Australia.

When it comes to more formal and institutionalised types of worship, the preference for or the use of the heritage language is far less clear-cut. Woods (2004) extensively studied various Christian-based ethnic churches in Australia including Anglican, Baptist, Catholic, Methodist, Lutheran, Orthodox, Reformed and Uniting churches. Whereas some ethnolinguistic groups – Latvians and Indonesians – continued to use the heritage language for services, many other groups had almost completely switched to English for most elements of the services. In his review of religion as a site of language contact, Spolsky (2003) notes that some religions have a close link to a specific language or language variety. This is, for example, the case for Islam and its close link to Classical Arabic (Quranic Arabic). As a result of this close link between language and religion, the domain of religious worship continues to be one of LM, albeit involving a variety of Arabic that is not used in everyday context. We shall elaborate on this in Chapter 8.

The domain of education

The use and presence of the heritage language in the educational domain is also characterised by enormous diversity. This diversity is the result of many factors, including the type of setting, i.e., territorial minority or immigrant community; the type of school, i.e., community or mainstream school and the linguistic 'nature' of the country, i.e., officially monolingual or bi- or multilingual. It is further influenced by the existence and/or endorsement of national, regional and international policies and charters about 'mother tongue' education. For example, the Council of Europe's European Charter for Regional and Minority Languages is a charter designed

> on the one hand to protect and promote regional and minority languages as a threatened aspect of Europe's cultural heritage and on the other hand to enable speakers of a regional or minority language to use it in private and public life. (www.coe.int/t/dg4/education/ minlang/aboutcharter/default_en.asp, accessed June 2015)

It sets out eight fundamental principles and provides a choice of sixty-eight concrete undertakings in seven areas of public life that European states should abide by, if they ratify the Charter. Whether or not to ratify the Charter is left entirely up to the state. For example, while Spain has ratified the Charter, France has not, leading to different arrangements for the Basque language in these countries.

In the case of European territorial minority settings whose states or polities have ratified the Charter and have taken steps to make minority language education available, this has supported LM (e.g., Broeder and Extra 1999; Gorter and Cenoz 2011; Jaspaert and Kroon 1991; see also Chapter 8). The positive influence on LM of the educational domain in migration settings is less straightforward. In fact, mainstream education in such settings has been and continues to be in most cases a powerful agent of linguistic assimilation and LS (e.g., Baker and Prys Jones 1998, for a history of bilingual education in the United States). Although some state systems supported or support some heritage language teaching (as a medium or a subject of instruction), the majority of these programs are geared towards transitional bilingualism, i.e., to aid transition to linguistic assimilation into the majority language. In Chapter 8 we shall elaborate on the type of educational programs found in mainstream education that are more geared towards LM.

When it comes to education or educational programs initiated and run by the heritage language community itself, there is some evidence that they aid LM, especially with regard to literacy (e.g., Clyne 1991; Fishman 1980; Monheit 1975; Peyton et al. 2001). However, there is enormous variation in the quantity and quality of exposure students have to the heritage language in such programs, leading to variable results with regard to LM.

The domain of work

The world of work for immigrant minorities (and to a large extent also for regional minorities) is often the domain that requires the sole or dominant use of the majority language. In fact, the official rhetoric of many societies, including those supportive of linguistic diversity and multilingualism, is that minorities and immigrants need to learn the majority or dominant language in order to fully participate in society, especially in employment. In fact, even in multilingual workplaces – on the shop floor as well as the board room – the majority language (or another widely used language) functions not only as official medium of communication but also as a lingua franca for workers not sharing the same language. An exploration of several Australian workplaces that employed people from a variety of language backgrounds revealed that the use of English – the majority language – was reinforced mainly because it acted as a lingua franca between workers as well as between workers and various levels of management (e.g., Clyne 1994; Clyne and Ball 1990). Exceptions are sometimes found in workplaces where a particular ethnolinguistic group 'dominates'. Goldstein's (1997) study of Portuguese factory workers in Canada showed that Portuguese not only could continue as the main language on the shop floor but also functioned as a language of solidarity between the workers. Another work environment where the minority or heritage language may have a prominent place is that of small businesses, shops and certain trades. Their customer or client base is often made up of people from the same or similar ethnolinguistic groups, promoting the use of the heritage language. Many large cities around the world are host to thousands of such businesses – delis, corner shops, hair salons, barbers, dry cleaners, phone shops, butchers, bakers, accountants, small law firms, and so on – in which personnel serve their clients and customers in many heritage languages. If these are family businesses in which the younger generation also works or assists, then they do act as a way to enhance LM. However, other than this sector of employment, the work domain is not associated with LM.

6.2.5   Common trends in LM and LS? Some summative observations

A fitting conclusion and summary of this chapter is the observation made by Fishman in 1965, which stresses the importance of the family and home as the alpha and omega for LM:

> In many studies of multilingual behaviour the family domain has proved to be a very crucial one. Multilingualism often begins in the family and depends upon it for encouragement if not for protection. In other cases, multilingualism withdraws into the family domain after it has been displaced from other domains in which it was previously encountered. (Fishman 1965: 76)

This statement has been borne out by the majority of studies examining LM in our two main settings. When it comes to the role of other contexts and domains in the process of LM or LS, results of research point towards variability or diversity rather than commonality. How these domains and contexts can be used in pursuit of LM will be explored further in Chapter 8. With regard to speaker characteristics, it is age and/or generation and type of marriage that are influential in determining patterns of LM or LS. Exogamy is most commonly associated with LS. In the context of immigrant settings, the first generation is more likely to maintain the heritage language than subsequent generations. In territorial minority settings LM is found more among old(er) members rather than younger ones.

However, the majority of factors that have been discovered and examined in relation to LM or LS seldom have the same impact across the many different settings or linguistic groups. We have shown that some factors will enhance LM in some situations or groups, whereas they may have the opposite effect in other contexts (e.g., gender). As a result, the study of LM and LS can be said to be successful in identifying the many triggers and causes of LS or LM but has not yet been able to come up with a convincing model or theory that can predict, reliably, which factors or combination of factors lead to a specific outcome across diverse settings and communities. Nevertheless, several models have been developed to account in particular for intergroup differences and we discuss the main ones in the next chapter.

POINTS FOR DISCUSSION AND TASKS

1. Discuss the following statement: Gender is more likely to be a factor influencing LM in rural minority settings than in cities with large immigrant populations.
2. Find out if there have been studies examining whether a person's income has an impact on his or her use of a minority language. If so, what are their findings? If there are no studies, how would you go about investigating this factor?
3. In immigrant settings it has been observed that LS is lowest among older first-generation speakers and among younger second-generation speakers. What do you think would be a pattern in third-generation speakers? Find evidence for your answer.
4. In this chapter we made a statement that in territorial minority settings, the presence of education in the minority language aids LM. Select four studies undertaken in the following regions – Basque Country, Brittany, Friesland and Guernsey – to provide support for this statement or to refute it.
5. The transactional domain is another domain in which the heritage or minority language is in direct competition with the majority language. Identify a setting or context in which this domain is more likely to aid LM rather than promote LS.
6. Do you agree with the observation made by scholars that LS is the societal norm and that it is often completed within three generations?

7. In this chapter we reviewed some common trends and patterns in terms of LM and LS relating to individual characteristics: age, gender, generation and marital situation. In your opinion, which show the greatest commonality across settings and groups, and why do you think that is the case?

SUGGESTIONS FOR FURTHER READING

Common trends

Clyne, Michael. 1982. *Multilingual Australia*. Melbourne: River Seine Publications.

    1991. *Community languages: the Australian experience*. Cambridge: Cambridge University Press.

These two books provide a detailed discussion of the impact of socio-demographic factors on LM and LS in the Australian context. They also examine the domains that are most commonly associated with LM and those that facilitate shift.

Gender

Burton, Pauline, Ketaki K. Dyson and Shirley Ardener. Eds. 1994. *Bilingual women: anthropological approaches to second language use*. Oxford: Berg.

Holmes, Janet. 1993. Immigrant women and language maintenance in Australia and New Zealand. *International Journal of Applied Linguistics* 3.2: 159–179.

Pauwels, Anne. 1997. The role of gender in immigrant language maintenance in Australia. In W. Wölck and A. De Houwer (eds.), *Recent studies in contact linguistics*. Bonn: Dümmler Verlag, 276–286.

Pavlenko, Aneta, Adrian Blackledge, Ingrid Piller and Maria Teutsch-Dwyer. Eds. 2001. *Multilingualism, second language learning, and gender*. Berlin and New York: Mouton de Gruyter.

These four references provide an insight into the role of gender in LM and bi- and multilingualism.

Endogamy and exogamy

Pauwels, Anne. 1985. The role of mixed marriages in language shift in the Dutch community. In M. Clyne (ed.), *Australia, meeting place of languages*. Canberra: ANU-RSPS, 39–55.

Yamamoto, Masayo. 2001. *Language use in interlingual families: a Japanese English sociolinguistic study*. Clevedon: Multilingual Matters.

For suggested reading in relation to domains, see Chapter 8.

7 Understanding the dynamics of language maintenance and shift

The existence of intergroup or interethnic differences in maintenance or shift rates is probably the most consistent finding emanating from the multitude of studies. Some linguistic minorities or ethnolinguistic groups maintain their language better than other groups, despite being exposed to the same environment. For example, Polish Australians maintain their language more and longer than Dutch Australians in the same Australian environment. Another observation regarding interethnic or intergroup differences in LM or LS rates relates to a specific group managing to maintain its language in very diverse settings. The Greek diaspora around the world is an example of this. Conversely, there are ethnolinguistic groups whose LM or LS rates are quite susceptible to the environment in which they find themselves. This could be said, for example, of Turkish immigrants in Australia in contrast to those living in the Netherlands or Germany. They seem to maintain their language better in the latter countries. It also applies to Basque people living in Basque territories of France and Spain. In the previous chapter we delved into some trends that seem to be common across heritage and territorial linguistic minorities. These related mainly to personal characteristics, i.e., sociodemographic factors, and to the contexts (domains) that promote LM or LS. Here, the focus is mainly on the group level in an attempt to shed light on these intergroup differences. In particular, we review a number of approaches that have attempted to identify factors influencing language behaviour at the group level. In most cases, the models developed are in fact taxonomies or typologies focusing on group factors. Some of these are described as 'theories' because their proposers contend that they are able not only to enhance our understanding of specific language-use patterns but also to predict whether a group is likely to maintain its language.

7.2   TAXONOMIES OF GROUP FACTORS INFLUENCING LM AND LS

7.2.1   Kloss' clear-cut and ambivalent factors

One of the first approaches to understanding differences in the language behaviour and language-use patterns of ethnolinguistic groups was Kloss' (1966) study of German-American language maintenance efforts during the late nineteenth and first half of the twentieth century. In this paper Kloss created a list of two types of factors that contribute to shaping the dynamics of LM or LS. He referred to them as clear-cut and ambivalent factors.

Clear-cut factors

Kloss identified several factors operating at group level that, in his opinion, clearly support LM, at least in the context of German-American immigrants and their offspring in the early twentieth century. They are (1) the socioreligious segregation of the group, (2) the group's early point of immigration into the new territory, (3) the existence of linguistic enclaves within that territory, (4) membership of a denomination with parochial schools and (5) the group's pre-emigration experience with LM.

Socioreligious segregation refers to a group that wishes to maintain its separation for sociocultural religious reasons. It continues to operate as a self-sufficient entity within a larger setting. This factor has been merged with the third factor – linguistic enclaves – by the majority of scholars using Kloss' typology in other contexts.

Early point of immigration into the new territory refers to the early arrival of the group in question into the new territory. The group may have migrated somewhat before or possibly at the same time as another group that has become the majority. This did indeed apply to some of the early German settlements in the United States. Kloss argues that an early arrival makes it possible for the group to establish its own structures in which its language, culture and practices continue to dominate.

The existence of linguistic enclaves. Where an ethnolinguistic group maintains little contact with its surrounding community, for whatever reason, and is relatively self-sufficient, this creates an optimal situation for long-term maintenance of the language. In Chapter 2 we mentioned that *Sprachinseln* – linguistic enclaves – may have been the first context in which the study of LM took place.

Membership of a denomination with parochial schools refers to the group belonging to a religious denomination or organisation that provides some form of schooling for its (child) members. This schooling is done through the medium of the heritage or minority language.

Pre-emigration experience with LM. According to Kloss, when a group has come from an environment in which it was already a linguistic minority or in which it was exposed to competition with another language, then it has gained experience in dealing with LM. This experience will bear positively on LM in the new environment.

Ambivalent factors

Kloss' list of ambivalent factors that concern the group rather than the individual includes (1) numerical strength of the group, (2) the linguistic and cultural similarity of the group to the majority or dominant group, (3) the attitude of the majority to the 'minority' language and/or the group and (4) a bundle of factors called 'sociocultural' characteristics. He maintained that these factors were ambivalent, as they have been shown to contribute to LM and to LS.

Numerical strength of the group. Groups that are numerically stronger may be better placed to maintain the language, as there are more people with whom and contexts and occasions in which to use the language. Being larger also means that contact with other groups, especially the majority group, is more difficult to avoid. Large groups are also more likely to be geographically dispersed, making it more difficult for their members to have frequent contact with each other. Such communities, even if not geographically dispersed, may develop less of a sense of community based around language because there may be other characteristics that take precedence for group membership. Smaller groups that are geographically less dispersed allow for denser networks and more frequent contact, but if they are quite small and not close knit, the changes of LM may be very limited. It is clear from this description that numerical strength is difficult to separate from related elements such as settlement patterns or geographical distribution.

The linguistic and cultural similarity of the group to the majority. If the minority group is linguistically and culturally quite similar to the majority, it may be more difficult for the group to maintain a separate linguistic and cultural identity than a group that is quite different in these areas. Yet a group's linguistic and cultural similarity may also mean that it will have less difficulty learning the majority language, giving it more time to devote to maintenance of the heritage (or minority) language. In settings where English is the majority language, this factor overwhelmingly favours LS: Dutch, German and

Scandinavian immigrant groups whose languages and cultures have greater affinity with English are amongst the groups with the lowest LM rate.

The attitude of the majority to the minority language and/or group. Maintaining a language that arouses suspicion or triggers other negative reactions from (members of) the majority group is often too much to bear for minority groups. There are many examples of languages that have become reviled as a result of war and various forms of xenophobia. In some cases the pressure has been so strong that it has led to language death (see Chapter 2). However, in some cases such adverse conditions have made the group more resilient in its maintenance efforts. A more tolerant majority attitude towards the minority or heritage language minority may assist that group to maintain the language better, although it may also lead to indifference, even apathy, leading to LS.

Sociocultural characteristics. Kloss used this phrase to cover a range of features pertaining to a group that may influence how it views the importance or relevance of LM. They include, for example, the role of the family and the link between language and specific cultural practices. Unfortunately, Kloss did not elaborate much on these but only mentioned their importance. Yet elements of this factor are often critical in understanding LM differences between ethnolinguistic groups. If language is seen by a specific group as relatively peripheral for it to maintain its identity as a group, then that group is unlikely to expend much effort on keeping the language going. If, on the other hand, there is a very strong link between language, religious practices and a group's identity, then efforts to maintain the language, at least for religious purposes, will be much stronger.

7.2.2 Testing and expanding Kloss' list of factors

Following the publication of this list of factors, scholars working in other migrant settings tested not only whether these factors were applicable elsewhere but also whether they belonged to the same type, i.e., clear-cut or ambivalent. Clyne's testing of these factors in the Australian immigrant context is one of the most extensive (e.g., Clyne 1979, 1982, 1991). In terms of clear-cut factors, not only has Clyne's work shown that some of these work towards LM only if they are combined, but he has also identified some further factors that, in his opinion, clearly promote LM. With regard to the former, Clyne's Australian work on various immigrant groups including Kloss' focal group – Germans – has shown that a group's early point of migration leads to LM only if it goes hand in hand with linguistic enclaves in a rural and relatively isolated settlement. When he tested the clear-cut nature of the fourth factor – i.e., membership of denominations with parochial schools – and the fifth factor – i.e., premigration LM experience – he found them to be ambivalent rather than clear-cut in the Australian context. For the fourth factor he refers to work undertaken by Kipp (1980) on two branches of the German Lutheran Church in rural Victoria, Australia. Members of the United Evangelical Lutheran Church of Australia, which conducted its Saturday school (i.e., parochial school) in German and had a strong emphasis on German language and culture maintenance, did not use or maintain German as well as those belonging to the other branch, the Evangelical Lutheran Church of Australia, which conducted its classes bilingually and was less focused on the continued use of German. With regard to the fifth factor Clyne (1982: 30) provides several examples that show its ambivalent rather than clear-cut nature:

> While *Volksdeutsche* exposed to language contact in eastern and central Europe or the Middle East prior to their arrival in Australia maintained German more than German and Austrian migrants . . ., the bilingual Sorbs (speaking a Slavic mother tongue) settled in 19th century German settlements in South Australia and Victoria adopted German instead of Sorbian. While multilinguals from Egypt have kept their languages, Frisian-Dutch-English trilinguals have generally shifted to English (Clyne 1982: 30).

With regard to additional clear-cut factors, Clyne (1982) identifies one operating at group level and two pertaining more to personal characteristics. He contends that *the status and usefulness of the ethnic language in education and world-wide communication* is a clear-cut factor promoting LM. In his view, a community whose language rates highly on these scales will be more inclined to maintain it than one whose language does not have such status. In my view, the clear-cut nature of the factor is doubtful. For example, German ranks much higher than Polish on both these scales in many immigrant settings, yet overall speaking, Polish is much better maintained than German. The two other factors he identifies as clear-cut are exogamy and the presence of grandparents. In Chapter 6, we confirmed the clear-cut nature of the former factor: exogamy promotes LS. The presence of grandparents does indeed promote the use of the heritage language, although it assumes that grandparents' knowledge of the majority language is minimal or their willingness to use it in the family is low (see also Chapter 8).

Clyne's extensive work on Kloss' typology in the Australian context not only led to the addition of two clear-cut factors mentioned here but also included a refinement of one ambivalent factor. His

Census-based language work assisted in clarifying the factor 'linguistic and cultural similarity of the group to the majority': 'it seems the *cultural* similarity is a more important factor than *linguistic* similarity, and that the former is a fairly clear-cut factor' (Clyne 1982: 35). A similar observation was made by Fishman et al. (1985).

Clyne has not been the only scholar identifying or expanding the list of factors that can influence the process of LM or LS. However, the value of identifying further factors, with the majority of these being ambivalent, is rather limited in terms of increasing the predictability LM or LS. Yet they do help in refining and understanding the complex dynamics that surround the process of LM and LS.

Although Kloss' typology is arguably one of the most influential early attempts at identifying factors that support LM or accelerate LS, it is by no means the only one. Edwards (1992: 38) mentions that other pioneers of the field such as Ferguson (1962), Stewart (1962) and Haugen (1972) have all produced lists, typologies or taxonomies of factors and variables that could shed light on the dynamics of LM and LS. Haugen's list became known as the 'ecology of language' approach and has been a reference point for many LM and LS investigations and for further work on typologies (e.g., Haarmann 1986). Edwards (1992: 37–38), in his attempt to establish a typology of minority language situations, regrets that 'these typologies have not, however, been systematically exploited', and he calls for the development of 'a framework of variables which could serve to illuminate contexts of maintenance or shift'. Such comprehensive typologies may be particularly helpful in identifying which particular combinations of factors can speed up or reduce the process of LS.

7.3 LANGUAGE AS A CORE VALUE

7.3.1 The core value theory

An approach that has had considerable impact on LM studies, especially in Australia but also to some extent elsewhere, has become known as the 'core value' theory. Its pioneering proponent in the context of LM work is the sociologist J. J. Smolicz, whose work was focused on trying to account for interethnic differences in LM and LS rates in Australia (e.g., Smolicz 1980, 1981; Smolicz and Secombe 1985). According to Smolicz and Secombe (1985: 11) 'the term "core value" refers to those values that are regarded as forming the most fundamental components or heartland of a group's culture, and act as identifying values which are symbolic of the group and its membership'. It is the set of core values that gives a group its distinctive identity. Not abiding by these values or rejecting them may lead to the exclusion of a member from the group. Similarly, a group's distinctive identity may be threatened if its core values are at risk. The values and/or beliefs that make up the core set may vary considerably from group to group. Smolicz and colleagues do not elaborate on these but implicitly refer to such elements as religious beliefs, family cohesion and specific cultural traditions (see, e.g., Kloss' sociocultural characteristics). Their main focus, however, is on language as a core value and its potential impact on LM. If a group assigns core value to its language, then it follows that its distinctive identity is threatened if it cannot maintain that language. The group will then, according to this theory, make significant efforts to keep its language going, most likely resulting in a higher LM rate. Conversely, a group whose set of core values does not include language may be less concerned about its loss, as it may impact only marginally on its distinctive identity. Smolicz in collaboration with various colleagues (e.g., Smolicz and Secombe 1985, 1989; Smolicz et al. 2001) illustrated this theory by describing the language behaviour and attitudes of various ethnolinguistic groups in Australia, including Chinese, Croatian, Greek, Indian, Italian, Latvian, Polish, Ukrainian and Welsh groups. For example, the authors established that groups such as the Chinese and Greeks in Australia see language as a core value. They then looked at their LM rates (based on Census data) and found that these groups have indeed (relatively) high levels of LM. This 'correlation' thus provides evidence of the link between language as core value and LM and 'proves' the predictive power of the core value theory. Its relative simplicity and alleged predictive power made it attractive to researchers to 'explain' interethnic variation in LM rates, especially when the various groups operated in a similar environment and faced similar external conditions.

7.3.2 Some weaknesses in the core value theory

Its relative simplicity did, however, also trigger a level of scepticism leading to further investigations that exposed several flaws in the theory, seriously undermining its predictive powers (e.g., Clyne 1988, 1991; Kennedy 2015; Kouzmin 1988). The most extensive criticism was undertaken by Clyne (1991), who highlighted three main problems with the theory: (1) a concern regarding the definition of what constitutes a group, (2) a concern that the theory does not address the reality of multiple group membership and (3) a concern that it cannot account for changing rates of LM in a group triggered by such phenomena as ethnic revivals. Clyne (1991) exemplified these concerns through a variety of Australian case studies. Here we will highlight only the main elements of these three problems and refer the reader to Clyne (1991) for an in-depth discussion.

Problematic definition of 'group'

In many of his writings Smolicz alternates between terms such as 'group', 'cultural group' and 'ethnic group' when he discusses the concept of core value. Although the definition of core value mentioned previously (Smolicz and Secombe 1985: 11) is in relation to the term 'group', a few paragraphs further, reference is made to 'cultural groups', e.g., 'Cultural groups differ in the extent to which they emphasise their native tongues as core values'. Yet most of the examples that he gives to illustrate his theory are of groups normally referred to as 'ethnic groups'. Clyne (1991) contends that Smolicz' use of the term 'ethnic group' is one that is couched in the ideologies of nineteenth-century state and nationhood in which an equation between language, ethnicity and nationhood was propagated, hence the importance of language in the make-up of an ethnic group. According to Clyne (1991: 94) more recent treatises and discussions around ethnicity downplay the language element in the definition of an ethnic group, leading him to pose the following question: 'To what extent is there a clash between the two aspects, language as the basis of a group and language as a possible carrier of the group?' Through an extensive case study of German in Australia he shows that there is a significant weakness in the core value theory as it builds upon an assumption of the linguistic homogeneity of an ethnic group or on the ethnic homogeneity of a language group.

Difficulty of dealing with multiple group membership

This criticism is closely linked to the first criticism. Most people identify themselves as belonging to a number of groups, ranging from those based on sociodemographic features (e.g., age, gender, class, nationality) to those linked to various pursuits (e.g., music lover, football fan, stamp collector). Depending on the situation a particular kind of group membership may take precedence over another and may therefore influence how we behave linguistically. This has been well documented in a multitude of sociolinguistic studies. In migrant and minority language settings this may affect to what extent language is seen as a marker of identity. Clyne (1991) illustrates this complexity around language as a core value in the context of multiple group membership with the case of German-speaking Jewish refugees from Nazi Germany living in Australia.

Core value theory and changes in attitudes towards LM

Clyne (1991) questions the extent to which a group can change its core values. Can language be dropped as a core value or, conversely, become a core value when it was not one before? This questioning comes in the context of phenomena such as 'ethnic revivals' (e.g., Fishman 1983b, Fishman et al. 1985) that have seen relatively sudden increases in the number of people belonging to an ethnolinguistic group claiming use of their heritage language. Clyne (1991: 104) comments that

> if previously, say, Maltese was not a core value in Maltese culture, can it suddenly become one because of the impact of Australian attitudes? Does it mean that the Maltese cultural core value system has changed? Or that language has become a core value in Maltese-Australian culture?

At stake here is the extent to which core values are long-term and stable features of a group's identity. If they are, then they are unlikely to change dramatically because of changes in the external environments. It could then be concluded that this theory cannot account for a situation such as that of the Maltese described by Clyne (1991). If, on the other hand, core values can be subject to occasional changes, then the predictive power of the theory would be diminished because of this fluctuation.

These criticisms of the core value theory have substantially reduced its impact as a predictive model of interethnic differences in LM and LS rates. Its main value now lies in having identified another major factor that can influence LM.

7.4 ETHNOLINGUISTIC VITALITY

In 1977, Howard Giles, Richard Bourhis and Don Taylor wrote a paper entitled 'Towards a theory of languages in ethnic group relations'. The paper was an attempt to develop 'a theoretical framework for understanding the interrelationship among language, ethnicity and intergroup relations' (Giles et al. 1977: 308). It brings together and builds upon related theories – Tajfel's theory of intergroup relations (Tajfel 1974) and Giles' speech accommodation theory (Giles 1973). This theoretical framework is couched within a social psychological approach to the study of language and multilingualism. Not unlike other frameworks and taxonomies, it has been subjected to significant criticism, some of which we will review later in this section. Notwithstanding that, the theory has had a significant impact on the field of LM and LS, with many studies of immigrant and minority language communities adopting a social psychological approach and seeking explanations of observed linguistic behaviour in terms of a group's ethnolinguistic vitality.

In this key paper, the authors describe ethnolinguistic vitality as follows: 'the vitality of an ethnolinguistic group is that which makes a group likely to behave as a distinctive and active collective entity in intergroup situations' (Giles et al. 1977: 308). If a group displays little vitality, for whatever reason, it will disintegrate as a group and no longer operate as a distinctive entity. On the other hand, groups with high vitality have a much better chance of survival in contact situations than those with low vitality. In its original version, the theory of ethnolinguistic vitality identified a set of structural variables that shape a group's low or high degree of vitality: they were variables linked to status of the ethnolinguistic group, to its demography and to the institutional support it receives in its environment. Each of these variables is further broken down into several factors. Figure 7.1 presents the taxonomy of variables and related factors that make up the notion of (ethnolinguistic) vitality. The authors then discuss each of these factors and how they could contribute to or signal high or low vitality.

In later work, Giles and colleagues stressed the importance of a group's subjective assessment of its vitality: 'group members' subjective assessment of ingroup/outgroup vitality may be as important in determining socio-linguistic and interethnic behaviour as the group's objective vitality' (Harwood et al. 1994: 175). This led to the distinction between objective and subjective ethnolinguistic vitality, both comprised of (roughly) the same variables and factors. When this framework is applied to questions of LM or LS, the assertion is that the higher a group scores on both aspects of ethnolinguistic vitality, the more likely it is that it will maintain or will be able to maintain its language.

7.4.1   Some criticisms of the ethnolinguistic vitality theory

Early and strong critics of the theory, at least in its original form, were the scholars Husband and Saifullah Khan (1982). Their criticism was primarily directed at what they described as flawed specifications in the concept of (ethnolinguistic) vitality. They also criticised the variables or 'tools of analysis' used as inexact and not sufficiently independent. Furthermore, they commented that the authors did not address the question of differential weighting of variables and factors.

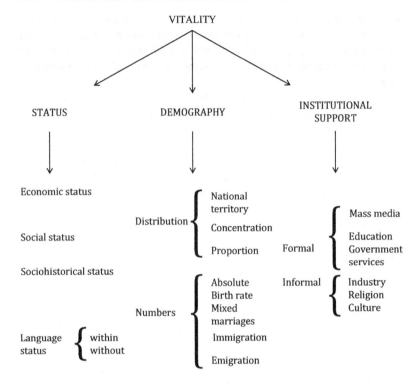

Figure 7.1: A taxonomy of the structural variables affecting ethnolinguistic vitality.
Source: Giles et al. (1977: 309).

Their conclusion was that the theory achieves only a relatively simplistic analysis of group situations. A strong rebuttal of this criticism was made by some of the authors (e.g., Johnson et al. 1983). Other criticisms have come from Haarmann (1986), who focused on terminological issues, and Clyne (1991: 89), who criticised its restricted applicability. He felt that the model was not attuned to the Australian situation, as it relied on 'relatively stable minority situations (such as Welsh-English)' and could therefore not deal well with constantly changing linguistic scenarios. Tollefson's (1991) criticism focused on the issue of power: he alleged that the theory of ethnolinguistic vitality was based on variables, characteristics and institutions that are relevant from a majority perspective (i.e., the dominant group), and that the theory ignored important historical and structural variables.

Despite these criticisms, the theory continues to flourish and its proponents continue to suggest revisions and refinements to strengthen it as a framework for understanding language and language behaviour in intergroup situations (e.g., Ehala 2010).

7.5   OTHER FRAMEWORKS AND APPROACHES

The models and typologies outlined in the previous sections are associated with a structural-functional approach to the study of language and multilingualism. Although this approach continues to be central to the study of LM and LS, more recent work on multilingualism (including on LM and LS) has seen a shift towards more interactionist and critical approaches (e.g., Heller 2007). The interactionist approaches build upon the work of Blom and Gumperz (1972) and tend to foreground the importance of social networks as a concept in understanding differential patterns of LM and LS. For example, Stoessel (2002) promotes a focus on social network to analyse language-use patterns in bi- and multilingual situations, as it allows for more fine-grained analysis. Furthermore, social network theory is also seen as being able to explain differences in LM and LS because 'a person's social networks affect the vitality of the community language and its likelihood to succumb to language shift' (García 2003: 25). Although the social network approach has become more prominent in more recent work, it is not a new approach. Gal's (1979) pioneering study on LS in Oberwart, Austria, reveals how membership of various social networks influences language use and choices.

Social network has shown to be particularly useful in explaining differences in language-use patterns at the level of the individual. It is less well geared to explaining differences observed at the level of groups. After all, the focus is on the kind of networks – e.g., dense, uniplex, multiplex – which an individual participates in and on linking that to the language practices that prevail in these networks.

The critical approach to the study of multilingualism presents a more radical departure to analysing and understanding the dynamics of multilingualism as well as of LM and LS. We shall come back to that in Chapter 10.

7.6   WORKING TOWARDS A PREDICTIVE MODEL?

Developing models and theories that assist in understanding and, where possible, predicting future behaviour is a *sine qua non* of academic research. Research in the field of LM and LS is no exception. Yet the discussions here reveal that the situation regarding the development of a predictive model can be best described as ongoing. There is no doubt that the continual explorations of variables, factors, forces and measures affecting how individuals and groups behave linguistically in intergroup settings will assist in refining our understanding of the dynamics of LM and LS. In particular, it will highlight the complexity and immense diversity of responses of groups to these phenomena. Although there seems to be a consensus among scholars that working towards a predictive model is not futile, many are doubtful of a successful attainment. This is not surprising given the very dynamic nature of most factors and forces involved in the process. In the final chapter of the book we explore this further by questioning whether it is still worthwhile to speak of LM and LS in many settings (especially large urban ones) where fluidity rather than stability is the prevailing linguistic constellation. However, these changes should not be a reason to give up one's pursuit. In 1992 Edwards had already written,

> Clearly, much more work needs to be done before a useful typology results. I think the work is worthwhile... I believe that a comprehensive typology would be a useful tool for description and comparison, leading to more conceptualisation of minority language situations, and perhaps permitting predictions to be made concerning shift/maintenance outcomes (Edwards 1992: 51).

POINTS FOR DISCUSSION AND TASKS

1. Numerical strength of the group is seen as an ambivalent factor in LM or LS. Select one group that has settled in two countries, e.g., Italians in the United States and Australia, Polish in Canada and the United States or Koreans in the United States and New Zealand. Examine their LM or LS patterns and compare them in terms of numerical strength in the two countries and whether they are similar or different.

2. Clyne (1982: 35) commented that 'it seems the *cultural* similarity is a more important factor than *linguistic* similarity, and that the former is a fairly clear-cut factor'. Examine this statement in a setting other than Australia or the United States, drawing upon relevant data to prove or disprove this statement.

3. Does the core value theory also apply to a territorial minority group? How does it explain the differential rates of LM in Basque people living in France and Spain?

4. In your opinion, what are the strengths of the theory of ethno-linguistic vitality? Explain why.
5. Identify a study that has used a social network approach to examining patterns of LM and LS. In your opinion, does it explain satisfactorily differences observed at group level?
6. Comment on Edwards' (1992) statement:

> Clearly, much more work needs to be done before a useful typology results. I think the work *is* worthwhile... I believe that a comprehensive typology would be a useful tool for description and comparison, leading to more conceptualisation of minority language situations, and perhaps permitting predictions to be made concerning shift/maintenance outcomes.

Do you agree with him? Why or why not?

SUGGESTIONS FOR FURTHER READING

The following are key texts for the various typologies and frameworks.

Edwards, John. 1992. Sociopolitical aspects of language maintenance and loss. Towards a typology of minority language situations. In J. Fase, K. Jaspaert and S. Kroon (eds.), *Maintenance and loss of minority languages*. Amsterdam: John Benjamins, 37–54.

Giles, Howard, Richard Y. Bourhis and Donald M. Taylor. 1977. Towards a theory of language in ethnic group relations. In H. Giles (ed.), *Language, ethnicity and intergroup relations*. London: Academic Press, 307–348.

Haarmann, Harald. 1986. *Language in ethnicity*. Berlin: Mouton de Gruyter.

Heller, Monica. Ed. 2007. *Bilingualism: a social approach*. Basingstoke: Palgrave Macmillan.

Kloss, Heinz. 1966. German American language maintenance efforts. In J. Fishman et al. (eds.), *Language loyalty in the United States*. The Hague: Mouton, 206–252.

Smolicz, Jerzy J. 1980. Language as a core value of culture. *Journal of Applied Linguistics* 11.1: 1–13.

Smolicz, Jerzy J., and Margaret Secombe. 1985. Community languages, core values and cultural maintenance: the Australian experience with special reference to Greek, Latvian and Polish groups. In M. Clyne (ed.), *Australia, meeting place of languages*. Canberra: Pacific Linguistics, 11–38.

Stoessel, Saskia. 2002. Investigating the role of social networks in language maintenance and shift. *International Journal of the Sociology of Language* 153: 93–131.

PART IV
Language maintenance efforts and reversing language shift

8 Efforts, agencies and institutions for language maintenance

In this part, we move beyond description and discussion of the dynamics of LM and LS to focus on the efforts, actions and initiatives of individuals, families, groups and the communities themselves to maintain their minority or heritage language and pass it on to future generations. Part III has two chapters. Chapter 8 is mainly occupied with documenting the kinds of activities and initiatives that minority and heritage language communities *themselves* are known to undertake in pursuit of LM. Sections 8.1 to 8.5 describe these efforts around the main domains of the home or family (Section 8.1), the community-based school (Section 8.2), religion (Section 8.3), secular community groups (Section 8.4) and the media (Section 8.5). In Section 8.6 we present some examples of how the majority or dominant community assists in LM in relation to schooling and the media. Inevitably, there is some overlap between Chapter 8 and Chapter 6 (to some extent, also Chapter 7) as they all deal with investigating the central question – Who speaks what language to whom, where and to what end? – and describing and analysing patterns of language use in relation to the key domains mentioned above.

In Chapter 9 we tackle two questions pertinent to LM: Can LS be reversed? Here, we will draw upon Fishman's Graded Intergeneration Disruption Scale to seek a response. The other question – Should LS be reversed? – deals with a more controversial topic, at least for languages that will disappear or be lost, if they are not maintained. In the context of this book, this affects territorial minority languages rather than heritage languages in migrant settings.

8.1 KEEPING THE HERITAGE OR MINORITY LANGUAGE GOING IN THE FAMILY

Throughout this book and in line with the dominant opinions of LM scholars we have stressed the key role that the family plays in efforts to maintain and pass on the heritage or minority language to future generations. So what can or do families do to keep the heritage or minority language alive? In the next sections we discuss various strategies, initiatives and practices found in families living in situations where there are pressures to shift to the dominant language(s) of the nation. Before that it is worthwhile clarifying our use of the term 'family' in the context of language maintenance efforts.

8.1.1   Defining family

What constitutes a family is, like other social organisational units, highly variable across cultures and across times. Blood ties tended to be a fundamental component of defining a family, although this was never universal and is losing its centrality due to changes in laws linked to marriage, adoption and other child-rearing practices. Increasingly the family is best seen as a community of practice (Lave and Wenger 1991) in which adults engage in child rearing. The adults may or may not be the biological parents of the children. Children may move between family units, either as a result of the initial family unit breaking up or because of child-rearing practices. Terms such as 'blended families', 'transnational families' and 'foster families' have arisen to describe newer constellations of family. Within the study of LM it is true that there has been limited problematisation of the term 'family'. In most LM studies to date there is little mention or discussion of family units that do not comply with the heteronormative view. The two dominant constellations of family described in such studies are those of the 'nuclear family' and the 'extended family'. The former refers to a social unit made up of (usually biological) parents and their children, whereas the latter is used to describe social units in which other (blood-related) family members such as grandparents, uncles, nieces or nephews are found. Implicit in these two types of family units is the fact that they live under the 'same roof' or at least in close proximity. The other distinction that has been recognised in LM studies concerns the ethnolinguistic make-up of the family, i.e., whether the parents belong to the same or a different ethnolinguistic group. Our discussion next will therefore be based largely on these types of family units. Another observation to make in relation to heritage language settings is that most studies discuss LM efforts in families where parents belong to the first generation and their children to the second generation. There is still a relative scarcity of studies that look beyond this scenario to explore how parents belonging to subsequent generations try to pass on the heritage language to the next generation.

Families keen to ensure that their children continue to speak the heritage or minority language have devised various practices to achieve this. Preferences and opportunities do vary significantly according to the family situation. Where both parents speak the same heritage or minority language a dominant strategy has been to keep the language going as the primary or, at least, the preferred means of communication within the unit. In families where parents do not share the same language(s) and may not have (much) competence in each other's language(s), the focus tends to be more on creating opportunities to use the heritage or minority language. Within the latter type of family a distinction is usually made between families where one parent is a speaker of the dominant language and where both parents are speakers of different heritage or minority languages.

8.1.2 An early start

Whatever family constellation is involved, an early start, preferably from birth, has been identified as a key element in laying the groundwork for a successful outcome in terms of both linguistic proficiency and continued use (e.g., Bialystok 2001; Grosjean 2008; Homel et al. 1987; McCardie and Hoff 2006; Saunders 1982; see also references in Chapter 6). An early start not only facilitates the process of gaining more advanced levels of linguistic competence (at least verbal) but also establishes bilingualism as a normal state of affairs. Preschool-age children are less likely to question the linguistic choices of their parents or of their familial environment in such a way that it jeopardises their bilingual development. If they do, parents can take the opportunity to reinforce positive views of bilingualism. Parents tend to be quite creative and ingenious in their responses. I recall a colleague telling me about his experience with his four-year-old daughter's question, 'Why do I have to speak two languages and other kids don't?' My colleague knew that his response would be critical in her continued acceptance of speaking two languages. Although he was not someone usually stuck for answers, he felt he could not provide his usual thoughtful responses. He ended up saying to her, 'Well, what do you think is better, one bar of chocolate or two bars?' To his surprise, and perhaps relief, his daughter considered it a most appropriate answer to her question and did not bring up the matter again until well in her teens. Early exposure to bilingualism and its treatment as a normal state of affairs has been shown to assist children in accepting their bilingualism when they are increasingly exposed to the wider society whose linguistic norms do not favour bilingualism, multilingualism or the linguistic practices associated with these phenomena.

In the context of the maintenance of minority languages, the preferred option is to ensure that the minority language is the main language of the family and of family-based interactions. This is also the obvious or only choice for immigrant parents, especially if they have limited competence in the language of their new environment. Making the heritage language the main language of the family requires much more thought and determination in contexts where one or both parents are (fluent) speakers of the dominant language. This applies to many second-generation parents in transnational and immigrant contexts and to some parents of minority languages. While such parents may have adequate knowledge of the heritage or minority language, they are used to communicating with each other in the dominant or majority language. These parents often rely on others, especially grandparents or other older relatives, to provide the heritage or minority language input to their offspring. Another option for an early start in such situations involves simultaneous bilingual language acquisition in which one of the parents opts to use the minority or heritage language to the child(ren) and the other uses the dominant language. This mode of early bilingualism is generally known as the 'one parent, one language' model.

8.1.3 The 'one parent, one language' model

In the 'one parent, one language' model, a child is exposed to and immersed in two languages from birth. The most common iteration of this model is where one parent consistently uses the heritage or minority language with the child and the other parent uses the majority language. There are, however, some variations on this model, some of which have existed for centuries and others that reflect more recent developments in family situations. For example, a regular child carer, for example, a nanny, *au pair* or grandparent, may be the one providing the heritage or minority language input, and the parents speak the majority language with the child(ren).

Ronjat's (1913) study of his son's bilingual (French-German) development is probably one of the first documented cases of the 'one parent, one language' model. He advocated a strict separation of the languages by parent and believed that transgression and deviation from this would have negative effects on the child's bilingual development. This insistence on a clear, if not strict, separation of the two languages to aid and achieve bilingual competence continues to receive widespread support, especially in advice to parents considering raising children bilingually. For example, Döpke (1994), who is an academic and bilingual consultant, provides the following advice to parents:

Language learning is most effective if the language is tied to particular people. The language we use is part of what defines our relationship to a particular person. In that way, language is self-perpetuating. Changing to another language calls the relationship into question ... Consistency in language use is extremely important. Many adults find that very difficult. They frequently fall back into English (if they live in Australia, for example) because this is the language they speak to everybody else. This way the child is placed in a situation like the following: *Mummy speaks English or Greek to me and everybody else speaks English to me. Consequently I can choose to speak English or Greek to Mummy, but because I hear English much more than Greek, English is easier to use. So why should I use Greek?* However, if the parent can get used to only speaking the minority language himself when interacting with the child, then the following scenario is the one that presents itself to the child: *Daddy speaks English to most people, but with me he only speaks Italian. I love Daddy and I like him to spend special time with me. I want to do everything Daddy does and I also want to speak like him.* In order for the adult to feel confident about using the minority language with the child it is best to make a decision to never speak anything but this particular language with the child and to start this as soon as the child is born or from the first time you have contact with a child if she is not your own. (www.bilingualoptions.com.au/consTXT2%20L1.pdf, accessed on 25 May 2015)

There is also some evidence (e.g., Lanza 1997) that children whose parents most closely abide by this model were considered to be (much) more active bilinguals (i.e., they produce more utterances in both languages) than those whose parents conformed less with the principle of language separation. Supporters of this model have shown that it is relatively successful in getting young children to be active or productive bilinguals. Furthermore, if one of the languages involved is the dominant or majority language, there is the added sociopsychological advantage of not being seen as a linguistic out-sider in the eyes of the majority. Yet others consider that to be a disadvantage as the dominant language enters or intrudes into a domain seen as the 'last refuge' for the use and maintenance of the heritage or minority language. Despite some successes and its relative popularity, the model has also attracted considerable criticism for a variety of reasons (e.g., Lyon 1996; Romaine 1995): it has been described as an elitist model catering largely to the bilingual needs or desires of the middle and professional classes. It is also considered artificial as in the 'real world' the majority of children growing up in bi- and multilingual settings engage in frequent code-switching and code-mixing and manage to become and stay bilingual. Another criticism concerns the lack of clear evidence that this model produces consistent positive results. The criticism of elitism is directed at the fact that many studies of this model involve children whose parent or parents are linguists or language experts with a professional interest in bilingualism (e.g., Hoffman 1985; Kielhoefer and Jonekeit 1983; Kravin 1992; Leopold 1939–1949; Porsché 1983; Ronjat 1913; Saunders 1988; Taeschner 1983). Also, the case studies not involving linguists as parents nevertheless focus mainly on families that could be labelled professional and/or middle class. My own experience in contributing to community seminars and workshops on bilingualism in Australia, Great Britain and Germany confirms this impression: parents attending these (free) seminars and interested in the 'one parent, one language model' belonged largely to the professional classes and were highly educated. The other criticism – its artificiality – is directed at the model prescribing strict separation of languages thus (deliberately) avoiding many of the typical features and practices of bilinguals: code-switching and -mixing and other contact phenomena. This approach is said to run counter to what bilinguals do with their languages. Its artificiality is believed to make it not only unrealistic but also unsustainable. This weakness is acknowledged by proponents of the model but countered with the observation that the need to provide the child with as much input as possible in an environment that is overwhelmingly disposed to the majority language justifies trying to limit the practices that involve mixing (Döpke 1998).

On balance, it could be said that the use of 'one parent, one language' model to promote bilingual language acquisition in a heritage or minority language setting has worked and continues to work for specific types of families and under special circumstances. It may not be realistic or suited for the majority of families trying to keep a heritage or minority language going. Furthermore, the relative paucity of studies investigating the impact of this model on continued maintenance of the heritage or minority language beyond childhood into in adolescence and adulthood makes it difficult to assess its role in long-term LM (see, however, Saunders 1988). Despite these criticisms, a number of studies of the 'one parent, one language' model, mentioned previously, provide detailed insights into strategies and practices used with young children that facilitate and support the acquisition of the heritage or minority language in the family, even outside the 'one parent, one language' model. In the next sections, we briefly discuss three of these: (1) consistency in language choice, (2) (positive) reinforcement of appropriate language choices by the child and (3) providing (positive) corrective feedback.

8.1.4 Consistency in language choice

Studies of other approaches to early bilingualism may not have observed or endorsed the strict separation of languages by parents but they have certainly documented that consistency in the use of the heritage or minority language aids the child or children's use of that language. Consistency does not have to imply constant use of the heritage or community language in all family situations or contexts. For example, in the presence of visitors or playmates who are not speakers of the heritage or minority language, parents may decide to switch to the use of the majority language to address their child. Best results are obtained when consistency of use (with or without the use of contact features) is coupled with persistence; i.e., parents insist that the child responds or communicates in the heritage or minority language and they persist in continuing to use the heritage or minority language, even if the child does not (yet) respond in it.

8.1.5 Positive reinforcement of appropriate language choices

Providing positive reinforcement of appropriate language choices is not a strategy unique to the heritage or minority language context. It is used in first-language acquisition and in second- and foreign-language learning. Praising and complimenting the child on being able to use the right utterance, word or phrase in the heritage or minority language acts as a stimulus for continued use. Sometimes, such reinforcement may involve not acceding to a request or ignoring a comment/demand until the appropriate language is used.

8.1.6 Providing corrective feedback

The provision of corrective feedback is another tactic or strategy widely used in second-language learning and first-language acquisition. In a heritage or minority language situation this can cover both metalinguistic comments along the lines 'No, that is not what mummy says, that is a daddy word, what does mummy say? or 'That is not what we say in this family, we use ...' and repetition by the parent of a child's utterance in the appropriate language.

8.1.7 Creating a language-rich environment for the heritage and minority language

Studies looking at bilingual language acquisition involving a heritage or minority language have highlighted the importance of having or creating a (minority/heritage) language-rich environment to aid both the acquisition process and the long-term use of that language, at least in the home or family domain. The issue of LM arises in language situations where there is competition between languages, with one or more languages losing ground against a more dominant or majority language. If the language disappears from the heartland of the family, the chances of the language being passed on to the next generation are (drastically) diminished, even futile. Of course, there is considerable variation for individuals and communities in their opportunities to speak, hear or be immersed in the minority or heritage language outside the home; for example, a Puerto Rican child living in a New York neighbourhood in which many Puerto Ricans and other Spanish speakers have settled can access a much wider network of Spanish speakers than a child of a Vietnamese family living in a remote country town in Australia. The creation of a language-rich home environment will be critical for children in the Vietnamese family, but it is not a negligible matter for the Puerto Rican child either. Generally, it is the family, mainly parents or grandparents, who are responsible for the acquisition process. They also remain key players in maintaining the language beyond the initial years. Although there is no direct relationship between quantity of language input and the acquisition of proficiency, limited exposure to a variety of structures, registers and uses of language does diminish a learner's ability to generate new structures, acquire a rich vocabulary and build up communicative competence in a language (e.g., Doughty 2003; Ortega 2011). If children are exposed only to a few formulaic routines in the heritage or minority language, it is hard to imagine that they can move beyond this formulaic use of the language. In most cases the home and the family environment constitute the main 'language laboratory' for young children, in which they hear, absorb and experiment with language structures, functions and uses. Providing the child with direct verbal input continues to be most important; if this can be done by an array of family members and other speakers of the heritage or minority language, this not only expands the input but also diversifies it, leading to contact with more structures and ways of speaking. In this regard, so-called extended families are better placed than small nuclear families to deliver this. Particularly important is the presence of speakers who prefer, by either necessity or choice, to speak the heritage or minority language. In practice, these tend to be speakers less comfortable with or proficient in the majority language, such as older people who have grown up speaking the language or, in the case of migrant families, overseas visitors. Grandparents, in particular, have played and continue to play a major role in heritage or minority LM. In many cultures they play a significant role in child rearing by having daily contact with their grandchildren. Furthermore, the greater participation of women in the paid workforce, by choice or necessity, also means that grandparents are often called upon to undertake some child-minding and child-rearing duties. Their influence on steering language use is felt among not only young children but also adolescents and young adults. The latter may no longer use or may even refuse to use the heritage or minority language with their parents but will accede to using it with grandparents. Overseas visitors from the 'homeland', including young adults, often have a similar effect in stimulating heritage language use among the younger generation. Parents have commented that the visits of overseas cousins or other younger relatives and acquaintance have given a boost, albeit usually temporary, to their children's use of the heritage language.

Another facet of creating a language-rich environment in the home involves exposing the child to or immersing him or her in the sounds and signs of the heritage language environment. Until the advent of the internet, this immersion largely consisted of the occasional voices of visitors and relatives, the sounds of some radio broadcasts and other audio-recordings in the heritage or minority language and the presence of reading material (books, magazines), games and other such materials. In fact, interviews with parents wishing to keep the heritage language alive in an immigrant setting revealed that they were constantly on the lookout for audiovisual resources appropriate for young children. Accessing such material was often a major enterprise for those who had migrated to far-flung places; overseas visitors were asked to bring along audio- and videotapes suitable for children. Parents visiting their homeland brought back suitcases full of language materials. Parents' clubs and groups were set up to exchange resources and local libraries were raided for the few resources they held in the heritage language. In the case of the maintenance of a minority language, the problem was sometimes more acute: appropriate resources were scarce or even nonexistent. The arrival of the internet in many homes around the world has radically changed this or has the potential to do so: it provides instant access to a rich variety of written and oral resources that assist families in creating a language-rich environment: films, videos, music, narrated stories, news reports, cartoons, comics, fairytales, games and puzzles that stimulate language use. The internet has also facilitated the expansion of direct contact with the language through offering cheap and instant channels of communication (audio and video-enabled) with heritage language speakers around the world. In Chapter 10 we shall look in more detail at this new 'domain' and how it can be particularly beneficial for older children and young adults in keeping the heritage language alive.

Another major advance in facilitating the acquisition and the maintenance of the heritage language in families is the (much) greater affordability of transnational travel: for many migrants and refugees of early and mid-twentieth-century large-scale migration movements such as those following World War II, the financial burden of travel to the homeland was too immense to undertake more than once in a lifetime and often meant saving up for many years. Furthermore, until the 1960s most long-distance travel across oceans involved long sea voyages that few could afford financially or time-wise. This has changed radically, so that many families can now travel regularly across the world, either to the homeland or to other places to visit heritage language-speaking relatives and communities. In places like Australia this has given rise to a greater number of children – the second generation – travelling to and living in their parental homeland for a considerable period of time. Interestingly, many of them return to *their* homeland after a few years. This often leads to a big boost in heritage language use in the family setting and an overall enrichment of heritage language environment for the family. For a language-rich environment to be truly effective, it needs to be accompanied by a positive attitude towards the heritage or minority language.

8.1.8 Displaying positive attitudes towards the heritage or minority language

This may seem like very straightforward advice that makes common sense. Yet the evidence from studies around the world clearly shows that this is often a very challenging task for minority or immigrant language families wishing to engage in LM. This is the case not only for families living in an environment hostile to the idea of minority LM but also for those not faced with such external and public hostility. Surveys of attitudes that individuals and communities hold towards their heritage or minority language and its maintenance generally reveal positive attitudes, with many desiring to pass on the heritage or minority language to the next generation. Even in communities and groups for whom language is not a 'core' value or whose LS rates are very high, attitudes continue to be positive (e.g., Bennett 1990; Pauwels 1980). Yet where commitment questions have been built into these surveys, responses are far less promising: the support for active steps to keep language going in the family reduces markedly (e.g., Bennett 1990). In interviews many parents reveal the challenge of modelling and displaying a positive view of the heritage language or minority and its maintenance. For example, Tuominen (1999: 59) presents the case of parents wishing to keep Russian going in the family:

> [Russian-speaking parents with two children]
> MOTHER: In the home we want to save it.
> AKT: Is it a rule then to speak Russian in the home?
> FATHER: We would like it to be, but . . .

Furthermore, immigrant and minority parents are often exposed to opinions, beliefs and advice held or given by professionals in education, health and social services that discourage the use or maintenance of the heritage or minority language. These include viewing bilingual language acquisition as too strenuous and taxing for most children, thus leading to language and other learning difficulties (e.g., Pauwels 1994, for opinions and beliefs about bilingualism held by health professionals). Although there is a significant amount of research in second and bilingual language acquisition that not only dismisses some of these claims but also reveals both cognitive and educational advantages of bilingualism, these research outcomes seem to be trickling down only (very) slowly into the training of these professions. These beliefs and opinions about the negative impact of LM and bilingualism on learning and language development per se continue to influence speakers of minority languages, especially in immigrant contexts, as parents try to come to grips with a new environment, a new language and a different culture. Faced with these (often well-meaning but ill-informed) 'professional' opinions, many immigrant parents do not have the confidence to project a positive view of their language or its maintenance. Perhaps more successful has been the work undertaken by researchers in collaboration with communities and some educators to provide basic guides and information on raising children bilingually. These are then distributed via health centres, community centres, (ethnic) schools and other avenues that can reach parents and others involved in bilingual upbringing. In fact there are now also numerous websites across the world providing detailed information on the subject (e.g., www.bilingualism-matters.ppls.ed.ac.uk, http://multilingual parenting.com/). Anecdotal evidence collected from researchers working in minority and immigrant settings (e.g., Wales, the Sami community in Norway, migrant communities in Australia, Canada, the United States, Germany and Scandinavia) reveals that an increasing number of immigrant and minority language parents (who are not all middle class!) are accessing family-oriented websites that provide information about bilingual upbringing.

A suitable final comment about LM in the family is that the multitude of studies concerned with bilingual language acquisition in families has revealed a plethora of practices, routines and strategies to encourage young children to learn and use the minority or heritage language. Ultimately, what works or does not work depends on the needs, contexts and experiences of each individual family. Some families who belong to groups with a history of migration and diaspora may continue to rely on practices that worked for previous generations; other families with such experience may be more willing to experiment with new routines or approaches.

8.1.9 Moving beyond the family

There is a clear consensus about the critical role that the family and the home environment play in the process of sustaining a heritage or minority language. In the case of families who are relatively isolated with no or limited access to networks of heritage or minority language speakers, the responsibility or 'burden' of LM weighs heavily on the home and family environment. For them, the activities and strategies outlined here are their main way of keeping the language going and passing it on to the next generation (however, see Chapter 10 for more recent developments).

For other families, there may be a range of other opportunities outside the home to foster LM. These will of course vary according to the setting in which the families operate. A migrant family settled in a neighbourhood populated by members of the same ethnolinguistic community will have different possibilities for the use of the heritage language than an immigrant family who belongs to a close-knit religious community that uses the heritage language mainly for religious ceremonies. A minority family living in an area where there are few other minority language speakers but where the children have opportunity to learn the minority language in the school is presented with a different LM scenario from that for a family living in the heartland of a linguistic minority but where there is no provision for schooling in the minority language. In the next sections (Sections 8.2 to 8.5) we review a number of contexts, agencies or institutions that are or can be associated with the heritage or minority language. Although some of these are not set up for the purpose of LM, they nevertheless facilitate the continued use of the language. Here we focus on four major 'agencies' that the community itself initiates and supports, with or without support from the majority: schools, religious institutions, organised leisure or culture groups and the media. Initiatives and support structures organised by the state or majority are reviewed in Section 8.6.

8.2 COMMUNITY SCHOOLS

In this context the word 'school' refers primarily to an educational agency or establishment set up by the linguistic minority or ethnic (migrant) community in order to pass on knowledge and practices, including language, associated with the community in question. There are numerous designations for such schools; 'ethnic group' schools, coined by Fishman et al. (1966), was one of the first labels to be used in the context of immigrant minorities. Other labels since then include ethnic schools, ethnic community schools, mother tongue schools, Saturday schools, heritage language schools and supplementary schools. Here we shall use the terms 'community schools' or 'community language schools' to emphasise that they are an initiative of a specific community rather than the state. In some countries the heritage language can also be learned within the wider public school system, although more often as a foreign language with limited or no accommodation to those students who use it as heritage language (see Section 8.6).

8.2.1 Language learning in community schools

There is enormous variety in how communities organise educational activities for their children, ranging from fully fledged educational establishments that offer a comprehensive curriculum to a regular gathering in a community hall or even a private dwelling to undertake lessons. Fishman et al. (1966) distinguished between three types of community schools:

- Schools that run throughout the day and that offer a comprehensive ethnocultural curriculum involving language, culture, history and religion.
- Schools that operate outside the formal school day, after hours and usually a few times per week.
- Schools that operate on weekends.

These three types continue to be dominant in the organisation of community schooling, although there is now a greater diversity within each of these, especially in the context of heritage language learning (see, e.g., García et al. 2013, for the United States; Jaspaert and Kroon 1991, for Europe). Although language may not be primary or sole focus of some community schools, especially those offering a more comprehensive cultural heritage educational package or those more focused on religious instruction, the heritage or minority language tends to feature in all such forms of schooling. Sometimes this may be limited to a special register or language variety such as Quranic Arabic in

Islamic or Quran schools, or Church Slavonic in community schools organised by Russian Orthodox communities. Community schools are primarily intended for children of the heritage or minority language communities, although they may also be open to adults from these minorities or people from other groups. Most community schools try to cater to children between the ages of six and eighteen, with the majority catering to primary-aged children.

How language learning is organised in such community school settings is also characterised by enormous diversity. In some cases students enhance linguistic skills or learn their language through intensive immersion-type educational activities or daily language classes, whereas others will learn the language for a few hours once per week in the private home of a community member. Resources, both material and human, are also widely variable; some communities rely heavily on the goodwill of some individuals prepared to spend a few hours teaching the heritage or minority language to children. These volunteers are often parents or community members with limited if any teacher training. They 'self-qualify' on the grounds that they are speakers of the language. This scenario tends to occur in small communities – of immigrants or territorial minorities – where there are limited community resources to sustain language learning. In other communities, especially those with a long history of migration, the homeland may provide assistance for the teaching of the language to the children of its diasporic population. This may include supplying teachers trained in the homeland and providing both the curriculum and teaching materials. Italy and Greece are examples of states that continue to provide language learning support to its diasporic communities. In yet other groups, often those who have been settled for a long time in a specific country, the teaching staff may be drawn from qualified local language teachers, many of whom belong to the ethnolinguistic group themselves. Clyne (1991) mentions that this is the case for German heritage language classes in Australia. This can also be said to apply to many of the teachers providing heritage language classes in Spanish in the United States (e.g., Valdés et al. 1980). In some countries the teaching of students, even outside the formal state-sanctioned education system, is heavily regulated. This covers matters such as obtaining police clearance to work with children, being certified by the local authorities as a teacher and demonstrating knowledge of the educational practices in the country. Such regulatory frameworks have a mixed impact on the teaching that takes place in schools run by heritage and minority communities. For communities, especially those in migrant settings that can comply with the regulations, the result is often beneficial: the teachers are better acquainted with the educational context within which most of their students grow up. They will also have acquired a range of pedagogical skills that assist them in the classroom. Yet their pedagogical and possibly ideological accommodation to the dominant educational philosophies and approaches may be seen as diluting the distinctiveness of the sociocultural, philosophical knowledge and practices linked to the specific ethnolinguistic group. Sometimes, communities are simply unable or unwilling to work within such a framework. Although such a scenario does not lead categorically to a lesser commitment by the students to language learning, the teaching styles adopted by the staff and their pedagogical approaches may be experienced as quite alien, sometimes reducing their motivation or engagement with the learning process. There are of course also countries and societies whose assimilationist policies discourage and even forbid the setup of community-based educational organisations dedicated to passing on ethno-specific traditions (e.g., linguistic, cultural, religious). This was the case in Australia in relation to German following the outbreak of both world wars (e.g., Ozolins 1993). Many territorial minority language communities in Europe have been exposed to this situation during past centuries (e.g., Skutnabb-Kangas 2000). In such oppressive environments language learning activities will have operated or tend to operate clandestinely, often limiting accessibility to only a minority of potential learners.

8.2.2 Community schools as an instrument of language maintenance

There is now a wealth of studies that have explored almost every aspect and angle of community-based language learning in many societies, especially those with large migrant populations and those with 'recognised' linguistic minorities. There have been studies of the types of language instruction found in community schools, the curriculum and language learning syllabus, the nature and training of teaching staff, the language practices in the classroom and students' and parental attitudes to the community-based language learning (e.g., Clyne and Fernandez 2008; Cummins 1981, 1983; Davis 1999; García et al. 2013; Hornberger 2005; Lee and Shin 2008; Peyton et al. 2001; Trifonas and Aravossitas 2014; Wiley 2005). As expected, given the diversity in community-based language learning opportunities and activities coupled with differences between ethnolinguistic communities, the results and insights obtained from these studies are similarly diverse, divergent and sometimes even conflicting. Given this multitude and diversity of findings, an overview of these within the context of this book is simply not feasible. However, with regard to the central issue of this book – LM and LS – the results of this growing body of research allow us to make some general observations about the role of community schools. In Chapter 6, we already mentioned that most studies provide some evidence for the positive role of community schools in the process of LM, albeit with many provisos linked to the elements mentioned before. Let us look at two observations that highlight the positive role of community-based language learning in LM.

The role of community schools in the acquisition of literacy in the heritage or minority language

The acquisition of literacy, whether for a first, second or other language, is usually associated with the domain of formal education. The school is the place in which most children learn to read and write and in which they are introduced to more formal aspects of language. This is also the case for the majority of community schools: learning to read and write in the heritage or minority language is a desired goal of the learning process. To what extent this goal is achieved will depend on a range of factors, including the amount of time devoted to language learning (time on task) and the type and exposure to the heritage or minority language the student has had before joining the school. Community language programs usually cater for a mixture of students; in a migrant setting, there could be immigrant children who were born in the home country but had no or minimal exposure to formal schooling. It could also include second-generation children who use or are exposed to the heritage language in the home environment. Other participants in this setting may be children who are sent to the school to acquire some skills in the heritage language, as the home environment no longer provides such exposure. Children who attend such classes in territorial minority language settings may also be quite diverse in terms of their exposure to, use of, and proficiency in the minority language. Although there is no clear evidence that literacy acquisition leads to LM, there are observations and suggestions that it enhances the possibility of LM. It provides the learner with greater opportunities to access a wealth of resources, both textual and oral, and it provides a solid base for passing the language to the subsequent generation. This also applies to some groups for whom the question of literacy development is more complex because the spoken variety is very different from their (assigned or chosen) language of literacy. This includes, for example, groups whose language situation is characterised by a form of diglossia in which there are clearly distinctive varieties for speaking, reading and writing (e.g., Arabic) as well as communities that may share the same or similar spoken varieties (e.g., Punjabi) but whose language of literacy is associated different scripts, i.e., the Gurmukhi/Shamukhi/Majhi scripts for Punjabi.

Enhancing the link between language and identity among peers

Participating in language learning in a community-based setting places the learner in an environment of peers who share many of the language and other cultural and social experiences of the learner. These shared characteristics and experiences around the heritage or minority language – both positive and negative ones – can create a sense of solidarity among students. The community school can thus provide a 'safe' environment in which students can experiment with and negotiate new affiliations and identities around the heritage or minority language, bilingualism and other cultural or ethnic markers. For many students it may be the only environment in which they can utter both positive and negative feelings linked to the heritage or minority language, at least to their peers. For others, contact with peers in the community school setting makes them realise that the heritage or minority language is not simply a language limited to their family or to older people, but that it has a much wider reach and value outside the home. Although there is no unambiguous evidence that children who have undertaken language learning in community-based contexts maintain the heritage or minority language better than those without such experience, there is an increasing number of observations from research projects that community-based language learning provides a safe space for students to forge identities linked to the heritage or minority language and to experiment with various linguistic practices. These two elements create a positive condition not only for future LM but also for a better understanding of linguistic diversity and multilingualism. In their research on language and identity in some complementary schools in Leicester, United Kingdom, Creese et al. (2006: 40–41) comment on this latter observation:

> We view complementary schooling as providing an important
> context for students to explore identity positions and create
> narratives in new and imaginative ways … Nancy Hornberger (2001)
> has argued for the necessity of bilingual spaces and havens
> in dominant monolingual environments. We see complementary
> schools as places where the dominant ideologies around bilingualism
> are contested and where young people are able to explore identity
> positions more safely. Interestingly, our findings are that
> complementary schools do not enforce singular and essentialised
> ethnic or heritage identities but instead provide a context for

students to combine their different life experiences in more fluid ethnicities with flexible bilingualism. Bilingualism becomes a key resource in negotiating these complex identities.

A recent detailed report on the impact of supplementary schools (i.e., community schools) on pupils' academic attainment in the United Kingdom (based on research undertaken by the Institute of Policy Studies, London Metropolitan University, in collaboration with the National Centre for Social Research and Bryson Purdon Research), Maylor et al. (2010) echoed the observations made by Creese et al. (2006). Their key findings with respect to the students attending such schools were:

- the development of positive attitudes towards education (including more focused, attentive, better behaved and more motivated learners);
- positive identity reinforcement;
- an increase in self-esteem/self-awareness;
- increased confidence in asking questions/speaking out aloud as well as socialising with others in and outside school;
- a better understanding of one's cultural background (heritage, language, religion);
- increased community/mother tongue language skills. (Maylor et al. 2010: 12)

By way of summary we could say that participating in community-based language schools or programs is more likely to have a positive than an adverse effect on LM, at least in the short term. Unfortunately, the link between participation in language learning in such schools or programs and long-term LM has not yet been thoroughly researched. Some inferences between the two can be made, though: in minority language settings, children who have attended such classes and have acquired some literacy may be better placed and more willing to continue speaking the minority language. In the immigrant context, there may be some link between attendance at community schools and greater levels of LM in the second generation. For example, many Greek parents insist that their children attend 'Greek' school, and many do so. Rates of LM among second- and third-generation Greek Australians are also quite a bit higher than those of similar generations in groups with a lesser tradition of or insistence on such schooling. Clyne (1991: 66) showed that 88.3 percent of second-generation and 48.5 percent of third-generation Greek Australians still made some use of Greek, whereas second- and third-generation German Australians, for example, had much lower rates: 27.3 percent for the second generation and 1.3 percent for the third generation.

8.3　THE RELIGIOUS DOMAIN

Religious differences, intolerance, oppression and even persecution have long been a major cause or reason for people to leave their territory; prominent examples in the western world are the seventeenth-century Puritans from England, who became known as 'Pilgrim fathers' and belonged to early settlers in America, Jews in various parts of the world and the Amish and Mennonites who escaped religious oppression in Germany. Some of these were able to establish new communities in other parts of the world where they enjoyed greater religious freedom (e.g., the early Puritans in America), whereas others found that their migration and resettlement did not do much to alleviate religious intolerance (e.g., some Jewish communities in South America). Sometimes the church (as an institution) also played a considerable role in determining the resettlement destinations for migrants. Postwar migration from the Netherlands to the 'new world' is a clear example of this: the various (Christian) churches set up migration agencies to send their members and parishioners to different parts of the new world, with the majority of Calvinist, other Reformed and Protestant migrants going to North America and (Roman) Catholics more likely to end up in Australia and New Zealand. Of course, there are also territorial minorities for whom religion is very important and a possible cause of friction with majority groups in the territory. Byrnes (1999) presents two such case studies from the French regions of Alsace and Roussillon.

In the migrant context, individuals, groups and entire communities may adopt different approaches to the maintenance of religious practices in the new environment: those whose exodus was mainly for religious reasons may be more committed to keeping their religious practices intact than those whose religious beliefs were more peripheral to the migratory reason. In the former case this may lead to the group becoming not only a linguistic minority but also a religious minority. This is, for example, the case with groups such as the Amish. Even if a group's religious denomination is already represented or established in the new environment, the (migrant) group may decide not to 'join' or 'merge' with it but keep its own ethnocultural version. For example, the Uniate Catholic Churches associated in Australia with Lebanese Maronite and Ukrainian immigrants have maintained their own practices rather than merged with those associated with the Roman Catholic Churches in Australia (Lewins 1978). Others were more open or susceptible to adapting to the local (dominant) version of their religious denomination, ultimately leading to their full integration into it. This process involves initially offering services through the heritage language with a gradual transition to the full use of the majority language.

Here we are specifically interested in the link between language and the conduct of religious activities. If a particular language is intricately linked to religious practices, then the continued knowledge of this language is an essential part of being a believer. If there is no such a strong link between language and religion, then (full) participation in various forms of worship is not denied by limited or no knowledge of that language. Researchers investigating the role of religion in LM (e.g., Clyne 1991; Klarberg 1976; Omoniyi and Fishman 2006; Woods 2004) usually place communities on a continuum in terms of the importance they attach to the use of specific language for religious worship. Followers of Islam (Muslim communities) are often identified as representative of the very strong link between language and religion, whereas certain branches of Roman Catholicism and 'Protestantism' are likely to be situated at the other end of the continuum. The majority of (world) religions and their various cultural expressions tend to lie somewhere in between these two extremes: they may continue to use a special language, sometimes seen as a sacred language or register for very specific religious rituals such as incantations and recitations, but perform other ceremonies and religious activities in either the heritage language or the language of the new environment. Another important factor that impacts on which language(s) will be used in communal worship is the group's attitude to keeping the next generations in the congregation and attracting new (outside) members to the congregation. Some communities are particularly concerned that continued insistence on the use of the heritage language for religious worship will lead to the departure of the younger generation, who often have no or limited proficiency in that language. The (Dutch) Reformed Church (a church based on Calvinist doctrines) in Australia is a clear example of this orientation. Because of its concern about losing younger members and its desire to attract new members not belonging to the Dutch Australian community, the Reformed Church has abandoned its use of Dutch for religious ceremonies, although it still ran some separate services in Dutch for elderly Dutch-born parishioners (Overberg 1981). For Australia, Clyne (1991: 132) undertook a survey of churches associated with ethnic and immigrant groups to identify what role the heritage language played in worship and other religious practices. Four major patterns emerged:

1. *Rapid assimilation*: The group in question does not set up its own parishes, temples or other places of worship. It may provide, on

its own or in association with an established church in Australia, some services in the heritage languages mainly for the benefit of newly arrived migrants.

2. *Transitional assimilation*: This category contains those communities that do not subscribe to a close link between language and religion. Although their religious practices may differ from that of the majority, the aim is to 'de-ethnicise' their practices so that they can be accessed by all. Services in the heritage language are merely transitional.

3. *Structural bi- or multilingualism*: 'This model provides for self-contained ethnic congregations conducting different community language or bilingual services within a wider English-dominated denomination' (Clyne 1991: 132).

4. *Pluralism*: This model represents those denominations and religions in which there is a close relationship between language and religion. In most cases, the heritage language continues to be the language also used for religious practices.

For communities and groups that have a desire to maintain all or some of their religious practices in heritage or minority languages, let us examine how this domain can assist in the maintenance of the language.

8.3.1 The heritage or minority language as the liturgical language

Where the heritage or minority language is used to perform the ceremonies and rituals associated with the religion, worshippers will be exposed to hearing the language regularly. Although this may often be a more formal register of the language, there is nevertheless regular contact with the language. For example, in many Christian Churches the interpretation and explanation of Bible passages are central elements of a church service; this is usually done through a sermon in the heritage or minority language by the priest, vicar or other religious leader. In other congregations the sharing of personal experiences is an important aspect of worship; here the believers not only hear but also use the heritage or minority language in a formal religious context. Of course, some religions assign a special 'sacred' status to an ancient language that may or may not be related to the heritage or minority used by the community; this was or is Latin for some Roman Catholics, Old Church Slavonic for some eastern Orthodox Churches, Sanskrit for Hinduism, Quranic Arabic for Muslims and Ancient Hebrew for Jewish believers, to name but a few examples. Where such languages or varieties are not radically or significantly different from the one(s) used by the community, they may act as an indirect stimulus for LM, especially for the younger generations. As attendance and participation in such religious ceremonies require the learning of the religious language, classes are provided by the community to familiarise the young with the rituals and to learn the language. Today, this is most prevalent in relation to followers of Islam (i.e., the existence of Quranic schools). These schools and classes cater primarily, though not exclusively, to students belonging to heritage and minority language communities that share these religious practices. The language of instruction and possibly the informal language used by pupils inside and outside the classroom may be the heritage or minority language. Thus the participation in religious instruction and services may enhance LM. For example, Gogonas (2012) examined LM among second-generation adolescents of Arabic-speaking background. He found that those who belonged to the Coptic religion experienced a significantly greater shift away from Arabic that those who were Muslims.

8.3.2 The use of the heritage or minority language for personal religious expression

Questionnaire-based surveys and in-depth interviews with members of linguistic minorities and heritage language communities have revealed that the heritage or minority language is the preferred code for communing with deities through personal prayers, incantations, requests, confessions and other personal interactions. Respondents have commented that they continue to use this language for these internal, private conversations even if they have completely shifted to the majority language in other domains. As mentioned in Chapter 6, my own work with Dutch migrants in Australia, a community notorious for its very low level of LM, found that many parents and grandparents still taught their children and grandchildren to say prayers in Dutch. Indeed, some of the children whom I interviewed could still recite (fragments of) prayers in Dutch (Pauwels 1980, 1983).

8.3.3 The congregation as a heritage or minority language–based community of practice

Perhaps the most profound impact religion can have on LM is as a practice in which a set of people regularly comes together to share in religion-focused communion. Often the formal worship event is accompanied by various other activities, including social and cultural ones: Sunday school for young children, Bible classes, preparations for special festivals, religion-inspired trips such as pilgrimages, processions and so on. These activities provide opportunities for worshippers to engage more freely with each other in the heritage or minority language.

8.4 SECULAR COMMUNITY-BASED ORGANISATIONS

Many migrant and minority communities establish organisations, clubs and societies that help them maintain, foster and strengthen social and ethnocultural traditions and practices associated with the group. In the case of migrant communities, these societies and organisations often also act to ease the transition into the new society by providing a temporary haven or refuge from the stresses of the settlement process. As expected, there is enormous variety in these organisations, as they reflect the very diversity of traditions and interests of communities around the world.

8.4.1 Clubs and societies

In migrant settings, some such societies are set up to attract migrants from a specific region rather than from the entire homeland. Good examples are the many regional clubs and societies that Italian migrants set up in their new environments. For many Italians a regional association is more important and more relevant than a national one, as many of their traditions including language are also regionally based (e.g., Auer 1991; Harney 1998; Huber 1977). Another interesting example is regionally based clubs that focus primarily on the rites, rituals and ceremonies linked to an important regional festival or tradition. For example, migrants from the Limburg province in the Netherlands continue to engage in the elaborate activities surrounding the pre-Lent festival, known around the world as Carnevale, Carnival or Mardi Gras. In Australia they have set up a number of clubs entirely devoted to this festival: members select an annual Prins Karnival (Carnival Prince) who will preside over the celebrations and will undertake ceremonial duties linked to the festival throughout the year. These celebrations still involve the use of the Limburg dialect, at least in a ritual way, thus implicitly supporting LM. Furthermore, there is a plethora of clubs and societies that focus on a tradition, activity, skill, craft or pastime 'typically' associated with or important to an ethnic, regional or national group; these range from clubs whose focus is on card and board games (e.g., Mah Jong, Klaverjassen, Shogi, Crokinole, Scopa), folk dancing, sports (petanque, dragon boat racing) or crafts (paper art, calligraphy) to societies devoted to various art and cultural pastimes including theatre, book and film clubs and music societies.

8.4.2   Heritage or minority language use in secular societies ▬▬▬

The extent to which these clubs and societies support or even encourage LM is also very variable. There are a number of factors that play a role in whether such organisations act as LM vehicles or not. These are not dissimilar from those affecting the role of religion in LM. Two major factors are (1) the type of activity associated with the club and (2) the type of members such organisations target or attract. Some activities clearly involve the use of heritage or minority language; for example, engaging in theatre performances or attending film and book reading clubs require the participants to use or, at least, to understand the heritage or minority language. These can be seen to actively support LM, and the people engaging in them do so frequently to keep up or enhance their skills in the heritage or minority language. Many other activities in clubs and societies can involve some use of the heritage or minority language and thus peripherally support LM. Some of these uses can be limited to various forms of formulaic language such as the linguistic routines associated with card games (e.g., dealing of cards, the calling of hands, describing moves), the names of specific dances or dance moves, sports and other games, reciting poems or singing songs. These uses can extend to instructions and explanations of how to undertake a certain craft or execute a certain task. Meetings of societies and clubs are another speech event in which the heritage or minority language can be used. Clyne and Manton (1979) examined the meeting routines in twenty different types of societies and clubs of four ethnic communities in Melbourne (Dutch, German-speaking, Greek and Italian) and identified three dominant patterns of language use: (1) sole or dominant use of the heritage language, (2) dominant use of English or (3) a mixture of both. Although the heritage language was still reported as the main language of meetings, there was significant variation among the four ethnolinguistic groups: only 42 percent of Dutch organisations claimed to still use Dutch, whereas this was 68 percent for the Greek ones, 65 percent for the Italian ones and 55 percent for the German ones. Conversely, the sole or dominant use of English was highest among the Dutch (37%) and lowest amongst the Greek societies (13%). All groups also reported the use of a mixture of the heritage language and English, with the highest percentage – 25 percent – claimed by the German societies. My own work (Pauwels 1986) on meeting routines in Dutch and German societies in Australia provided a further breakdown in terms of the language used by the chair and the committee members and the language used in meeting agendas and minutes. The overall results echoed the findings by Clyne and Manton (1979), with Dutch organisations using the heritage language least. This investigation also showed that the chairperson tends to be the one using the heritage language most and that agendas and minutes tended to be written in the language preferred or used by the chair.

The other factor that influences the degree to which such organisations assist LM is the audience or membership they target or attract. In the case of migrant organisations, they tend to cater more to members of the first generation. This is often the result of their original purpose, i.e., to support, socially and culturally, the newly arrived migrants in their settlement process. This orientation towards and attraction of older generations is perhaps less obvious in minority language organisations, although the type of activity may also be geared more towards an older generation. Clyne (1991) commented that most younger (second-generation) members joined or participated in ethnic clubs and societies in Australia only if the activity or pastime was clearly geared towards them: while clubs often provided activities geared towards the very young, they did not do so well in terms of adolescents. However, some communities organise summer camps or have youth groups (especially scouting organisations) catering to this age group. Another dilemma faced by many secular organisations is the choice of language: if LS is already quite advanced in the heritage or minority language community, especially amongst the younger generations, then continuing to hold functions and activities in that language may exclude the very people whom they wish to attract as members. Overall, most secular community clubs and societies play a limited role in direct support for LM: while they continue to provide an environment or a community of practice in which first-generation or older people can socialise in their heritage or minority language, they seldom act as a vehicle for LM for younger generations. Clyne (1991: 138) makes this general observation about the role of such organisations in LM:

> The need for an ethnic support group may diminish over time. It may increase temporarily with the ageing of the first generation or for some economic or political reason. Subsequently it may be taken over by new vintage migrants or by a second generation committed to language maintenance. Or the second generation may wish to continue the organization but mainly in English.

8.5 THE DOMAIN OF MINORITY MEDIA

Here we focus on those media that are produced by the minority or migrant groups themselves. Until recently, this domain consisted mainly of various forms of print media – newspapers, magazines and bulletins – and some electronic media, notably radio stations and television channels. However, this domain has expanded extensively with the advent of the internet. Both immigrant and territorial linguistic minorities now use the internet – websites and social media – extensively to support their culture, language or other traditions (e.g., Amant and Kelsey 2012; Sheyholislami 2011; Tagg 2015). Here we focus on the more traditional or older media – print and broadcasting – and come back to the internet and social media in Chapter 10.

The role of the minority media in LM is not dissimilar from that associated with religious practices: depending on the community in question, the availability of such media in the heritage or minority language may be motivated by a desire to keep the language going or to cater to individuals with no or minimum competence in the majority language (this is mainly the case in immigrant settings). However, such media may see the use of the heritage or minority language as a by-product of the main focus: reporting news and relating events that are of particular interest to the minority community. In the case of immigrant or diasporic communities there is also often a desire to receive news about the homeland. Furthermore, the minority media also tend to highlight or foreground information and news that is particularly relevant or interesting to a specific community. Irrespective of the primary goals of minority media, they do tend to make use of the heritage or minority language, as noted by Riggins (1992: 3): 'what better strategy could there be for ensuring minority survival than the development of their own media conveying their own point of view *in their own language?*' (emphasis added). So, if or when such media make use of the heritage or minority language, even if it is not their primary focus, they can assist in LM. The continued use of the heritage or minority language in these media can, however, also be seen as limiting: if younger generations have limited literacy or other linguistic competencies in the heritage or minority language, then they may turn away from these media because of the language barrier.

8.5.1 The print media

Ethno-specific and minority group print media have probably been in existence for as long as there have been minorities and migrant communities. Such groups have been publishing their own newspapers, news sheets and bulletins to provide both local news and news from the homeland for centuries. This is also the case for other 'regional' minorities who produced or continue to produce news sheets, often in defiance of the majority group (e.g., Kurds in Turkey; Sheyholislami 2011). Although it is impossible to know or even to make a reasonable guess of how many such newspapers have been or are in circulation, their number is likely to be in the thousands and will cover many of the world's languages. For some of the 'Anglophone' migration destinations of the past few centuries there are some tentative figures or guesses: for Australia, Clyne (1991) estimated that there were more than 120 newspapers in more than thirty community languages being locally produced by the 1990s. In 2009, New America Media reported the existence of more than 2500 ethnic media organisations producing newspapers or magazines in many heritage languages in the United States. Canada is said to have more than 250 ethnic newspapers covering more than forty ethnolinguistic communities. Based on the findings of a European Community (EU)-funded project, Minorities and Their Media in the EU: A Mapping, a similar picture emerges for many of the EU countries, (e.g., www.lse.ac.uk/media@lse/research/EMTEL/ minorities/reports.html, accessed 15 August 2014). Undoubtedly, many such publications will also circulate in other continents even if they have not yet been documented to the same extent.

If these newspapers and other print-based news materials use the heritage or minority language, they can be or become important vehicles for LM (Cormack and Hourigan 2007). In the case of migrant communities, the content of articles and reports is usually a mixture of local (ethnic community), national, international and homeland news. Some articles in the heritage language are sourced or reprinted from homeland newspapers, while others are produced by local reporters. Sometimes this is accompanied by a difference in linguistic forms and expressions: whereas the homeland articles are normally written in the standard version of the heritage language, local news items, readers' letters and sometimes even editorials may be written in a more local version of the heritage language. The former provide heritage language readers with an opportunity to keep abreast of linguistic innovations and to keep in touch with the 'preferred' variety for literacy – the standard language. The latter often contain a number of features typical of contact varieties: there are lexical transfers from the dominant/majority language to denote concepts, objects or events typical of the new environment. Sometimes grammatical constructions reflect the influence from the contact language, leading to disapproving comments from some readers. Semantic transfers are also likely to occur but are not so easily spotted by the readers (e.g., Clyne 1991). Another linguistic problem faced by some heritage language newspapers, at least in the time before digital production, concerned the typesetting of the paper. This task was often undertaken by or outsourced to people who had no or limited knowledge of the language. As a result the presence of typographical errors was often quite high, leading to negative reactions from the readership. Nevertheless, studies of immigrant families and minority groups have shown that locally produced print media are a feature in quite a few households. They are read primarily by the first generation (in the case of migrants) and by the older generations (in the case of regional minorities). It is therefore not surprising to see an increase in such newspapers becoming bilingual to accommodate younger generations with limited knowledge of the heritage or minority languages. Sometimes this involves translation of the same news items or stories, and sometimes some news items are published only in the majority language alongside others solely written in the heritage or minority language. There is also evidence of code-mixing in some print media. Although the lack of literacy skills may be a reason for the younger generations turning away from these print media, their disinterest is more likely to be due to the content covered in the paper. Since the advent of the internet, an increasing number of heritage and minority language speakers now have online access to an array of newspapers and other publications. This development may have reduced the need for and the role of locally produced print media in cultural and linguistic maintenance.

8.5.2 Audiovisual media: broadcasting

Before the internet, radio and television broadcasting were the other main media that minority communities used to inform and entertain, often using the heritage or minority language. Of course the use of such languages in broadcasts was often forbidden or banned by the majority population; this happened especially during war time. Where and when their use was not forbidden, a range of communities seized the opportunity to launch radio and later television programs to service the minority or heritage language community. Some even set up radio and television stations. Similar to the print media, ethnic or minority broadcasting was seldom set up with LM as the main purpose. However, because many such broadcasts do use the heritage or minority language, they can contribute to LM. In contrast to print media, access to radio and television broadcasts is not restricted to those with literacy skills in the language. In fact, they offer the opportunity to listen to the language so that people who can no longer speak the language still have a chance to maintain or even enhance their receptive skills in the language. Yet, especially in the case of heritage languages, the main audience for radio broadcasts tends to be older listeners, usually first generation and those with limited skills in the majority language. Although there are some programs targeting young children, there are very few programs for adolescents, limiting their role in LM. The audiences for minority television broadcasts tend to be wider, as the visual aspects may reduce communication barriers for less competent language users, with some providing subtitles in the majority language. The quality and quantity of these broadcasts vary widely depending on the resources available to community. In some cases the community's broadcasts are limited to thirty- to sixty-minute weekly programs that were produced in the homeland. At the other end of the spectrum we see communities owning radio and television stations that are able to broadcast twenty-four hours a day, combining local and imported news items, music and other entertainment, all in the heritage or minority language (e.g., Browne and Uribe-Jongbloed 2013; Cormack and Hourigan 2007; Kelly-Holmes 2001). The increased accessibility of satellite TV has also altered, in some cases quite radically, the opportunities for migrant and diasporic communities to immerse themselves in the heritage language: they are able to listen and watch programs as varied as the daily news, weather forecasts, game shows, sports events, 'soaps' and many films. In LM terms, this expansion has made heritage language television more attractive to a younger audience in such communities and has also given the entire community more access to a greater diversity of language varieties. Indeed the types of languages now used in minority and heritage language radio and television broadcasts are very varied, depending on the origin or sourcing of the programs. This is especially the case for heritage languages. The language varieties used in homeland programs will be those typifying homeland language use, often the formal spoken variety of the standard language, and in some cases a more colloquial or regional variety of the language. Locally produced programs, on the other hand, may feature the standard variety of the heritage language but with local features or various forms of code-switching and code-mixing involving the heritage and the majority languages.

8.6 BEYOND THE COMMUNITY: MAJORITY SUPPORT FOR LM

The concepts of a linguistic minority and a minority language are inexorably linked to the emergence and rise of the nation-state and its concomitant ideologies desirous of the unification of (ethnic) people, territory, language and culture (e.g., May 2011). Where these elements were not aligned, then specific actions would be taken to 'resolve' this nonalignment. These included drastic measures such as the elimination or eradication of groups that would or could not align to this ideology and the expulsion of such groups. Other measures involved various forms of assimilation with physical or other penalties for nonobservance. Modes and methods of linguistic oppression are indeed multifarious and have been studied as early as 1918 (Barker 1918, on the German Empire) as well as led to detailed discussions of linguistic (human) rights (e.g., Pupavac 2012; Skutnabb-Kangas et al. 1995). Although the denial of linguistic rights and linguistic oppression continues to be widespread to this date, the rise of minority rights and ethnic revival movements, particularly in the 'westernised' world, has led to some nation-states providing some rights and/or status to the languages of linguistic minorities. The reactions and actions of nation-states to these demands are too diverse to cover in this book focused on LM. We therefore refer the reader to the multitude of texts that cover this topic, e.g., Coulmas (1991), Craith (2005), Grin (2003), Mowbray (2012), Orman (2008), Ramanathan (2013) and Spolsky (2004). Here we restrict ourselves to some general observations that are pertinent to our discussion about majority or state support for LM. Those nation-states that are willing to recognise and/or support linguistic minorities tend to differentiate between indigenous or autochthonous minorities and those that are considered allochthonous, including immigrants and nomadic people. With regard to the former minorities, state actions and reactions can include recognition of the minority language as an official language of the state or of a specific region with concomitant support for its use in education and other public institutions. It can, however, also be limited to mere tolerance to its continued use in the public sphere. With regard to the languages of nonindigenous minorities, few if any states provide formal recognition of these with specific rights enshrined in law. Rather, there may be an acknowledgement of their existence in the nation-state and an attitude of tolerance towards their continued existence. For these languages, the main form of state support is usually of a transitional nature, for example, the provision of some (public) services – health, law, education – in a range of heritage languages for newly arrived migrants. Sometimes their role and continued existence is dealt with through formal policies, especially in relation to education. In this book we will not elaborate further on the various policies that nation-states have developed to support minority or heritage languages but will provide some references to key texts in the Further Reading section. Here we will give some examples of majority (state) support for the continued use and/ or maintenance of minority and heritage languages in two domains: education and the media.

8.6.1 Supporting heritage and minority languages in education ▪

Besides the domain of family and home, education is possibly the most vital domain for ensuring that the next generation acquires and maintains the minority or heritage language. State support for this domain can therefore constitute a (major) contribution to LM. As expected, such support can vary considerably not only from state (country) to state but also across languages and language situations. This diversity has started to be captured in the ever-growing volume of studies that provide detailed descriptions and discussions of educational programs, actions and initiatives around the world that benefit from some level of state (official) support or endorsement (for general overviews, see, e.g, Baker and Prys Jones 1998; Bratt-Paulston 1988; Cummins 1983; Wright et al. 2015; and for some region-specific ones, see, e.g., Baldauf 2005 and Lo Bianco 2009, for Australia; Ceñoz and Gorter 2010 and Extra and Gorter 2001, for Europe; Peyton et al. 2001, for the United States, Canada and Europe; and Wiley et al. 2014 for the United States). As even the survey studies have difficulty capturing the diversity, our discussion next will reflect only some very general trends in the types of state support that is extended to heritage and minority language education. State support tends to vary according to the following parameters: (1) target group, (2) type of language community and (3) goal of program.

Target group

In terms of the target group, the main distinction is made between programs (however limited or expansive) targeting minority or heritage language speakers 'exclusively' and those that are also accessible by others. Although the boundaries between these two types are not overly rigid, they nevertheless exist.

Type of community

With regard the second parameter, some distinction can be made between educational provision for regional, autochthonous communities and for nonindigenous, migrant and diasporic (sometimes including nomadic) communities. Here the boundaries are even more porous, especially at the lower end of support. For example, state support for minority and heritage languages may be limited to a small financial subsidy to community-based programs. In that context there may be little difference between these types of communities. At the higher end of support, differences may be more pronounced. While a state may support the minority language through comprehensive provision of primary and secondary schooling in the minority language, this kind of support is seldom, if ever, extended to nonindigenous language communities.

Goal of program

In the context of LM the key distinction is between programs that are seen as transitional and those whose goal is enrichment and/or oriented to maintenance. Transitional programs provide various forms of minority or heritage language learning, mainly in the early years of schooling, to ease the student's transition from his or her minority or heritage language into the majority language. Conversely, enrichment programs aim to further develop the student's knowledge and proficiency in the heritage or minority language, in tandem with the majority language. Within either type of program, there may be various models to achieve the goals. These include, for example, language as subject programs varying in intensity from a few to many hours per week. There are also a number of content-based language learning programs, including those that involve long- or short-term full or partial immersion (modelled after the Canadian French-English immersion programs) or based on the European Content and Language Integrated Learning model, generally known as CLIL.

A general observation about state support for LM-oriented programs is that the regional minorities that have achieved some recognition or rights are the more likely candidates to receive ongoing support for LM language programs. European examples include Basque in the autonomous Basque region in Spain; Frisian in the province of Friesland, the Netherlands; and Welsh in Wales. Such support is far less likely in the case of regional minorities lacking recognition or for heritage language communities. In the latter case, state support is primarily of a transitional nature. The majority of state-supported heritage language programs in many European countries and in traditional immigrant destinations such as Australia, Canada, New Zealand and the United States belong to this type and mainly target first-generation (overseas-born) speakers of heritage languages. Where the state provides support for nontransitional language learning, it tends to target the school population as a whole rather than heritage learners. In reality, however, heritage language learners tend to make up a large proportion of such programs, especially if the heritage language is not perceived as having instrumental value or is not considered a world language. When it comes to judging these latter programs in terms of their contribution to LM, the outcomes are quite varied. Variability of outcomes is linked not only to the model of language learning, e.g., language as subject versus content-based language learning, or to their duration, e.g., availability during a few years of the schooling period only as opposed to availability during the entire schooling period, but also to the recognition given to such programs. This refers to the recognition of minority or heritage language study as a genuine school subject in mainstream education; such study is seen to carry the same weight or 'prestige' as that of the study of any other 'foreign language' and is therefore treated in the same way when it comes to examinations. It is in this respect that many states/countries still fall short of genuine support, especially for heritage languages. While they may be offered as subjects at lower levels in the schooling system, they are not available when it comes to assessment practices that lead to certification or entry into further or higher education. This applies to most European countries, including those whose school populations boast a tremendous linguistic diversity. On the other hand, Australia and some US states provide some heritage language learners with final exams in their heritage language that count towards their overall school results and entry into further study. Although a majority of these programs are language-as-subject programs and may not be as rich in language as various immersion-type programs, they do contribute to LM because of the recognition they obtain within mainstream education. It is, however, not surprising that the full immersion programs along the lines of those undertaken in the Basque region (e.g., Ceñoz and Gorter 2010) not only lead to advanced proficiency levels, but also make a significant contribution to LM in regional minority settings.

8.6.2 Supporting heritage and minority languages through the state-supported media

The types of support that the state provides or provided for linguistic minorities and groups through the media run parallel to those described for the field of education: transitional and enrichment. The former is to facilitate the assimilation or integration of the linguistic minorities by providing them with essential information in their heritage or minority language. Media provisions under this category tend to be minimal and are clearly not oriented towards LM. Typical examples include radio or television announcements about civic matters in a range of minority or heritage languages. Sometimes mainstream print media may also have sections, seen as specifically relevant to a linguistic minority group, in that language. In immigrant societies the transitional character of these media provisions is clearly demonstrated by the constant change in languages that feature in such media.

There are also cases where mainstream media, operating with state funds, provide some ongoing support for programs, channels or stations that broadcast in minority or heritage languages. Territorial minority groups that have achieved some degree of national recognition (through law or other means) may demand or be entitled to dedicated media – usually radio and television – in their language. For example, Omrop Fryslân (Broadcaster Friesland), in the Netherlands, provides radio and television broadcasts in the Frisian language. In Italy, the regional government of Udine provides some support for Friulian broadcasts. In the United Kingdom, the state-funded broadcaster BBC has a special channel for programs in Scottish Gaelic and a regional channel for Wales. It is not surprising that there is great variation across communities in terms of the quantity and quality of minority language programs. In some cases the programs in the minority language are limited to some regional news broadcasts a few times a day, whereas in others there is a constant flow of programs, including entertainment and educational programs. Some television broadcasts will also cater to those with more limited knowledge of the language by employing subtitles.

State support for enrichment or maintenance-oriented media for heritage languages is not widespread. Where it exists, it is usually the result of constant lobbying by migrant communities combined with a more positive majority attitude towards multiculturalism and linguistic diversity. This is the case in Australia where these factors have led to the establishment of the Special Broadcasting Service (SBS) that is partially state funded (e.g., Clyne 1982, 1991, 2005). Its initial orientation in the 1980s was transitional, but it has moved to become oriented towards enrichment. The radio branch of SBS is more specifically focused on LM, as it broadcasts in seventy-four different languages that can be listened to across the country. Its television stations, on the other hand, do not have a clear focus on LM: about 55 percent of broadcasts are in English, with the remaining 45 percent made up of fifty languages. The broadcasts in heritage languages largely consist of (imported) films and documentary and educational programs that provide subtitles to make them also accessible to non-heritage language speakers. With the advent of and greater access to satellite and online media in a plethora of languages, the role of state-supported media in heritage languages is less about actual support to language resources but more about symbolic support that demonstrates the value of multilingualism.

POINTS FOR DISCUSSION AND TASKS

1. In your opinion, do you think that one-child families have a better or worse chance for passing on the heritage or minority language than those with multiple children? Consider the advantages of each type of family in terms of LM.

2. In migrant settings, LM institutions and agencies (other than community schools) do not cater well to adolescents. What is the reason for that? What sorts of agencies or activities could communities develop that could be more focused on this age group?

3. If you live in an area where some heritage language communities have settled, investigate if they have set up some form of community-based language education (or classes). If so, what type of program is it, and to whom does it cater? If they have not set up such a program, explore the reasons for this absence.

4. Investigate whether participation in community-based language programs has had a positive impact on a second- or third-generation member of a heritage community. Select some adults belonging to the same heritage language community. Investigate if those who participated in community-based language learning have maintained the heritage language better than those who did not attend such classes.

5. A number of religions prepare their young members in a variety of ways to become full members of the congregation or religious community; sometimes this involves learning to read the sacred texts associated with the religion (e.g., Talmud, Koran, Bible, Vedas) and attending classes in which religious education takes place. Select a religion associated with a linguistic minority or heritage language community in your country. Investigate the language practices that occur in this type of religious education. Do they contribute to LM?

6. In this chapter we mentioned that 'ethno-specific and minority group print media have probably been in existence for as long as there have been minorities, migrant communities and print media'. Select a territorial or immigrant linguistic minority with which you are familiar or that is found in your region. Explore what sort of community-based media its members have developed and how these have operated. Do they make use of the heritage or minority language? If they have been existence for several decades, even centuries, have they changed in terms of language(s) used? If so, what has been the trend?

7. It is sometimes claimed that certain sports activities are a good way of engaging younger people with their community and with their minority or heritage language. Identify these types of sporting activities and examine the veracity of this claim.
8. Is there another agency, domain or network not mentioned in this chapter that could be associated with the use of a minority or heritage language and that could promote LM?
9. Only a number of European countries belonging to the European Union have ratified the European Charter for Regional or Minority Languages. Examine whether three of these – Austria, the Netherlands and Poland – have taken action in terms of supporting minority language education, and identify which minorities and which rights in education are being supported.
10. Investigate for the same countries as in Point 9 whether they provide any educational support for heritage languages (i.e., immigrant languages).

SUGGESTIONS FOR FURTHER READING

The topics dealt with in this chapter are very wide ranging and have generated not only a multitude of studies but also overviews of such studies. The list below is therefore very eclectic but should help readers identify texts on each of these topics and areas of research.

LM efforts in the family

Caldas, Stephen. 2006. *Raising bilingual-biliterate children in monolingual cultures*. Clevedon: Multilingual Matters.
Döpke, Susanne. 1992. *One parent, one language: an interactional approach*. Amsterdam: John Benjamins.
Lanza, Elizabeth. 2009. Multilingualism and the family. In P. Auer and Li Wei (eds.), *Handbook of multilingualism and multilingual communication*. Berlin: Mouton de Gruyter, 45–67.
Okita, Toshie. 2002. *Invisible work: bilingualism, language choice and childrearing in intermarried families*. Amsterdam: John Benjamins.
Pauwels, Anne. 2005. Maintaining the community language in Australia: challenges and roles for families. *International Journal of Bilingual Education and Bilingualism* 8: 124–31.
Zentella, Ana. 1997. *Growing up bilingual: Puerto Rican children in New York*. Malden, MA: Blackwell.

Some texts mentioned above also contain references to guides for parents to assist with raising children bi- or multilingually.

Community-based language education

Beynon, June, and Katherine Toohey. 1991. Heritage language education in British Columbia: policy and programmes. *Canadian Modern Language Review* 47.4: 606–616.

Creese Angela, Arvind, Bhatt, Nirmala Bhojani and Peter Martin. 2006. Multicultural, heritage and learner identities in complementary schools. *Language and Education* 20.1: 23–43.

Extra, Guus. 2009. From minority programmes to multilingual education. In P. Auer and Li Wei (eds.), *Handbook of multilingualism and multilingual communication*. Berlin: Mouton de Gruyter, 175–206.

Extra, Guus, and Durk Gorter. Eds. 2001. *The other languages of Europe: demographic, sociolinguistic and educational perspectives*. Clevedon: Multilingual Matters.

García, Ofelia, Zeena Zalharia and Bahar Otcu. Eds. 2013. *Bilingual community education and multilingualis: beyond heritage languages in a global city*. Bristol: Multilingual Matters.

LM efforts in the context of religion

Omoniyi, Tope, and Joshua Fishman. Eds. 2006. *Explorations in the sociology of language and religion*. Amsterdam: John Benjamins.

Rosowsky, Andrey. 2008. *Heavenly readings: liturgical literacy in a multilingual context*. Clevedon: Multilingual Matters.

Woods, Anya. 2004. *Medium or message: language and faith in ethnic churches*. Clevedon: Multilingual Matters.

LM and secular community organisations

García, Ofelia, and Joshua A. Fishman. Eds. 2002 *The multilingual apple: languages in New York City*, second edition. Berlin: Mouton de Gruyter.

Pauwels, Anne. 1986. *Immigrant dialects and language maintenance in Australia*. Dordrecht: Foris Publications.

Potowski, Kim, and Jason Rothman. Eds. 2011. *Bilingual youth*. Amsterdam: John Benjamins.

LM and community-based media

Cormack, Mike, and Niamh Hourigan. Eds. 2007. *Minority language media*. Clevedon: Multilingual Matters.

Georgiou, Myria. N.d. Mapping minorities and their media: the national context – the UK. www.lse.ac.uk/media@lse/research/EMTEL/minorities/papers/ukreport.pdf, accessed 30 June 2015.

Johnson, Melissa. 2000. How ethnic are US ethnic media? The case of Latina magazines. *Mass Communication and Society* 2.2/3: 229–248.

9 Reversing language shift

In this chapter we address two questions relating to LS: (1) *Can* LS be reversed? (2) *Should* LS be reversed? The first question very much builds upon the previous chapter in which we discussed at length the diverse efforts that families and communities are known to undertake to keep their language(s) going. To what extent such efforts have been successful in *reversing* LS is a question to which there has been no clear response to date. There is no doubt that some of the efforts and initiatives discussed in Chapter 8 have been of assistance in slowing down the rate of LS or in keeping the minority or heritage language alive in select domains or for special functions. Furthermore, in Chapters 6 and 7 we identified a range of individual and group factors and forces that could provide a positive disposition to LM and thus slow down LS. Yet the general consensus amongst LM researchers working in migrant settings is one that sees LS as the inevitable result of such language contact. Furthermore, its process is often completed within three generations, especially in communities with limited recourse to LM institutions. These observations and findings can also be said to apply to many territorial minority settings, especially when they are a minority without status, legally enshrined or not. Given the view of the inevitability of LS, at least for migrant communities, the task of reversing LS is particularly challenging. In the next section we will discuss the Graded Intergenerational Disruption Scale (GIDS) that has been developed by Joshua Fishman (1990) as an aid in diagnosing the state of a language, i.e., in ascertaining the degree of threat to or vitality of a language. The scale also includes the steps or stages the affected speech community needs to go to through to revitalise its language and, thus, reverse LS, which in some cases may imply bringing it back from near extinction. In the second part of this chapter we tackle briefly the question that often evokes strong feelings and reactions not only in the affected communities but also among the scholarly community, i.e., *Should* LS be reversed?

9.1 CAN LS BE REVERSED? THE GRADED INTERGENERATIONAL DISRUPTION SCALE

In 1990 Joshua Fishman (Fishman 1990) published a paper entitled 'What is reversing language shift (RLS) and how can it succeed?' in which he proposed a model that can guide a systemic approach to the question. This model is generally known as the Graded Intergenerational Disruption Scale. Fishman (1991) contains a more elaborate discussion of the GIDS together with a range of case studies of languages in need of revitalisation. By applying the GIDS he demonstrates why some of these languages and their communities can be considered so-called success stories, whereas most continue to struggle in their attempts at reversing LS. Of his twelve case studies, only three – Modern Hebrew in Israel, French in Quebec and Catalan in Spain – represent in his opinion (more or less) success stories. The other cases – Irish Gaelic in Ireland; Basque in Spain and France; Frisian in the Netherlands; Navajo, Spanish and Yiddish in the United States; Maori in New Zealand and Aboriginal and Immigrant Languages in Australia – are assessed as continuing to be problematic in terms of achieving or making significant progress in revitalisation or LS reversal. Here it is not our intention to discuss these case studies but to present the GIDS in its role as a (still) powerful tool to assist language communities, activists and possibly policy makers in assessing in which stage of endangerment the language finds itself, and which steps need to be taken to reverse LS.

Before we present the GIDS, it should be noted that it is not the only framework that has been developed in relation to language revitalisation or the reversal of LS. For example, Gorter (2007) reviews three other models, known as the Euromosaic framework (Nelde, Strubell and Williams 1996), the European Charter for Regional or Minority Languages and the vitality factors developed by a UNESCO ad hoc group in 2003 (for details, see Gorter 2007). He provides a comparison between the frameworks (including the GIDS) and concludes that 'each has its strengths, but further work needs to be done and there is also considerable value in knowing more about individual cases' (Gorter 2007, no page numbering). Here we focus on the GIDS, as it has been and continues to be the framework widely applied across various minority language settings.

9.1.1 The stages of the GIDS

Fishman identifies eight stages or steps in his GIDS, with Stage 8 representing the most threatened and Stage 1 the least threatened stage of a language.

Stage 8: At this stage only a few isolated speakers may be left, so that little interaction in the language takes place. Further, the language may be in need of almost full or partial reconstruction, implying that the first task is to document it before it can be acquired again, even by adults. Most languages listed in the 2015 version of the web-based language catalogue Ethnologue as 'in trouble' (1531) or 'dying' (916) would find themselves in this stage. The languages, language communities and settings that are subject of this book do not fall into this stage; that is much more the domain of the study of endangered languages (e.g., Austin and Sallabank 2011; Farfán and Ramallo 2010; Grenoble and Whaley 1998; Nettle and Romaine 2000).

Stage 7: At this stage the language is used almost exclusively by older speakers to communicate amongst themselves. This implies that there is no intergenerational transmission to speak of, because parents use the majority or dominant language in interaction with their offspring. If we regard immigrant speech communities as separate speech communities (i.e., not part of the overall language community), then a significant number of such communities can be said to be in this stage. Within the migrant setting a number of scenarios represent Stage 7. The most dramatic one affects first-generation families where the parents born and raised outside the new setting do not continue using the heritage language with their children, but switch to the majority language as the main language for family interaction. The heritage language may survive somewhat when parents talk to elderly relatives, friends or community members, but there is no evidence of intergenerational transmission. Studies of Dutch-born migrants to the 'new world' (North America, Australia and New Zealand) have been found to represent this scenario (e.g., Clyne 1982, 1991; Klatter-Folmer and Kroon 1997; Pauwels 1980, 1986, 2013; Willemyns 2013). A frequently occurring scenario of Stage 7 in migrant settings is that found in second-generation families across a variety of ethnolinguistic groups. In these families the parents were born and raised in the new setting. Although they may have been raised in a family where the heritage language was still quite prominent, they neither use nor transmit that language to their third-generation children. Sometimes these third-generation children may still hear the language as used by elderly relatives, but they do not use it themselves as they cannot speak it. In relation to territorial minority settings, Stage 7 is also widespread, especially if the linguistic minority does not have any legal protection or status within the polity. To achieve any form of revitalisation there must be intergenerational transmission. Hence, communities that find themselves in this stage must try to reintroduce the heritage or minority language as a medium of intergenerational communication.

Stage 6: At this stage the heritage or minority language is still used as an informal language in a variety of (minority) community contexts and for intergenerational communication. In fact Fishman (1991: 92) suggests that 'Xish [the minority language, *author's comment*] is the normal language of informal, spoken interaction between and within all three generations of the family, with Yish [the majority language, *author's comment*] being reserved for matters of greater formality or technicality than those that are common fare of daily family life.' According to Fishman (1991: 92) this stage is 'an extremely crucial stage for Xish because the lion's share of the world's intergeneration-ally continuous languages are at this very stage and to continue to survive and, in most cases, without going on to the subsequent ("higher") stages'. In other words, for many languages (especially oral ones) reaching this stage may in fact represent a successful reversal of LS. However, the challenge within this stage is to ensure that this intergenerational transmission continues beyond the first three gener-ations in both migrant and territorial minority settings. The youngest generation must continue with the practice of using the minority or heritage language with the next generation and so on. This is becoming increasingly difficult because of changes in familial structures as well as a much greater degree of voluntary or forced mobility for many people. The three-generation family living together or in close vicinity is not so common any longer in many parts of the world. Similarly, the clustering of families and friends in a specific neighbourhood also occurs less frequently due to higher mobility. In Chapter 10, we shall discuss whether new communication technologies can assist in over-coming the barrier of communication across vast distances. In terms of the migrant setting, this stage applies primarily to more recently migrated families who still rely quite heavily on their heritage lan-guage to communicate.

Stage 5: In this stage not only is the minority or heritage language used orally in a broad spectrum of community-related domains, but there is also evidence of literacy amongst many members of the com-munity and there is an opportunity to acquire literacy in that language. For the adult population this means that they can access written sources in their language – books and other print media. For the younger generation there is an opportunity to acquire literacy. In most instances the latter is achieved through community-initiated and -supported schooling ranging from occasional language lessons offered by a volunteer to regular classes geared to the acquisition of literacy, as we have discussed in Chapter 8. Migrant and territorial minority communities vary greatly in their efforts to provide literacy opportunities to the younger generation (e.g., García et al. 2013; Valdés et al. 2006, for examples of the breadth of community language schooling).

Stage 4: At this stage the heritage or minority language is starting to make inroads into the domain of mainstream education. There are several scenarios for its entry into mainstream education. Initially the teaching of the heritage or minority language may be financed, wholly or in part, through the community itself or agencies associated with it. Another scenario is where the majority (state) provides a specific time-bound grant for a small-scale introduction of the language in mainstream education. In most polities participation in such programs is then restricted to minority group members. In some cases, especially in the context of territorial minorities, the state may provide ongoing support for the teaching of the language throughout the years of schooling. Even though we discussed a range of these scenarios in Chapter 8, we should note that few communities, especially in migrant settings, could be said to have reached this stage. In fact, the provision of heritage language in mainstream education, whether sponsored by the community itself or supported by governmental agencies, can occur even where there is limited or sometimes no intergenerational transmission of the heritage or minority language. It is not uncommon for some communities to 'hand over' responsibility for heritage or minority language learning to the education system (see Section 8.6.1).

Stage 3: This stage is concerned with the increasing use of the heritage or minority language 'in the lower work sphere (outside of the Xish neighbourhood/community) involving interaction between Xmen and Ymen' (Fishman 1991: 103). While there may already be use of the heritage or minority language in shops, businesses and on the shop floor during Stages 6 and 5, this would be to communicate with fellow speakers (Fishman's 'Xmen'). In Stage 3 its use is extended to communication with members of other groups, including the majority (Fishman's 'Ymen'). This expansion is linked mainly to enterprises and workplaces run or dominated by the minority group or in minority-dominated areas. Important in this stage is that the minority or heritage language will start to be used by majority members when dealing with members of the minority. In Fishman's (1991: 104) words: 'when Yish businessmen are serving the local Xish public, RLS [reversing language shift] efforts must be oriented to requesting that this service be in Xish.' Generally speaking, there are few if any migrant communities that find themselves in this stage. Sometimes there may be some evidence of majority members using the heritage language (occasionally) in business or transactional settings – this occurs primarily in restaurants and cafes and sometimes also in small shops (e.g., in a delicatessen) where the majority language customer places orders or undertakes a transaction in the heritage language. However, this is an entirely voluntary action, and most restaurant or shopkeepers would not (dare to) insist on the heritage language. There is some evidence that territorial linguistic minorities may have been somewhat more successful in reaching this stage. Fishman (1991) provides the example of Catalan (in Spain) as having reached this stage.

Stage 2: In this stage the heritage or minority language is starting to be available and used in the mass media as well as for specific services such as health, financial and housing offered through majority institutions and agencies, including government-sponsored ones. This expansion may involve the availability of interpreters so that minority members can be served in their language in contexts such as the courts and hospitals. It may involve the provision of written information about various services in the minority language. With regard to the mass media, this could involve setting up specific radio and television stations dedicated to the language or the provision of a certain amount of broadcasting time for the language. Here we need to note again the fact that some of these services can be present in our two main settings without the minority or heritage language community having reached that stage. In fact, modern societies with large immigrant populations often start providing translation and interpreting services in other languages. They may even provide some news media as well as government and other public services in such languages. However, in the majority of cases, these are transitional measures until the migrant community is able to function in the majority language, as we have seen in Chapter 8.

Stage 1: The ultimate stage in the trajectory of reversing LS involves the minority or heritage language being used in the higher echelons of education, employment and government and being widespread in the mass media. If a community can reach this stage, then it is likely that its language will obtain some degree of 'protection' through legislation. The community is also likely to have obtained some cultural and/ or economic autonomy. Fishman (1991: 107) warns that this stage

> represents the end of a long and difficult haul, but, most certainly, it does not represent the end of RLS problems and concerns. Indeed, the problems at this stage of the GIDS are often particularly aggravated and politicized ones, but there are definite advantages to being at this stage as well.

Fishman (1991: 395) provided a tabular representation of his GIDS scale, as shown in Table 9.1. The table shows not only the eight stages

Table 9.1 *Stages of reversing language shift*

Severity of intergenerational dislocation

(Read from the bottom up)

1. Education, work sphere, mass media and governmental operations at higher and nation-wide levels.
2. Local/regional mass media and governmental services.
3. Local/regional (i.e., nonneighborhood) work sphere, among both Xmen and Ymen.
4. b. Public schools for Xish children, offering some instruction via Xish, but substantially under Yish curricular and staffing control.
   a. Schools in lieu of compulsory education and substantially under Xish curricular and staffing control.

II *RLS to transcend diglossia, subsequent to its attainment*

5. Schools for literacy acquisition, for the old and for the young, and not in lieu of compulsory education.
6. The intergenerational and demographically concentrated home–family–neighborhood: the basis for mother tongue transmission.
7. Cultural interaction in Xish primarily involving the community-based older generation.
8. Reconstructing Xish and adult acquisition of XSL.

I *RLS to attain diglossia (assuming prior ideological clarification)*

Source: From Fishman (1991: 395).

in the GIDS but also the two main phases: Phase 1 involves the minority language becoming involved in a diglossic relationship with the dominant or majority language. In the second phase of RLS, the minority language moves beyond a diglossic relationship and expands its functions and roles to attain fully recognised status.

9.2 SHOULD *LS* BE REVERSED?

This question has engendered much debate, inside and outside academia alike. Within academia, the discussion, not surprisingly, has focused on those languages and their communities that are at major risk of extinction. Indeed, most volumes that deal with endangered languages address this question (e.g., Austin and Sallabank 2011; Bradley and Bradley 2002; Crystal 2000; Farfán and Ramallo 2010; Grenoble and Whaley 1998; Janse and Tol 2003). Its importance in relation to endangered languages is further evidenced by the publication of a lengthy and comprehensive article on the matter in the leading linguistic journal *Language* in 1992. It is perhaps not surprising that those working in the field of endangered languages and territorial minority languages are more inclined to provide an affirmative rather than a negative response to question. With the possible exception of scholars whose primary or sole interest in the documentation of such languages is to pursue questions of linguistic typology and linguistic universals, most researchers feel engaged with the fate of the communities and their languages and tend to support their survival and revitalisation. The main argument proffered in favour of LS reversal is one that stresses the importance of linguistic diversity. Here a parallel is drawn with biodiversity. Krauss (1992), for example, compares endangerment and threat of extinction between the animal world and languages: he quotes that 7.4 percent of mammals and 2.7 percent of bird species are endangered compared with more than 50 percent of the world's languages being endangered. The former is considered a catastrophe, but the latter does not seem to raise the same feelings of loss amongst the wider community. Bernard (1996), who is also an advocate of LS reversal and revitalisation, expressed caution about these analogies between biological and linguistic diversity:

> The problem with our analogies is that they are based on speculation, not on empirical observation or on theoretical grounds. Biologists have empirical evidence that biodiversity is good for life on the planet in general. They have strong theoretical models for the mutual dependence of diverse species ... For all we know, there really is no comparison to be made between biodiversity and cultural diversity. For all we know, one language and one culture might be fine. (Bernard 1996: 141)

His argument in favour of linguistic diversity is also evolutionarily based but hinges on seeing languages as the main storage of knowledge that would be lost if the language is lost: 'We need only recognize that the knowledge generated by all those successfully adapting cultural groups over the millennia is stored in all those thousands of languages now spoken around the world' (Bernard 1996: 141). Drawing upon the frequently quoted facts about the number of speakers associated with the world's languages, i.e., that only 276 of 6000 languages account for the majority of speakers in the world (estimated to be five billion) and that 95 percent of the world's languages are spoken by a mere 5 percent of people, Bernard (1996: 142) comments: '95% of the cultural heterogeneity of the world – 95% of the *differences* in ways of seeing the world – is vested in under 5% of the people, and the problem gets worse every year.' Evolution-based arguments, are, however, also used to support a negative response to the question: language contact has been and continues to be a fundamental feature of human environ-ments around the world; for millennia, contact between languages has led to the creation of new languages and the disappearance of others because 'we should try to remember that – historically and linguistic-ally – change rather than stasis is the norm' (Edwards 2003: 38). In other words, LS and language death are 'natural' features of linguistic evolution. From this point of view reversing LS would be more a question of choice rather than necessity. Some scholars (e.g., Ladefoged 1992) have provided examples demonstrating that there are many individuals and indeed communities that are willing to embrace the new language and to make it their own.

A related yet different perspective on this matter of the right to or choice of LS reversal is couched within the framework of *linguistic human rights*. Skutnabb-Kangas et al. (1995: 1–2), for example, advo-cate that 'linguistic rights should be considered basic human rights'. They mention that speakers of majority languages around the world have these rights, but these seldom apply to linguistic minorities. Consequently, if LS is the result of forced abandonment of their lan-guage, then they should have the right to reinstitute or revive the language.

Reactions and responses to this question will continue to engender much debate, often highly emotive. This is not surprising given the diverse attitudes that people hold towards language, linguistic identity and linguistic rights. Polarised positions such as 'doing something is better than doing nothing' and 'intervention in linguistic matters can be worse than doing nothing, if there has been inadequate preparation across a wide spectrum of social life' (Edwards 2003: 43) will continue to frame debate around this topic.

POINTS FOR DISCUSSION AND TASKS

1. The Manx language (Isle of Man, United Kingdom) is said to be a success story of reversing LS. Find a number of studies dealing with the Manx language revival and apply the GIDS to see in which stage Manx was before LS was reversed, and identify the stage in which it finds itself today.
2. Choose a heritage language group that settled in a new environ-ment at least three generations ago, e.g., Italians in the United States, Germans in Brazil or Greeks in Australia. Identify in which stage the group finds itself, and whether there are

indications that it is moving closer to LS or that there are signs of a degree of LS reversal. Use the GIDS to identify the stages and the actions that have been taken (or not) to reverse LS.

3. The question 'should LS be reversed' has been debated less in the context of immigrant or diasporic languages. This is probably because the consequences of a migrant group giving up the use of its language do not lead to language death. However, what arguments could be presented to support reversing LS in these communities?

4. In his book *How new languages emerge*, Lightfoot (2006: 2) writes:

> Languages diversify, and not just languages that spread over large areas through conquest and other forms of social domination. The phenomenon, like language death, connects to the way that people identify themselves with groups, adopting modes of speech that characterize the group. People, teenagers from every generation, speak differently as they feel themselves to belong to a distinct group, just as they may dress differently or wear their hair differently. The tendency for languages to diversify reflects the fact that linguistic change is a constant of human experience.

Discuss this statement in the context of the need or desire to reverse LS.

SUGGESTED FURTHER READING

GIDS

Fishman, Joshua. 1990. What is reversing language shift (RLS) and how can it succeed? *Journal of Multilingual and Multicultural Development* 11.1–2: 5–36.

    1991. *Reversing language shift*. Clevedon: Multilingual Matters.

    Ed. 2001. *Can threatened languages be saved?* Clevedon: Multilingual Matters.

Other scales and frameworks

Gorter, Durk. 2007. *European minority languages: endangered or revived?* Ljouwert: Fryske Akademy. http://depot.knaw.nl/3856/1/21759.pdf, accessed 7 June 2015.

'Should LS be reversed?'

Edwards, John. 2007. Societal multilingualism: reality, recognition and response. In P. Auer and Li Wei (eds.), *Handbook of multilingualism and multilingual communication*. Berlin and New York: Mouton de Gruyter, 447–467.

Skutnabb-Kangas, Tove. 2012. Linguistic human rights. In L. M. Solan and P. M. Tiersma (eds.), *The Oxford handbook of language and the law*. Oxford: Oxford University Press, 235–247.

Tonkin, Humphrey, and Timothy Reagan. Eds. 2003. *Language in the 21st century*. Amsterdam: John Benjamins.

Volume 68, no. 1, of *Language* 1992 is dedicated to endangered languages. It also addresses the question of LS reversal and revitalisation/revival.

In Volume 68, no. 4, of *Language* 1992, Peter Ladefoged presented another view of the question.

PART V
Future developments in the study of language maintenance and shift

10   Opportunities and challenges for the future study of language maintenance and shift

LM and LS research is now in its seventh decade since its establishment as a dedicated field of study in the 1960s. Like other fields of specialist study, the field of LM and LS has changed over time, reflecting both internal and external developments in the discipline. The preceding chapters of this book have documented the main developments that took place between the 1960s and the late twentieth century. We have shown how a variety of disciplines not only became increasingly interested in this topic of study but also contributed to it through different methodological approaches and theoretical insights: they included but were not limited to (linguistic) anthropology, social psychology of language, sociology of language and sociolinguistics. Indeed, other disciplines such as demography, political science and even economics have made contributions (e.g., Grin and Vaillancourt 1997; Ozolins 1993; Veltman 1983; amongst others). As we mentioned in Chapter 2, scholars interested in the language situation of migrant communities in the 'new world', primarily North America, spearheaded the development of the field. Later, its geographical range expanded to other parts of the world – Europe, South America, parts of Asia and Southern Africa – where new waves of immigrants had settled. A particularly interesting development concerned the expansion of LM studies to migrant communities in Europe. Until the 1960s Europe had in fact been the major 'source' region for migration to the new world. Its citizens, communities and their language practices constituted the focus of the pioneering early studies in North America and Australia, e.g., studies of Norwegians, Swedes, Dutch, Germans, Greek, Italians and Poles. In the second half of the twentieth century, Europe changed its role from being the source *for* to the recipient *of* migration, as we described in Chapter 2. The other main setting for LM and LS research is that of territorial linguistic minorities around the world. However, this setting has become increasingly the subject of a separate branch of language contact studies: language endangerment. Unfortunately, an already large and still growing number of the languages of the world's linguistic minorities find themselves in this state. In these cases urgent linguistic documentation is the primary objective to be achieved before any revitalisation or revival can be undertaken. Questions of LM or LS within the territorial setting have therefore mainly focused on linguistic minorities that have not gone beyond Stage 6 in Fishman's Graded Intergenerational Disruption Scale. With the splitting of research on indigenous territorial minorities into studies of language endangerment and LM/LS, it is not surprising that the migrant and/or diasporic settings dominated and continue to dominate the LM and LS research scene. It is especially this setting that has faced some radical changes in more recent times, largely linked to the globalising forces of the late twentieth and early twenty-first century. These changes not only have the potential to impact on questions of LM or LS but also may require a reshaping if not a transformation of the field. Here we will examine the impact of two major changes linked to globalisation – mobility and communication technology – on the study of LM and LS.

10.1 GLOBALISATION AND THE STUDY OF MULTILINGUALISM

It has become impossible to avoid mentioning the impact that the globalising forces of the late twentieth and early twenty-first century are having on so many aspects of people's lives. For example, employment, education, trade and industry, consumer/customer services, security, communication and mobility are all elements that have undergone transformations as a result of globalising trends and forces. Such changes are also transforming the scientific and academic study of these phenomena, especially in disciplines whose focus is the human condition and societal relations. This includes studies of linguistic diversity and multilingualism (e.g., Aronin and Singleton 2008; Block 2005; Blommaert 2010; Heller 2007) in which LM and LS research is embedded. Two key elements of globalisation impact on constellations of multilingualism and therefore also on their study: mobility and communication.

10.2 FROM MIGRATION TO MOBILITY

10.2.1 Towards a new paradigm of mobility studies

The consequences of globalisation for mobility have been subject of a refocusing in sociological studies of space and social relations.

Sociologists Sheller and Urry (2006) argued that mobility (virtual and real) has fundamentally changed how 'the social' and relationships between people are studied. No longer is such study focused around a set of intense relations between individuals in *close physical proximity*, but social relations are seen as increasingly defined beyond established spatial and time boundaries: across local, regional and national boundaries as well as across real and virtual space and time. Similarly, contact between people now is often technologically mediated rather than involving real or 'here and now' face-to-face encounters. Later works by these authors and others (e.g., Adey et al. 2013; Cresswell 2006; Urry 2007) have therefore proposed a new paradigm of mobilities for the social sciences in which the concept of mobility is central. We could say that globalisation has affected both the scale and type of mobility. Many more people are regularly if not almost constantly 'on the move' over long distances in search of employment, education, trade, freedom or security. Because of enhanced transport facilities that enable regular long-distance travel, the boundaries between migration and commuting have become increasingly blurred (e.g., Eliasson et al. 2003). More than ever, these forms of mobility cut across class and other social strata of societies: from unskilled labourers and skilled workers needing to cross borders, legally or illegally in search of employment, to middle managers and senior executives of multinational companies traversing the globe to acquire more capital. Then there are the thousands of young people moving across the globe in search of an education that would give them the skills to operate in a global context. For many people, however, mobility does not result in 'permanent' settlement in a new location, the traditional focus for migration and indeed LM studies. Rather, they do not wish to or cannot resettle in a new location. Those not *wishing* to permanently resettle elsewhere tend to belong to the professional echelons of society working for private or public multinational and international agencies or who engage in mobility for educational reasons. Those who *cannot* resettle comprise a constantly growing group of people – many of them refugees from war-stricken or poverty-stricken parts of the world who are increasingly faced with closed borders. At the time of writing, the influx of refugees from Middle Eastern and African countries arriving in (ramshackle) boats on the Italian and Greek coast or via Turkey is creating disunity among European countries. Despite European agreements on freedom of movement, some countries are not allowing these refugees to enter, let alone to settle down. Despite their desire to settle they need to keep moving, giving rise to a type of enforced nomadism.

10.2.2 The new mobility and multilingualism ▬▬▬▬▬▬▬

These changes in mobility patterns very much affect linguistic matters. Of course multilingualism and linguistic diversity have long been the more widespread societal linguistic constellations across all parts of the world. However, the steep increase in various types of mobility in recent years has led not only to a much greater linguistic diversity but also to the heightened visibility of linguistic diversity. This is especially the case in countries and polities operating with monolingual regimes or ideologies, i.e., most so-called first world countries. Whereas extreme linguistic diversity was seen as a characteristic of sub-Saharan African countries or Pacific region countries such as Papua New Guinea or the Philippines, countries such as Australia, Canada, France, Germany, the United Kingdom and the United States are now quoted as housing hundreds of languages within their borders. This heightened visibility of multilingualism is particularly noticeable in large urbanised areas in these countries as they have become 'home' – temporary or longer term – to people from all parts of the globe. New York has been said to be home to around 800 languages (as reported by the BBC in 2012; www.bbc.com/news/magazine-20716344), more or less the same number as that quoted by Ethnologue for Papua New Guinea (851 languages). The increasingly multilingual character of such cities has given rise to a new field of research labelled 'linguistic landscapes' that is devoted to the examination of linguistic signs – street signs, shop signs, billboards, menu boards and so on – and their relevance and meaning (functional or symbolic) for linguistic communities (e.g., Backhaus 2007; Gorter et al. 2011; Landry and Bourhis 1997; Shohamy and Gorter 2009). In fact, the field now has its own journal, *Linguistic Landscape: An International Journal*.

Coming back to the linguistic 'superdiversity' of many cities, this is a matter not only of the presence of more languages but also of constantly changing linguistic *constellations* due to these new forms of mobility. With the exception of the officially sanctioned dominant language(s), the 'hierarchy' or prevalence of some minority languages may be subject to considerable change depending on the patterns of movement of their communities. Some communities may stay put and are joined by new waves of immigrants, whereas others move on or become dispersed within the urban agglomeration or beyond. Although Census surveys and other tools of linguistic demography may give us a glimpse into this heightened and changing diversity, it may not capture another important aspect of this situation: an increasing number of people with complex linguistic repertoires and linguistic histories. In his book *The sociolinguistics of globalization*, Blommaert (2010: 8–9) provides a poignant example of this by outlining the linguistic repertoires and language practices of a Nigerian family living in a suburb of Antwerp, Belgium:

> Thus, when a Nigerian woman goes to buy bread in a Turkish-owned bakery, the code for conducting this transaction will, for both, be a clearly non-native and very limited variety of local vernacular Dutch, mixed with some English, or German, words ... At home, the Nigerian family will have access to television, and the choice will go to English-medium channels, with an occasional foray, often initiated by the children, into Dutch-medium children's programmes. There will be a very low level of consumption of local printed media ... At the same time, telephone contact in native languages will be maintained with people back home and fellow migrants now living in Brussels, London or Paris. Occasionally, there will be mutual visits during which the African regional language might be the medium of communication among adults, while the children revert to vernacular forms of English to interact with each other. Their exposure to education environments in which different languages are the medium of instruction – Dutch and French, for instance – constrains the use of any other language.

Although people with complex linguistic repertoires that include or draw upon multiple languages have always been around, including in diasporic settings, there is no doubt that their presence has increased in light of the mobility trends outlined here. These changes present challenges to the dominant modus operandi in LM and LS research, which we will discuss in the final section of this chapter. Before that we shall look at the other key element affected by globalisation: technology-mediated communication.

10.3 COMMUNICATING VIA TECHNOLOGY

Keeping in touch, exchanging information and communicating with people living far away have become much easier due to advances in communication technologies. Cheap(er) long-distance telephony and mobile communication devices that allow for audio(visual) contact and the internet have largely done away with limitations imposed by vast distances. The internet has probably been the most revolutionary element in radically changing not only how we communicate, gather, access and exchange information but also how we socialise. The latter is increasingly shaped by social media tools available via the internet. The impact of the expansion of technology-mediated communication has not been ignored in language and linguistic research. Its impact is being investigated in many branches and fields of language research. Studies in these fields have examined such issues as how the internet has shaped language use, the speech genres that have developed or been affected by the internet, new linguistic forms and practices arising through computer-mediated communication, the creation of new linguistic identities and the extent to which social variables such as gender and age affect internet-based communication (for overviews, see e.g., Crystal 2001; Herring 2008; and the online journal Language@Internet, www.languageatinternet.org). It is clear that the internet together with other communication technologies present new and enhanced opportunities for LM, especially for diasporic, immigrant, transnational and other communities 'on the move'. In fact, the internet could be seen as both a tool for LM and an additional domain in which the minority or heritage language could be used.

10.3.1   The internet and LM

Scholars of LM identified the ability to regularly connect with one's linguistic 'heartland' as an important LM-enhancing factor (see Chapter 7). In the 'precyberspace' era this was mainly achieved via occasional contact with speakers from this linguistic 'heartland' through visits to and from the homeland and through the influx of new waves of migrants from the speech community. The positive impact of this factor was quite limited for those transnational and immigrant communities far removed from their home territories; this applied particularly to nineteenth- and twentieth-century migrants and refugees from Europe to various parts of the new world. As we have stated earlier, the cost and distance of travel were prohibitive for many migrants and their overseas relatives, minimising the positive impact of this factor. While the arrival of new waves of fellow speakers may have sparked increased use of and opportunities for heritage language use, these usually faded after a few years. The arrival of the internet and other forms of computer-mediated communication not only have made it easier, cheaper and quicker to keep in touch with speakers of one's language(s) around the world, but has also made a wealth of language resources, many of which are interactive, accessible to such communities. In Chapter 8, we described the many efforts parents make to create a rich heritage language environment for their children. In the pre-internet era this involved drawing upon the often minimal, locally available resources, listening to the occasional radio broadcasts in the heritage language, asking visitors to bring language materials from the homeland or subscribing to costly publications.

With the internet many such resources are instantly available. Also in most instances there is greater variety allowing individuals and communities to create an online or virtual heritage language environment. Of course for these resources to assist LM, they need to be accessed and used by the members of the speech communities. Although the multilingualism of the internet has become a topic of investigation in a growing number of studies (for an overview, see e.g., Leppänen and Peuronen 2012), there is much more to be done. In relation to LM it is important to examine whether and how minority and heritage language members use the internet to 'support' their languages and linguistic identities. Because of the relative dearth of such studies in the first decade of the twenty-first century (however, see references in the Suggested Further Reading section), I decided to examine the internet 'habits' of some Dutch Australians belonging to the second and third generations. It was my intention to find out whether they accessed information in the Dutch language and used the internet to communicate with other speakers of Dutch around the world. Next, I include a short description of this small-scale project and its findings to date to give an insight into how a group with 'low linguistic vitality' nevertheless exploits the internet to reignite some heritage language use.

LM in cyberspace: a Dutch-Australian study

In 2007 twenty-nine second-generation Dutch Australians, with whom or with whose parents I had worked before (for research published in Pauwels 1980 and 1983), agreed to participate in a brief study about their internet use. Unfortunately, only twelve people met the minimal selection criteria for inclusion. One was basic proficiency in at least one skill of Dutch, that is, speaking, listening, reading or writing. Their proficiency in Dutch was a matter of self-assessment (using the Common European Framework of Reference scales). The second criterion for inclusion was having regular access to the internet. These twelve participants were asked to provide information about their internet habits, with specific attention to their use of the internet that involved the use of Dutch. All twelve participants could be said to be very 'cyberactive', spending between three and six hours a day undertaking internet-based activities, although most of this time involved the use of English. They estimated that they spent between 1 and 5 percent of their internet time on Dutch-related activities. Table 10.1 summarises their internet-based activities and use with regard to Dutch.

Table 10.1 *Dutch-based internet uses and activities by informants*

Type of internet uses (Dutch)	Number of informants (12 total)
[1] Browsing and accessing Dutch-language websites	12
[2] Accessing online audio materials	10
[3] Accessing online video materials (film, TV etc.)	8
[4] Accessing online text-based materials (newspapers, magazines, books etc.)	8
[5] Playing games, mainly card games	8
[6] Audio and video calling	8
[7] Email and asynchronous communication	6
[8] Social networking	5
[9] Online language-learning materials	4

All twelve participants regularly accessed and browsed through websites [1] that were in Dutch. Popular websites (other than those covered in the other categories) were those related to tourism in the Netherlands: transport timetables, weather forecasts, shopping, cultural events and places. Other popular sites were mainly sports related: Dutch football club and ice-skating websites. Although some of these now have English versions, pages for fans, for example, are provided only in Dutch. In most cases this type of internet use did not require more than very basic literacy skills: websites often have extensive visual materials that assist a reader with basic skills in understanding the message. Accessing online audio [2] and video materials [3] was also an activity frequently undertaken by most participants. As can be expected, a wide variety of programs was accessed, with those less proficient in Dutch preferring less linguistically demanding ones (e.g., music programs, football match commentaries). The same observation applied to those using the internet to access print media [4]. Other uses of the internet in which a majority of participants engaged regularly were online card games [5] and audio and video calls [6]. The online games that involved some use of Dutch were mainly popular Dutch card games, such as Klaverjassen and Hartenjagen. Audio- and video-calling was extremely popular, with many claiming to use it almost weekly, primarily to communicate with family and friends in the Netherlands. Most participants seemed to make an attempt to use (some) Dutch in these interactions, especially if their interlocutors were elderly.

Others – those who spent some time living in the Netherlands – often engaged in them as an LM measure, i.e., to keep their Dutch alive. For example, one regular Skype user commented: 'I look forward to my weekly call with [*name*]. We catch up on gossip and I just love using Dutch to a Dutchy [*sic*] it makes me feel part of that world'. Internet activities [7] and [8] that require or involve some writing – e.g., entering information in or writing entries for social media such as Facebook, Twitter, email and blogs – are used by fewer participants in this project, most likely because of their limited skills in writing Dutch. In fact, their participation in social media sites seemed restricted to reading Dutch-language entries of their Facebook followers and friends. If they write something, it is mainly formulaic language such as greetings. Those using email do so to correspond mainly with some elderly family and friends in the Netherlands, but the messages tend to be very brief and rely heavily on formulaic language. Finally, four participants commented that they used the internet specifically as a tool to improve their Dutch-language skills. This involved accessing online dictionaries and course and test materials for Dutch, including speech samples.

In addition to questions about their internet use, they were also asked why they engaged in internet-based activities that involved Dutch. While LM was seldom mentioned as the main reason, the most popular response (10 out of 12) can be paraphrased as 'It allows me to immerse myself in a Dutch world as part of my identity'. It seemed that engaging with the Dutch language continues to be seen as an important part of their identity. Furthermore, the internet was also judged to be an easy and 'safe' option to engage with some use of Dutch. One participant who had spent some time in the Netherlands wrote,

> After my time in the Netherlands I felt more confident using some Dutch but now without being surrounded by Dutch there is no need and no motivation. But I do like to keep in touch with Dutch and the internet is such an easy way and safe – no need to worry about getting it wrong!

This small-scale investigation has shown that the internet is seen as a helpful tool to continue engaging with a heritage language without too much effort. Indeed these participants come from a community with limited interest and effort in LM, yet there is evidence that they keep in touch with the language because of the opportunities the internet offers them. It is therefore likely that groups with a greater commitment to LM may benefit even more from the LM opportunities associated with the internet.

10.3.2   Is the internet replacing other LM efforts? ▬▬▬▬▬▬▬

Another question worth asking is whether the ubiquity of the internet and its huge potential to provide a language-rich virtual environment is affecting other LM institutions and activities. As we do not yet have enough information about the online practices of linguistic minorities vis-à-vis their languages, it is difficult to give more than a very speculative answer to this question. An institution that is unlikely to see its role and potential for LM usurped by the internet is that associated with religion and other forms of worship. Community-based language education, a key component in LM, is also unlikely to disappear in the face of internet resources. Although there is some evidence, including in our Dutch Australian case study, that some individuals will use internet language-learning resources to enhance their heritage language learning, these tend to be adults rather than children. In fact, the internet may enhance community-based language education by expanding not only the pool of language-learning materials but also the range and types of registers and styles linked to the language in question. In addition, it could be used to provide dispersed communities interested in LM with a tool and platform to offer online classes. Its impact may be felt more in relation to the production and availability of ethno-specific or minority media. Indeed, the internet provides access to a wealth of print and electronic media in a multitude of languages, so that members of heritage and minority language communities can read and view news in their language with great ease and at minimal cost. In some cases this may render locally produced print media obsolete. However, there is evidence that such outlets now also have an online presence, not unlike the mainstream media. Given the orientation of secular community organisations it is also unlikely that their existence would be 'threatened' by the social networking opportunities associated with the internet. Most such organisations have difficulty attracting younger members of the community, so that their role in LM for subsequent generations is rather limited. Of more interest in the context of LM would be to explore the extent to which internet-based networking through social media is creating a platform for younger members of heritage and minority language communities to engage with their peers. For example, in studies by Androutsopoulos (2006), Cunliffe and Herring (2005) and Lam (2004) there is evidence that young minority and heritage language speakers do use social media to create an online network. Even if these comments about the impact of the internet on other LM institutions are rather speculative, there are some indications that the internet enhances and creates further LM opportunities rather than threatens them. To turn these speculative observations into evidence, we need to engage in a detailed program of research about LM and the internet.

10.4   CHALLENGES FOR THE FUTURE STUDY OF LM AND LS

The radical changes in mobility patterns not only affect the linguistic landscapes of many cities and, sometimes, even countries around the world, they also reveal an increasing number of individuals with complex linguistic repertoires. In Section 10.2.2 we briefly mentioned the case of a Nigerian family living in Belgium (Blommaert 2010). Here we would like to provide two further vignettes of families and individuals* that illustrate the complex linguistic repertoires and multilingual practices that have now become much more prevalent as a result of increased mobility. The language practices described in these vignettes, drawn from my own work on multilingual families, similarly reveal some challenges to the dominant approaches of LM and LS studies presented in this book. We will use these examples to discuss the challenges to future studies of LM and to make some suggestions about reorienting such studies.

Vignette 1: the Tran family

This is the story of two Vietnam-born brothers – Hai and An – whose father, Tuan, an academic, sought asylum in Australia during a work-related visit to Australia. Unfortunately, he failed in his attempts to bring his wife and his two boys to Australia. His wife was terminally ill in Vietnam, and when she died, his two sons went to live with their uncle, Trac, and his wife, Mai. Trac and Mai, together with their nephews, fled Vietnam as boat refugees and ended up living in a suburb of Paris with a large migrant population. Their father was unsuccessful in his further attempts to reunite with his sons in Austra-lia. Hence, they continued to live with their aunt and uncle in France where they went to school and to university. Their father managed

---

* Names used in these vignettes are pseudonyms to protect the privacy of the participants.

Table 10.2 *Language repertoires of the Tran family*

Hai	French, Vietnamese, English, (Arabic)
Françoise	French, Arabic, English, (Vietnamese)
Jean-Marc	French, Arabic, English, (Vietnamese)
An	French, Vietnamese, English, Swedish, (Arabic)
Gitte	Vietnamese, Swedish, English, (French)
Birgit	Swedish, English, Vietnamese, (French)

brief visits to his sons but Tuan's main contact with them was via letters and phone calls. After university in France, Hai, the older son, undertook postgraduate study in England. An, the younger son, took up an internship in Sweden where he met Gitte, a Sweden-born Vietnamese woman whom he married and with whom he had one child, Birgit. Meanwhile Hai returned to Paris to marry his fiancée, Françoise, a French woman of Moroccan descent. They have one child, Jean-Marc. Both brothers and their families then moved to Australia under a skills migration scheme where they lived close to their father. However, both families returned to Europe a few years ago – Hai to France and An to Sweden – because of family and employment reasons. Since leaving Vietnam in mid-1970s, both brothers and their families have lived in three countries: Hai in France, England and Australia, and An in France, Sweden and Australia. They are very much a transnational family illustrative of new modes of mobility and new ways of communicating with each other. As a result of this mobility they acquired a number of languages and linguistic resources upon which they continue to regularly draw to communicate with each other. The order of languages shown in Table 10.2 reflects the family member's self-assessment of his or her competence in their respective languages. The bracketed languages are those in which the members judged themselves to have minimal competence, not enough to carry on a simple conversation or in which they had mainly receptive skills.

Although Tuan and Trac described themselves as largely 'monolingual' upon leaving Vietnam – they claimed to have basic French through schooling and a smattering of English – they and their offspring have become multilingual as a result of this mobility. The linguistic choices made by any member of this family group vary contextually, but they almost always involve drawing upon multiple languages, including languages in which they have minimal competence. The most prevalent linguistic practice within this extended family network is best described as extensive code-switching with contextual variations in terms of the (shared) languages or linguistic resources drawn upon. For example, regular email interaction between Hai and An is mainly in French although with occasional switches to English and Vietnamese. Birgit skypes with her cousin, Jean-Marc, in a mixture of English, Vietnamese and French. In a family gathering that brings together three generations, there is no 'lingua franca' but a constant moving between the various languages. After an interview, An emailed me about his language practices, as he felt that he had not expressed himself clearly enough:

> Hi Prof I have been thinking about your questions and the mess I made of them, not knowing which language I speak with members of my family, but it is really complicated. What we speak to each other, you know with our friends, *copains*, and our familly [*sic*]; my wife, my daughter, sometimes my brother and his family. I don't know it – we use a lot of languages specially when we [*sic*] together – with my uncle and aunt yes we speak more Vietnamese but there is also a lot of French. I try to remember it's difficult, we don't sort of think about the languages we speak – now it's Swedish to my wife but then other days it is mainly Vietnamese even some French and I don't think it changes because we talk about something else. I will give it some more thought but honestly I think we speak a bit of most of our languages all the time. Is that a problem? I sometimes worry when this colleague at work says to me – you know, you speak like Frech [*sic*] and swedish [*sic*] and English and Chinese (he thinks I speak Chinese) to this person on the phone, is that not confuisng [*sic*] for them?

An also reported that Birgit's school had invited her to participate in Vietnamese-language classes as part of a transitional bilingual program. He commented that Birgit came home from school excited and said: 'pappa I can learn Vietnamese if I want, the teacher said, but I said I want to learn more French but she said it had to be the language I spoke at home so I said yes we speak French at home, *langue maison*.'

Vignette 2: the aid workers

The second vignette concerns a family in which the parents are former aid workers who lived in Africa and Southeast Asia. They are both Dutch citizens. Theo, the father, is Dutch-born and comes from a Dutch 'ethnic' family. The mother, Marjolein, grew up in the Netherlands as the third daughter of Indonesian parents who had settled near Rotterdam after World War II. While Theo grew up in a household that was entirely Dutch-speaking, Marjolein's linguistic home environment included Bahasa (Indonesia), Dutch and some

Table 10.3 *Language repertoires of the aid workers and children*

Marjolein	Dutch, English, Amharic, Bahasa, (Punjabi)
Theo	Dutch, English, Amharic, French, (Punjabi)
Lili	Dutch, English, Amharic, (Punjabi, Urdu)
Abeba	Dutch, English, Amharic, (Punjabi, Urdu)

Sundanese. They met each other while on aid work in Ethiopia. There they acquired some Amharic mainly to interact with local people. Most communication with other aid workers was in English. They married in Ethiopia but went back to the Netherlands when they were expecting their first child, a girl – Lily. Dutch was the main language used in the family during this time. When Lily was two years old, they decided to adopt a young Ethiopian girl, Abeba, who was also two years old at the time, and they brought her to the Netherlands. Both parents felt it was important that their Ethiopian daughter learn her 'heritage' language. Increasingly the parents used both Dutch and basic Amharic to both girls and developed networks with Amharic speakers in the Netherlands to expose both girls and themselves to more Amharic. Dutch was the language of schooling, although the girls also learnt English as a foreign language. When the girls were nine their parents took up another aid assignment in Pakistan, in a Punjabi-speaking environment. Their schooling was largely in English with some instruction in Urdu. When the girls were twelve, the parents returned to Europe and have settled in London. The parents' and children's linguistic repertoires continue to include a number of languages that they draw upon in various ways, as shown in Table 10.3.

Interactions in this family group have seldom been limited to one language; instead, like the Tran family, they use multiple codes (languages) rather than a lingua franca. In their current location (London) family interactions largely involve translanguaging between English and Dutch, and some Amharic. The sisters also occasionally use some Punjabi and even Urdu with some school friends of Pakistani and Indian heritage. Marjolein continues using Bahasa to her relatives, both in the Netherlands and in Indonesia. She regularly skypes her mother and sister, who still live in the Netherlands. With her mother she uses primarily Bahasa and with her (older) sister it is a mixture of Dutch, Bahasa and some English. Her relatives in Indonesia now also have access to the internet, so she occasionally talks to them via Skype: with some older relatives she tries to use some Sundanese but relies mainly on Bahasa. Recently, both daughters have asked her to teach them some Bahasa after a visit from two of their Indonesian cousins: they want to continue chatting with them online. The Indonesian cousins know some English but not enough to interact with the girls.

The language practices of the families described in these vignettes and in Blommaert's example provide some challenges to LM as conceptualised within the main approaches presented in this book. Unlike the majority of language situations described in LM/LS research where contact is between two, possibly three languages, the language situation in these families involves the frequent use of multiple languages. Furthermore they constantly draw upon 'elements' of these languages to interact with each other and with other multilinguals who share some but not all of their languages. It seems that the standard question – who speaks what language to whom and when – is a difficult, even confusing one to answer by the members of these families, as An's comment, earlier, illustrates. Another feature of their language situation as a result of their mobility is that new languages are added to their repertoire and other ones recede in the background, only to become more prominent at a later stage. Although there may be situations, usually outside the family network, where they opt for a lingua franca, their contacts with relatives and close friends tend to favour a language practice previously known as code-switching (within a structuralist framework) but now increasingly described as *languaging* (Jørgensen 2008) or *translanguaging* (Garcia and Li Wei 2014). When it came to questions of linguistic identity or identification, the members of both families generally opted for one that stressed their multilinguality. For example, An, Hai and Marjolein indicated that the language(s) they 'inherited' from their parents was/were an important component of their linguistic identity in certain contexts but did not define them. In fact, Marjolein commented that Indonesian was her ethnic identity, something that was 'fixed' in biology, but it was not her linguistic identity, which she described as 'always changing'.

Another challenge relates to supporting LM efforts outside the family: most of the LM agencies and institutions described in Chapters 8 and 9 are primarily organised around a single language, mostly with a close link to ethnicity rather than around multiple languages. Furthermore, benefits in terms of LM arise only if individuals and groups are settled on a long-term basis so that they have regular access to them. These 'multilingual families' also pose a challenge to some support structures provided by the state for heritage language speakers. For example, the children's multilingual home environment caused confusion for the educational authorities in Sweden and the Netherlands, respectively.

In Sweden, Birgit could study only Vietnamese but not French because Vietnamese was considered her heritage language and the educational authorities do not seem able to cater to multilingual home environments. In the Netherlands only Abeba was entitled to Amharic but not her Dutch-born and 'ethnic' Dutch sister, Lily, who was considered to be Dutch-speaking with no need for home language support.

Although I have presented only two examples of family 'multilingualism' arising from new forms of mobility, these scenarios do not seem to be exceptional (or at least less exceptional) as I discovered after presenting the first vignette at a conference. Many academic and community members contacted me afterwards and provided me with even more complex examples of such family groups residing in Amsterdam, Barcelona, Berlin, Chicago, Madrid, Marseille, Moskou, Melbourne, New York and Toronto.

10.5   NEW DIRECTIONS FOR THE STUDY OF LM AND LS

These observations reveal that the linguistic situations of an increasing number of individuals, families and possibly groups are much more dynamic and fluid than before, in part because of their own increased mobility and in part because of the increased presence of multiple languages in many urban landscapes as well in cyberspace.

In light of these new mobilities and other factors associated with globalisation that impinge on communication, an increasing number of scholars are urging a rethinking of the focus on and approaches to studies of language in society, especially those dealing with multilingualism (e.g., Block 2005; Blommaert 2010; Blommaert and Rampton 2011; Gal 2006; Heller 2007; Lähteenmäki et al. 2011; Makoni and Pennycook 2007; Rampton 2006). For example, in the preface to his book *The sociolinguistics of globalization*, Blommaert (2010: xiii) writes:

> And I make this effort because I believe that globalization forces us –
> whether we like it or not – to an *aggiornamento* of our theoretical and
> methodological toolkit. Much as modernism defined most of the
> current widespread tools of our trade, the transition towards a
> different kind of social system forces us to redefine them.

Other sociolinguists working in the field of multilingualism have echoed these views, similarly proposing a rethinking or reconceptualisation of key concepts such as language and multilingualism. This reconceptualisation involves a move away from 'Saussurean' structuralism or structural-functional approaches to language to more critical approaches to the study of language, building upon 'Bakhtinian' deconstructionist framework (Bakhtin 1981). Central to this development is abandoning the view of languages as separate, autonomous codes, as 'bounded entities' according to Makoni and Pennycook (2007), and of multilingualism as a set of monolingualisms, i.e., the use of multiple languages seen as separable codes. Instead, people should be seen as engaging in a set of linguistic practices that, in the case of multilinguals, draw upon the resources of various codes – 'languages' in a conventional sense. Moving or switching between these resources associated with various codes that make up a speaker's linguistic repertoire is increasingly referred to as 'languaging' or 'translanguaging' as mentioned earlier. These shifts and reconceptualisations are seen as assisting in exploring the new linguistic constellations characterised by hybridity, mobility and fluidity and their impact on the language behaviour and practices of individuals and groups.

It should be recognised that, until recently, much research into LM and LS has worked with notions of language and bi- and multilingualism that align with a structuralist view. Thus the main focus of investigations has been on whether these 'bounded entities' are maintained, lost, or become mixed with another one or whether they have been (gradually) replaced by another one. This focus or view may indeed become more difficult to maintain as the central one in the contexts of increased linguistic diversity, hybridity and mobility outlined in previous sections. Of course, there continue to be linguistic situations involving several 'languages' that are less affected by the hypermobility associated with 'western' forms of globalisation and whose study may be less challenging to structural-functional approaches to LM and LS. For other situations, as outlined in the vignettes, it would be worthwhile to reflect on these reconceptualisations associated with critical approaches to the study of language in society, language contact and multilingualism. Do they assist in understanding the complexity of language choices to be made? Do they assist in examining the relationship between identity and multilingual practices and ultimately in understanding why some groups prefer or are able to continue operating with linguistic repertoires that draw upon many languages and others not? Perhaps terms like LM and LS are no longer appropriate to designate the processes of language changes described in this book. Or they could be reshaped or reconceptualised to more adequately reflect the 'new' linguistic constellations affecting so many individuals and groups. For example, rather than seeing LS as a process of (gradual or rapid) shift from one language to another language, we may conceive of it as a gradual reduction in the multilingual nature of a person's or a group's language repertoire or language practices. In other words, if a person or group draws upon multiple languages to communicate across multiple settings, 'domains', networks and so on, and, over time, there is a clear reduction in the languages or codes that make up the repertoire *and* no new languages or codes are added to this repertoire, then this would constitute a case of LS. Conversely, LM could be conceived as the maintenance of a multilingual repertoire even if the languages or codes upon which the individual or group draws change. These are questions that should be explored more fully to keep the study of LM and LS relevant to the rapidly changing linguistic scenarios that individuals as well as societies constantly face.

POINTS FOR DISCUSSION AND TASKS

1. Territorial minorities are possibly less affected by changing patterns of mobility than diasporic ones. For the latter, the internet has aided them in overcoming communication barriers due to distance. In your opinion, how does the internet facilitate LM in territorial minorities?
2. Does the internet offer the researcher of LM or LS new opportunities to study LM. If so, which ones?
3. Can the internet stimulate LM in people who have very little knowledge of their heritage or minority language?
4. In this chapter we presented some vignettes of families whose language practices demonstrate 'new' multilingualisms. Can you find some other examples of such families? Discuss what constitutes LM in these cases.
5. Discuss the following statements: 'The concept of LM is a product of an ideology that equates a language with a nation-state.' LM also assumes clear boundaries between languages, and thus it is no longer appropriate to discuss the language dynamics characterising so many groups and societies around the world.

SUGGESTED FURTHER READING

Mobility studies
Sheller, Mimi, and John Urry. 2006. The new mobilities paradigm. *Environment and Planning A* 38.2: 207–226.

Urry, John. 2007. *Mobilities*. Cambridge: Polity Press.

LM, multilingualism and the internet

Androutsopoulos, Iannis. 2006. Multilingualism, diaspora, and the internet: codes and identities on German-based diaspora websites. *Journal of Sociolinguistics* 10.4:429–450.

Cunliffe, Daniel, and Susan Herring. Eds. 2005. Minority languages, multimedia and the web. Special issue of the *New Review of Multimedia and Hypermedia* 11.2.

Danet, Brenda, and Susan Herring. Eds. 2003. The multilingual internet: language, culture and communication in instant messaging, email and chat. Special issue of the *Journal of Computer Mediated Communication* 9.1

Fitzgerald, Michael, and Robert Debski. 2006. Internet use by Polish Melburnians: implications for maintenance and teaching. *Language Learning & Technology* 10.1: 87–109.

Leppänen, Sirpa, and Saija Peuronen. 2012. Multilingualism on the internet. In M. Martin-Jones, A. Blackledge and A. Creese (eds.), *The Routledge handbook of multilingualism*. Abingdon: Routledge, 384–403.

Critical approaches to the study of multilingualism

Blommaert, Jan. 2010. *The sociolinguistics of globalization*. Cambridge: Cambridge University Press.

Heller, Monica. Ed. 2007. *Bilingualism: a social approach*. Basingstoke: Palgrave Macmillan.

Martin-Jones, Marilyn, Adrian Blackledge and Angela Creese. Eds. 2012. *The Routledge handbook of multilingualism*. Abingdon: Routledge.

References

Adey, Peter, David Bissell, Kevin Hannam, Peter Merriman and Mimi Sheller. Eds. 2013. *Handbook of mobilities*. London: Routledge.

Aikio, Marjut. 1992. Are women innovators in a shift to a second language? A case study of Reindeer Sami women and men. *International Journal of the Sociology of Language* 94.1: 43–62.

Ajzen, Icek, and Martin Fishbein. 2005. The influence of attitudes on behavior. In D. Albarracín, B. T. Johnson and M. P. Zanna (eds.), *The handbook of attitudes*. Mahwah, NJ: Erlbaum, 173–122.

Alladina, Safder, and Viv Edwards. Eds. 1991. *Multilingualism in the British Isles. The older mother tongues and Europe*. London: Longman.

Androutsopoulos, Jannis. 2006. Multilingualism, diaspora and the internet: Codes and identities on German-based diaspora sites. *Journal of Sociolinguistics* 10.4: 520–547.

Antonini, Rachele. 1999. Linguistic and social inequality: choosing between English and Gaelic in Gaeltacht areas. Unpublished MA thesis, Università di Bologna.

Arel, Dominique. 2002. Language use in censuses: backward- or forward-looking? In D. Kertzer and D. Arel (eds.), *Census and identity: the politics of race, ethnicity, and language in national censuses*. Cambridge: Cambridge University Press, 92–120.

Aronin, Larissa, and David Singleton. 2008. The complexity of multilingual contact and language use in times of globalization. *Conversarii. Studi Linguistici* 2: 33–47.

Auer Peter. 1991. Italian in Toronto: a preliminary comparative study on language use and maintenance. *Multilingua* 10: 403–440.

2003. Crossing the language border into Turkish? Uses of Turkish by non-Turks in Germany. In L. Mondada and S. Pekarek Doehler (eds.), *Plurilinguisme – Mehrsprachigkeit – Plurilingualism*. Tübingen: Francke, 73–93.

Auer, Peter, and Inci Dirim. 2003. Socio-cultural orientation, urban youth styles and the spontaneous acquisition of Turkish by non-Turkish adolescents in Germany. In J. K. Androutsopoulos and A. Georgakopoulou (eds.), *Discourse constructions of youth identities*. Amsterdam: John Benjamins, 223–246.

Auer, Peter, and Li Wei. Eds. 2009. *Handbook of multilingualism and multilingual communication*. Berlin: Mouton de Gruyter.

Austin, Peter, and Julia Sallabank. Eds. 2011. *The Cambridge handbook of endangered languages*. Cambridge: Cambridge University Press.

Backhaus, Peter. 2007. *Linguistic landscapes: a comparative study of urban multilingualism in Tokyo*. Clevedon: Multilingual Matters.

Baetens-Beardsmore, Hugo. 1982. *Bilingualism: basic principles*. Clevedon: Multilingual Matters.

Baker, Colin, and Sylvia Prys Jones. 1998. *Encyclopedia of bilingualism and bilingual education*. Clevedon: Multilingual Matters.

Bakhtin, Mikhail. 1981. *Le principle dialogique* [The dialogic principle]. Paris: Seuil.

Baldauf, Richard B. Jr. 2005. Micro language planning. In P. Bruthiaux, D. Atkinson, W. Eggington, W. Grabe and V. Ramanathan (eds.), *Directions in applied linguistics: essays in honor of Robert B. Kaplan*. Clevedon: Multilingual Matters, 227–239.

Bao, Ngu Tong, and Desmond Cahill. 2001. The settlers: Vietnamese. In. J. Jupp (ed.), *The Australian people: an encyclopedia of the nation, its people and their origins*. Cambridge: Cambridge University Press, 721–737.

Barker, Ernest. 1918. *Linguistic oppression in the German empire*. New York: Harper Brothers.

Barni, Monica, and Guus Extra. Eds. 2008. *Mapping linguistic diversity in multicultural contexts*. Berlin: Mouton de Gruyter.

Bennett, E. Jane. 1990. Attitudes of the second generation Dutch to language maintenance and ethnic identity. Unpublished PhD thesis, Monash University.

Bernard, Russell H. 1996. Language preservation and publishing. In N. Hornberger (ed.), *Indigenous literacies in the Americas: language planning from bottom up*. Berlin: Mouton de Gruyter, 139–156.

2006. *Research methods in anthropology: quantitative and qualitative approaches*. Oxford: Alta Mira Press.

Besemeres, Mary. 2002. *Translating one's self*. Oxford: Peter Lang.

2004. Different languages, different emotions: perspectives from autobiographical literature. *Journal of Multilingual and Multicultural Development* 25.2–3: 140–158.

Besemeres, Mary, and Anna Wierzbicka. Eds. 2007. *Translating lives: living with two languages and cultures*. St Lucia, QLD: University of Queensland Press.

Bettoni, Camilla, and John Gibbons. 1988. Linguistic purism and language shift: a guise-voice study of the Italian community in Sydney. *International Journal of the Sociology of Language* 72: 15–36.

Beynon, June, and Katherine Toohey. 1991. Heritage language education in British Columbia: policy and programmes. *Canadian Modern Language Review* 47.4: 606–616.

Bhatia, Tej K., and William C. Ritchie. Eds. 2004. *The handbook of bilingualism and multilingualism*. Malden, NJ: Wiley-Blackwell.

Eds. 2013. *The handbook of bilingualism and multilingualism*, second edition. Malden, NJ: Wiley-Blackwell.

Bialystok, Ellen. 2001. *Bilingualism in development*. Cambridge: Cambridge University Press.

Block, David. 2005. *Multilingual identities in a global city: London stories*. London: Palgrave.

Blom, Jan-Petter, and John Gumperz. 1972. Social meaning in linguistic structure: code-switching in Norway. In J. Gumperz and D. Hymes (eds.), *Directions in sociolinguistics: the ethnography of communication*. New York: Holt, Rinehart and Winston, 407–434.

Blommaert, Jan. 2010. *The sociolinguistics of globalization*. Cambridge: Cambridge University Press.

Blommaert, Jan, and Ben Rampton. 2011. Language and superdiversity. *Diversities* 13.2: 1–22.

Bourhis, Richard, and Howard Giles. 1976. The language of cooperation in Wales: a field study. *Language Sciences* 42: 13–16.

Bradley, David. 2002. Language attitudes: the key factor in language maintenance. In D. Bradley and M. Bradley (eds.), *Language endangerment and language maintenance: an active approach*. New York: Routledge, 1–10.

Bratt-Paulston, Christina. Ed. 1988. *International handbook on bilingualism and bilingual education*. Westport, CT: Greenwood Press.

Bratt-Paulston, Christina, Pow Chee Chen and Mary C. Connerty. 1993. Language regenesis: a conceptual overview of language revival, revitalization and reversal. *Journal of Multilingual and Multicultural Development* 14.4: 275–286.

Briggs, Charles L. 1986. *Learning how to ask: a sociolinguistic appraisal of the interview in social science research*. Cambridge: Cambridge University Press.

Broeder, Peter, and Guus Extra. Eds. 1999. *Language, ethnicity and education*. Clevedon: Multilingual Matters.

Browne, Donald R., and Enrique Uribe-Jongbloed. 2013. Introduction: ethnic/linguistic minority media – what their history reveals, how scholars have studied them and what we might ask next. In E. Haf Jones and E. Uribe-Jongbloed (eds.), *Minority languages and social media: participation, policy and perspectives*. Bristol: Multilingual Matters, 1–28.

Bull, Tove. 2002. The Sámi language(s), maintenance and intellectualisation. *Current Issues in Language Planning* 3.1: 28–39.

Burton, Pauline, Ketaki K. Dyson and Shirley Ardener. Eds. 1994. *Bilingual women: anthropological approaches to second language use*. Oxford: Berg.

Byrnes, Joseph. 1999. The relationship of linguistic practice to linguistic culture: language, religion, and education in Alsace and Roussillon 1860–1890. *Church History: Studies in Christianity and Culture* 68.3: 598–626.

Caldas, Stephen. 2006. *Raising bilingual-biliterate children in monolingual cultures*. Clevedon: Multilingual Matters.

Callan, Victor J., and Cynthia Gallois. 1982. Language attitudes of Italo-Australian and Greek-Australian bilinguals. *International Journal of Psychology* 17: 345–358.

Callan, Victor, Cynthia Gallois and Paula Forbes. 1983. Evaluative reactions to accented English: ethnicity, sex role and context. *Journal of Cross-Cultural Psychology* 14.4: 407–426.

Cameron, Deborah. 2003. Gender issues in language change. *Annual Review of Applied Linguistics* 23: 198–201.

Castonguay, Charles. 1982. Intermarriage and language shift in Canada, 1971 and 1976. *The Canadian Journal of Sociology/Cahiers Canadiens de Sociologie* 7.3: 263–277.

Cavallaro, Francesco. 2010. *Transgenerational language shift: from Sicilian and Italian to Australian English.* Melbourne: LaTrobe University.

Cavanaugh, Jillian R. 2006. Little women and vital champions: gendered language shift in a northern Italian town. *Journal of Linguistic Anthropology* 16.2: 196–210.

Ceñoz, Jasone, and Durk Gorter. 2010. The diversity of multilingualism in education. *International Journal of the Sociology of Language* 205: 37–53.

Clemente, Ignasi. 2008. Recording audio and video. In L. Wei and M. Moyer (eds.), *The Blackwell guide to research methods in bilingualism and multilingualism.* Oxford: Blackwell, 177–191.

Clyne, Michael. 1967. *Transference and triggering.* The Hague: Nijhoff.

1979. Factors promoting migrant language maintenance in Australia. In P. de Lacey and M. E. Poole (eds.), *Mosaic or melting pot?* Sydney: Harcourt Brace Jovanovich, 119–128.

1982. *Multilingual Australia.* Melbourne: River Seine.

1988. The German-Australian speech community: ethnic core values and language maintenance. *International Journal of the Sociology of Language* 72: 67–83.

1991. *Community languages: the Australian experience.* Cambridge: Cambridge University Press.

1994. *Intercultural communication at work.* Cambridge: Cambridge University Press.

2004. History of research on language contact. In U. Ammon, N. Dittmar, K.-J. Mattheier and P. Trudgill (eds.), *Sociolinguistics. An international handbook of the science of language and society/ Soziolinguistik. Ein internationales Handbuch zur Wissenschaft von Sprache und Gesellschaft.* Volume 1. Berlin and New York: Mouton de Gruyter, 799–805.

2005. *Australia's language potential.* Sydney: University of NSW Press.

Clyne, Michael, and Martin Ball. 1990. English as a lingua franca in Australia, especially in industry: a first progress report. *Australian Review of Applied Linguistics* series S 7: 1–15.

Clyne, Michael, and Suzanne Fernandez. 2008. Community language learning in Australia. In N. Hornberger (ed.), *Encyclopedia of language education*, second edition. Volume 4: *Second and foreign language educa-tion*. New York: Springer, 169–181.

Clyne, Michael, and Sandra Kipp. 1997. Trends and changes in home language use and shift in Australia, 1986–1996. *Journal of Multilingual and Multicultural Development* 18.6: 451–473.

2002. Australia's changing demography. *People and Place* 10.3: 29–35.

Clyne, Michael, and Susan Manton. 1979. Routines for conducting meet-ings in Australia: an inter-ethnic study. *Ethnic Studies* 3.1: 25–34.

Clyne, Michael, Suzanne Fernandez and Felicity Grey. 2004. Languages taken at school and languages spoken in the community: a compara-tive perspective. *Australian Review of Applied Linguistics* 27.2: 1–17.

Clyne, Michael, John Hajek and Sandra Kipp. 2008. Tale of two multilingual cities in a multilingual continent. *People and Place* 16.3: 1–8.

Codó, Eva. 2008. Interviews and questionnaires. In L. Wei and M. Moyer (eds.), *The Blackwell guide to research methods in bilingualism and multilin-gualism*. Oxford: Blackwell, 158–176.

Common European Framework of Reference. 2001. www.coe.int/t/dg4/lin guistic/cadre1_en.asp.

Cormack, Mike. 2006. The media, language maintenance and Gaelic. In W. McLeod (ed.), *Revitalising Gaelic in Scotland: policy, planning and public discourse*. Edinburgh: Dunedin Academic Press, 211–219.

Cormack, Mike, and Niamh Hourigan. Eds. 2007. *Minority language media*. Clevedon: Multilingual Matters.

Coulmas, Florian. Ed. 1991. *A language policy for the European community: prospects and quandaries*. Berlin and New York: Mouton de Gruyter.

Craith, Nic Mairead. 2005. *Europe and the politics of language: citizens, migrants and outsiders*. London: Palgrave Macmillan.

Creese Angela, Arvind Bhatt, Nirmala Bhojani and Peter Martin. 2006. Multicultural, heritage and learner identities in complementary schools. *Language and Education* 20.1: 23–43.

Cresswell, Tom. 2006. *On the move: mobility in the modern western world*. New York: Taylor & Francis.

Crystal, David. 2000. *Language death*. Cambridge: Cambridge University Press.

2001. *Language and the internet*. Cambridge: Cambridge University Press.

Cummins, Jim. 1981. *Bilingualism and minority language children*. Ontario: OISE.

1983. *Heritage language education: a literature review*. Toronto: Ministry of Education.

Cunliffe, Daniel, and Susan Herring. Eds. 2005. *Minority languages, multi-media and the web*. Special issue of *New Review of Multimedia and Hyper-media* 11.2.

Daan, Jo. 1987. *Ik was te bissie. Nederlanders and hun taal in de Verenigde Staten* [I was too busy. The Dutch and their language in the United States]. Zutphen: De Walburg Pers.

Danet, Brenda, and Susan Herring. Eds. 2003. The multilingual internet: language, culture, and communication in instant messaging, email and chat. Special issue of the *Journal of Computer-Mediated Communication* 9.1.

Davis, Kathryn. Ed. 1999. *Foreign language teaching and language minority education.* Honolulu: University of Hawai'i, SL & C Center.

Dejong, Gerald. 1975. *The Dutch in America, 1609–1974.* Boston: Twayne Publishers.

Denison, Norman, 1977. Language death or language suicide. *International Journal of the Sociology of Language* 12: 13–22.

De Vries, John. 1985. Some methodological aspects of self-report questions on language and ethnicity. *Journal of Multilingual and Multicultural Development* 6: 347–368.

    1990. On coming to our census: a layman's guide to demolinguistics. *Journal of Multilingual and Multicultural Development* 11.1–2: 57–76.

    1994. Canada's official language communities: an overview of the current demolinguistic situation. *International Journal of the Sociology of Language* 105–106: 37–68.

De Vries, John, and François Vallee. 1980. *Language use in Canada.* Ottawa: Ministry of Supply and Services.

De Walt, Kathleen M., and Billie R. De Walt. 2011. *Participant observation: a guide for fieldworkers,* second edition. Plymouth: Alta Mira Press.

Dollinger, Stefan. 2012. The written questionnaire as a sociolinguistic data gathering tool. *Journal of English Linguistics* 40.1: 74–110.

Döpke, Susanne. 1992. *One parent, one language: an interactional approach.* Amsterdam: John Benjamins.

    1994. Two languages in early childhood. Unpublished paper, Monash University. www.bilingualoptions.com.au/consTXT2%20L1.pdf, accessed June 2014.

    1998. Can the principle of 'one person – one language' be disregarded as unrealistically elitist? Unpublished paper, Monash University. www.bilingualoptions.com.au/consTXTelit.pdf, accessed June 2014.

Dorian, Nancy. 1973. Grammatical change in a dying dialect. *Language* 49: 413–38.

    1981. *Language death: the life cycle of a Scottish Gaelic dialect.* Philadelphia: University of Pennsylvania Press.

    Ed. 1992. *Investigating obsolescence: studies in language contraction and death.* Cambridge: Cambridge University Press.

Doughty, Cathy. 2003. Instructed SLA: constraints, compensation, and enhancement. In C. Doughty and M. Long (eds.), *The handbook of second language acquisition.* Oxford: Blackwell, 256–310.

Drager, Katie. 2014. Experimental methods in sociolinguistics. In J. Holmes and K. Hazen (eds.), *Research methods in sociolinguistics.* Oxford: Wiley Blackwell, 58–73.

Dressler, Wolfgang. 1972. On the phonology of language death. *Proceedings of the Chicago Linguistics Society* 8: 448–457.

Duan, Lei. 2004. A sociolinguistic study of language use and language attitudes among the Bai people in Jianchuan county, China. Unpublished Master's thesis, Payap University.

Dykman, E. 1999. Exploring second language acquisition and acculturation through autobiographical texts: a qualitative study of second language learners/authors. Unpublished doctoral dissertation, School of Education, New York University.

Eades, Diana. 2013. *Aboriginal ways of using English*. Canberra: Aboriginal Studies Press.

Edwards, John. 1992. Sociopolitical aspects of language maintenance and loss: towards a typology of minority language situations. In J. Fase, K. Jaspaert and S. Kroon (eds.), *Maintenance and loss of minority languages*. Amsterdam: John Benjamins, 37–54.

1994. *Multilingualism*. London: Routledge.

2003. Contextualising language rights. *Journal of Human Rights* 2.4: 551–571.

2007. Societal multilingualism: reality, recognition and response. In P. Auer and Li Wei (eds.), *Handbook of multilingualism and multilingual communication*. Berlin and New York: Mouton de Gruyter, 447–467.

2010. *Minority languages and group identity: cases and categories*. Amsterdam: John Benjamins.

Ed. 1998. *Language in Canada*. Cambridge: Cambridge University Press.

Ehala, Martin. 2010. Refining the notion of ethnolinguistic vitality. *International Journal of Multilingualism* 7.4: 363–378.

Eliasson, Kent, Urban Lindgren and Olle Westerlund. 2003. Geographical labour mobility: migration or commuting? *Regional Studies* 37.8: 827–837.

Enfield, Nick J., Paul Kockelman and Jack Sydell. Eds. 2014. *The Cambridge handbook of linguistic anthropology*. Cambridge: Cambridge University Press.

Erickson, F. 1982. Audiovisual records as a primary data source. *Sociological Methods and Research* 11.2: 213–232.

Extra, Guus. 2009. From minority programmes to multilingual education. In P. Auer and Li Wei (eds.), *Handbook of multilingualism and multilingual communication*. Berlin: Mouton de Gruyter, 175–206.

2010. Mapping linguistic diversity in multicultural contexts: Demolinguistic perspectives. In J. A. Fishman and O. García (eds.), *Handbook of language and ethnic identity: disciplinary and regional perspectives. Volume 1*. New York: Oxford University Press, 107–122.

Extra, Guus, and Durk Gorter. Eds. 2001. *The other languages of Europe*. Clevedon: Multilingual Matters.

Extra, Guus, and Ludo Verhoeven. Eds. 1993. *Immigrant languages in Europe*. Clevedon: Multilingual Matters.

Extra, Guus, and K. Yağmur. 2004. Demographic perspectives. In G. Extra and Y. Kutlay (eds.), *Urban multilingualism in Europe: immigrant minority languages at home and in school*. Clevedon: Multilingual Matters, 25–72.

Eds. 2004. *Urban multilingualism in Europe: immigrant minority languages at home and in school*. Clevedon: Multilingual Matters.

Farfán, José A. F., and Fernando Ramello. Eds. 2010. *New perspectives on endangered languages*. Amsterdam: John Benjamins.

Fasold, Ralph. 1984. *The sociolinguistics of society*. Oxford: Basil Blackwell.

Fehlen, Fernand. 2002. Luxembourg, a multilingual society at the Romance/Germanic language border. *Journal of Multilingual and Multicultural Development* 1–2: 80–97.

Ferguson, Charles. 1959. Diglossia. *Word* 15: 325–340.

1962. The language factor in national development. In F. Rice (ed.), *Study of the role of second languages in Asia, Africa, and South America*. Washington, DC: Center of Applied Linguistics, 8–14.

1966. National sociolinguistic profile formulas. In W. Bright (ed.), *Sociolinguistics*. The Hague: Mouton, 309–315.

1968. Language development. In J. A. Fishman, C. A. Ferguson and J. D. Gupta (eds.), *Language problems of developing nations*. New York: John Wiley & Sons, Inc., 27–35.

Ferguson, Charles, and Shirley Brice Heath. Eds. 1981. *Language in the USA*. Cambridge: Cambridge University Press.

Finnegan, Edward, and John R. Rickford. 2004. Eds. *Language in the USA: themes for the 21st century*. Cambridge: Cambridge University Press.

Fishman, Joshua. 1964. Language maintenance and language shift as a field of inquiry. A definition of the field and suggestions for its further development. *Linguistics – An Interdisciplinary Journal of the Language Sciences* 9: 32–70.

1965. Who speaks what language to whom and when? *La Linguistique* 2: 67–88.

1970. *Sociolinguistics: a brief introduction*. Rowley, MA: Newbury House.

1972. *The sociology of language: an interdisciplinary social science approach to language in society*. Rowley, MA: Newbury House.

1980. Bilingualism and biculturalism as individual and societal phenomena. *Journal of Multilingual and Multicultural Development* 1: 3–37.

1983a. Language and ethnicity in bilingual education. In J. Fishman (ed.), *Culture, ethnicity and identity*. New York: Academic Press, 127–138.

1983b. The rise and fall of the 'ethnic revival' in the USA. *Journal of Intercultural Studies* 4.3: 5–46.

1990. What is reversing language shift (RLS) and how can it succeed? *Journal of Multilingual and Multicultural Development* 11.1–2: 5–36.

1991. *Reversing language shift*. Clevedon: Multilingual Matters.

2013. Language maintenance, language shift, and reversing language shift. In T. K. Bhatia and W. C. Ritchie (eds.), *The handbook of bilingualism and multilingualism*. Oxford: Wiley-Blackwell, 466–494.

Fishman, Joshua A. Ed. 1968. *Readings in the sociology of language*. The Hague: Mouton.

Ed. 1971. *Advances in the sociology of language*. Volume 1. The Hague: Mouton.

Ed. 2001. *Can threatened languages be saved?* Clevedon: Multilingual Matters.

Fishman, Joshua, and Ofelia García. Eds. 2010/2011. *Handbook of language and ethnic identity*. Volumes 1 and 2. New York: Oxford University Press.

Fishman, Joshua A., Robert L. Cooper and R. Ma. 1971. *Bilingualism in the barrio*. Bloomington: Research Center for the Language Sciences, Indiana University.

Fishman, Joshua A., Vladimir C. Nahirny, John E. Hofman and Robert G. Hayden. Eds. 1966. *Language loyalty in the United States: the maintenance and perpetuation of non-English mother tongues by American ethnic and religious groups*. The Hague: Mouton.

Fishman, Joshua A., Michael H. Gertner, Esther G. Lowy and William G. Milán. Eds. 1985. *The rise and fall of ethnic revival*. Berlin: Mouton.

Fitzgerald, Michael, and Robert Debski. 2006. Internet use by Polish Melburnians: implications for maintenance and teaching. *Language Learning & Technology* 10.1: 87–109.

Folmer, Jetske. 1991. Language shift and language loss in a three generation Dutch family in New Zealand. Unpublished MA thesis, Tilburg University.

1992. Dutch immigrants in New Zeeland: a case study of language shift and language loss. *Australian Review of Applied Linguistics* 15.2: 1–18.

Gal, Susan. 1978. Peasant men can't get wives: language change and sex roles in a bilingual community. *Language in Society* 7.1: 1–16.

1979. *Language shift: social determinants of language shift in bilingual Austria*. San Francisco, CA: Academic Press.

2006. Minorities, migration and multilingualism: language ideologies in Europe. In P. Stevenson and C. Mar-Molinaro (eds.), *Language ideologies, practices and policies: language and the future of Europe*. London: Palgrave Macmillan, 13–27.

García, Mary Ellen. 2003. Recent research on language maintenance. *Annual Review of Applied Linguistics* 23: 22–43.

García, Ofelia, and Joshua A. Fishman. Eds. 2002. *The multilingual apple: languages in New York City*, second edition. Berlin: Mouton de Gruyter.

García, Ofelia, and Li Wei. 2014. *Translanguaging: language, bilingualism and education*. New York: Palgrave Macmillan.

García, Ofelia, Zeena Zalharia and Bahar Otcu. Eds. 2013. *Bilingual community education and multilingualis: beyond heritage languages in a global city*. Bristol: Multilingual Matters.

Gardner, Sheena, and Marilyn Martin-Jones. Eds. 2012. *Multilingualism, discourse and ethnography*. New York: Routledge.

Georgiou, Myria. No date. Mapping minorities and their media: the national context – the UK. www.lse.ac.uk/media@lse/research/EMTEL/minorities/papers/ukreport.pdf, accessed 30 June 2015.

Giles, Howard. 1973. Accent mobility: a model and some data. *Anthropological Linguistics* 15: 87–105.

Giles, Howard, and Peter Powesland. 1975. *Speech style and social evaluation.* London: Academic Press.

Giles, Howard, Richard Y. Bourhis and Donald M. Taylor. 1977. Towards a theory of language in ethnic group relations. In H. Giles (ed.), *Language, ethnicity and intergroup relations.* London: Academic Press, 307–348.

Giles, Howard, Philip M. Smith and Peter Robinson. 1980. Social psychological perspectives on language: prologue. In H. Giles, P. Robinson and P. M. Smith (eds.), *Language: social psychological perspectives.* Oxford: Pergamon Press, 1–7.

Giles, Howard, Peter Robinson and Philip M. Smith. Eds. 1980. *Language: social psychological perspectives.* Oxford: Pergamon Press.

Gogonas, Nikolaos. 2012. Religion as a core value in language maintenance: Arabic speakers in Greece. *International Migration* 50.2: 113–129.

Goldstein, Tara. 1997. *Two languages at work: bilingual life on the production floor.* Berlin: Mouton de Gruyter.

Gorter, Durk. 1994. A new sociolinguistic survey of the Frisian language situation. *Dutch Crossing: A Journal of Low Countries Studies* 18: 18–31.

  2007. *European minority languages: endangered or revived?* Ljouwert: Fryske Akademy. http://depot.knaw.nl/3856/1/21759.pdf, accessed 7 June 2015.

Gorter, Durk, and Jasone Ceñoz. 2011. Multilingual education for European minority languages: the Basque country and Friesland. *International Review of Education* 57.5: 651–666.

Gorter, Durk, and Guus Extra. Eds. 2008. *Multilingual Europe: facts and policies.* Berlin: Mouton de Gruyter.

Gorter, Durk, Jarich F. Hoekstra, Lammert G. Jansma and Jehennes Ytsma. Eds. 1990. *Fourth International Conference of Minority Languages.* Volume II: *Western and Eastern European Papers.* Clevedon: Multilingual Matters.

Gorter, Durk, Heiko F. Marten, Luk Van Mensel and Gabrielle Hogan-Brun. Eds. 2011. *Minority languages in the linguistic landscape.* Basingstoke: Palgrave Macmillan.

Grenoble, Lenore, and Lindsay J. Whaley. Eds. 1998. *Endangered languages.* Cambridge: Cambridge University Press.

Grin, François. 2003. Language planning and economics. *Current Issues in Language Planning* 4.1: 1–66.

Grin, François, and François Vaillancourt. 1997. The economics of multilingualism: overview of the literature and analytical framework. *Annual Review of Applied Linguistics* 17: 43–65.

Grosjean, François. 1982. *Living with two languages.* Cambridge, MA: Harvard University Press.

  2008. *Studying bilinguals.* Oxford: Oxford University Press.

Gumperz, John J. 1962. Types of linguistic communities. *Anthropological Linguistics* 4.1: 28–40.

Haarmann, Harald. 1986. *Language in ethnicity*. Berlin: Mouton de Gruyter.

Hall, Robert A. Jr. Ed. 1987. *Leonard Bloomfield: essays on his life and work*. Amsterdam: John Benjamins.

Hamers, Josiane, and Michel Blanc. 1983. *Bilinguality and bilingualism*. Cambridge: Cambridge University Press.

Harney, Nicholas. 1998. *Eh paesan: being Italian in Toronto*. Toronto: University of Toronto Press.

Harwood, Jake, Howard Giles and Richard Y. Bourhis. 1994. The genesis of vitality theory: historical patterns and discoursal dimensions. *International Journal of the Sociology of Language* 108: 167–206.

Hasselmo, Nils. 1961. *American Swedish*. Unpublished PhD dissertation, Harvard University.

1974. *Amerikasvenska* [American Swedish]. Lund: Esselte.

Haugen, Einar. 1938a. Language and immigration. *Norwegian-American Studies and Records* 10: 1–43.

1938b. Phonological shifting in American Norwegian. *Language* 14: 112–120.

1939. *Norsk i Amerika*. Oslo: J. W. Cappelens Forlag.

1953. *The Norwegian language in America: a study in bilingual behavior*. Philadelphia: University of Pennsylvania Press.

1956. *Bilingualism in the Americas: a bibliography and research guide*. University: University of Alabama Press.

1972. *The ecology of language: essays by Einar Haugen*, ed. Anwar S. Dil. Stanford, CA: Stanford University Press.

Heller, Monica. Ed. 2007. *Bilingualism: a social approach*. Basingstoke: Palgrave Macmillan.

Herring, Susan. 2008. Language and the internet. In W. Donsbach (ed.), *International encyclopedia of communication*. Oxford: Blackwell, 2640–2645.

Hickey, Raymond. Ed. 2010. *The handbook of language contact*. Malden, NJ: Wiley-Blackwell.

Hinton, Leanne. 2001. Involuntary language loss among immigrants: Asian-American linguistic autobiographies. In J. Alatis and A. Tan (eds.), *Language in our time: bilingual education and official English, Ebonics and standard English, immigration and the UNZ initiative*. Washington, DC: Georgetown University Press, 203–252.

Hoffmann, Christine. 1985. Language acquisition in two trilingual children. *Journal of Multilingual and Multicultural Development* 6: 479–495.

Hoffmann, Fernand. 1981. *Triglossia in Luxemburg*. In E. Haugen, J. D. McClure and D. Thomson (eds.), *Minority languages today*. Edinburgh: University Press, 201–207.

Holmes, Janet. 1993. Immigrant women and language maintenance in Australia and New Zealand. *International Journal of Applied Linguistics* 3.2: 159–179.

Holmes, Janet, and Kirk Hazen. Eds. 2014. *Research methods in sociolinguistics.* Oxford: Wiley-Blackwell.

Holmquist, Jonathan C. 1985. Social correlates of a linguistic variable: a study of a Spanish village. *Language in Society* 14.2: 191–203.

Homel, Peter, Michael Palij, Doris Aaronson. Eds. 1987. *Childhood bilingualism: aspects of linguistic, cognitive and social development.* New York: Lawrence Erlbaum.

Hornberger, Nancy. 2005. Opening and filling up implementational and ideological spaces in heritage language education. *Modern Language Journal* 89: 605–612.

Huber, Rina. 1977. *From pasta to pavlova: a comparative study of Italian settlers in Sydney and Griffith.* St Lucia: Queensland University Press.

Hunnicutt, Kay H., and Mario Castro. 2005. How census 2000 data suggest hostility toward Mexican-origin Arizonians. *Bilingual Research Journal* 20.1: 109–125.

Husband, Charles, and Verity Saifullah Khan. 1982. The viability of ethnolinguistic vitality: some creative doubts. *Journal of Multilingual and Multicultural Development* 3: 193–205.

Hymes, Dell. 1962. The ethnography of speaking. In T. Gladwin and W. C. Sturtevant (eds.), *Anthropology and human behavior.* Washington, DC: Anthropology Society of Washington.

Janse, Mark, and Tol Sijmen (with the assistance of Vincent Hendriks). Eds. 2003. *Language death and language maintenance: theoretical, practical and descriptive approaches.* Amsterdam: John Benjamins.

Jaspaert, Koen, and Sjaak Kroon. Eds. 1991. *Ethnic minority languages and education.* Amsterdam: Swets & Zeitlinger.

Johnson, Melissa. 2000. How ethnic are US ethnic media: the case of Latina magazines. *Mass Communication and Society* 2.2–3: 229–248.

Johnson, Patricia, Howard Giles and Richard Bourhis. 1983. The viability of ethnolinguistic vitality: a reply. *Journal of Multilingual and Multicultural Development* 4: 255–269.

Johnstone, Barbara. 2000. *Qualitative methods in sociolinguistics.* New York: Oxford University Press.

Johri, Rohri. 1998. Struck in the middle or clued up on both: language and identity among Korean, Dutch, Samoan immigrants in Dunedin. Unpublished PhD dissertation, University of Otago.

Jones, Kathryn, and Delyth Morris. 2007. Welsh-language socialization with the family. *Contemporary Wales* 20.1: 52–70.

Kamwangamalu, Nikonko. 2001. Ethnicity and language crossing in post-apartheid South Africa. *International Journal of the Sociology of Language* 152: 75–95.

Kelly-Holmes, Helen. Ed. 2001. *Minority language broadcasting: Breton and Irish.* Clevedon: Multilingual Matters.

Kennedy, Susan. 2015. Selective multiculturalism? Symbols of ethnic identity and core values theory. *Journal of Educational and Social Research* 5.1: 249–259.

Kielhöfer, Bernd, and Sylvie Jonekeit. 1983. *Zweisprachige Kindererziehung* [Bilingual upbringing of children]. Tübingen: Stauffenberg.

Kipp, Sandra. 1980. German language maintenance and language shift in some rural settlements. *ITL* 28: 69–80.

Kipp, Sandra, and Michael Clyne. 2003. Trends in the shift from community languages: insights from the 2001 census. *People and Place* 11: 33–41.

Kipp, Sandra, Michael Clyne and Anne Pauwels. 1995. *Immigration and Australia's language resources*. Canberra: Australian Government Publishing Service.

Klarberg, Manfred. 1976. Identity and communication: maintenance of Hebrew, decline of Yiddish. In M. Clyne (ed.), *Australia talks*. Canberra: ANU Press, 89–102.

Klatter-Folmer, Jetske, and Sjaak Kroon. Eds. 1997. *Dutch overseas: studies in maintenance and loss of Dutch as an immigrant language*. Tilburg: Tilburg University Press.

Kloss, Heinz. 1927. Spracherhaltung [language maintenance]. *Archiv für Politik und Geschichte* 8: 456–462.

   1966. German American language maintenance efforts. In J. Fishman et al. (eds.), *Language loyalty in the United States*. The Hague: Mouton, 206–252.

   Ed. 1985. *Deutsch als Muttersprache in Australien* [German as a mother tongue in the United States]. Stuttgart: Franz Steiner Verlag.

Kouzmin, Ludmila. 1988. Language use and language maintenance in two Russian communities in Australia. *International Journal of the Sociology of Language* 72: 51–65.

Kramsch, Claire. 2005. The multilingual experience: insights from language memoirs. *Transit* 1.1. http://transit.berkeley.edu/2005/kramsch/.

Krauss, Michael. 1992. The world's languages in crisis. *Language* 68: 4–10.

Kravin, Hanne. 1992. Erosion of a language in bilingual development. *Journal of Multilingual and Multicultural Development* 13: 307–325.

Kuhn, Walter. 1934. *Deutsche Sprachinsel-Forschung* [German Research on linguistic enclaves]. Leipzig: Hirzel.

Labov, William. 1971. Some principles of linguistic methodology. *Language in Society* 1: 97–120.

   1972. *Sociolinguistic patterns*. Oxford: Blackwell.

   1990. The intersection of sex and social class in the course of linguistic change. *Language Variation and Change* 2.2: 205–254.

Ladefoged, Peter. 1992. Another view of endangered languages. *Language* 68.4: 809–811.

Lähteenmäki, Mika, Piia Varis and Sirpa Leppänen. 2011. The shifting paradigm: towards a reconceptualisation of multilingualism. *Apples: Journal of Applied Language Studies* 5.1: 2–11.

Lam, Wan Shun Eva. 2004. Second language socialization in a bilingual chatroom: global and local considerations. *Language Learning and Technology* 8.3: 44–65.

Lambert, Wallace. 1967. A social psychology of bilingualism. *Journal of Social Issues* 23.2: 91–109.

Lambert, Wallace, et al. 1960. Evaluational reactions to spoken languages. *Journal of Abnormal and Social Psychology* 60: 44–51.

Landry, Rodrigue, and Richard Bourhis. 1997. Linguistic landscape and ethnolinguistic vitality: an empirical study. *Journal of Language and Social Psychology* 16.1: 23–49.

Lanza, Elizabeth. 1997. *Language mixing in infant bilingualism*. Oxford: Clarendon Press.

2009. Multilingualism and the family. In P. Auer and Li Wei (eds.), *Handbook of multilingualism and multilingual communication*. Berlin: Mouton de Gruyter, 45–67.

Lave, Jean, and Etienne Wenger. 1991. *Situated learning: legitimate peripheral participation*. Cambridge: Cambridge University Press.

Lawson, Sarah, and Itesh Sachdev. 2000. Codeswitching in Tunisia: attitudinal and behavioral dimensions. *Journal of Pragmatics* 32: 1343–1361.

2004. Identity, language use and attitudes: some Sylheti-Bangladeshi data from London, UK. *Journal of Language and Social Psychology* 23: 49–69.

Lee, Jin Sook, and Sarah J. Shin. 2008. Korean heritage language education in the United States: the current state, opportunities, and possibilities. *Heritage Language Journal* 6.2: 1–20.

Leopold, Werner. 1939–1949. *Speech development of a bilingual child*. Volumes 1–4. Evanston, IL: Northwestern University Press.

Leppänen, Sirpa, and Saija Peuronen. 2012. *Multilingualism on the internet*. In M. Martin-Jones, A. Blackledge and A. Creese (eds.), *The Routledge handbook of multilingualism*. Abingdon: Routledge, 384–403.

Lewins, Frank. 1978. *The myth of the universal church*. Canberra: ANU Press.

Li, David, and Elly Tse. 2002. One day in the life of a 'purist'. *International Journal of Bilingualism* 6.2: 147–202.

Lieberson, Stanley. 1963. *Ethnic patterns in American cities*. New York: Free Press.

1965. Bilingualism in Montreal: a demographic analysis. *American Journal of Sociology* 71.1: 10–25.

1966. Language questions in censuses. *Sociological Inquiry* 36.2: 262–279.

1980. Procedures for improving sociolinguistic surveys on language maintenance and language shift. *International Journal of the Sociology of Language* 25: 11–28.

Lightfoot, David. 2006. *How new languages emerge*. Cambridge: Cambridge University Press.

Linguistic Minorities Project [LMP]. 1985. *The other languages of England*. London: Routledge & Kegan Paul.

Lo Bianco, Joseph. 2009. *Second languages and Australian schooling*. Melbourne: ACER, Australian Education Review.

Luepke, Friederike, and Anne Storch. 2013. *Repertoires and choices in African languages*. Berlin: de Gruyter.

Lyon, Jean. 1996. *Becoming bilingual: language acquisition in a bilingual community*. Clevedon: Multilingual Matters.

McCardie, Peggy, and Erika Hoff. Eds. 2006. *Childhood bilingualism*. Clevedon: Multilingual Matters.

Mackey, William F., and Donald Cartwright. 1979. Geocoding language loss from Census data. In W. F. Mackey and J. Ornstein (eds.), *Sociolinguistic studies in language contact: methods and cases*. The Hague: Mouton, 69–98.

Mackey, William F., and Jacob Ornstein. Eds. 1979. *Sociolinguistic studies in language contact: methods and cases*. The Hague: Mouton.

MacKinnon, Kenneth M. 1977. Language shift and education: conservation of ethnolinguistic culture amongst schoolchildren of a Gaelic community. *Linguistics* 198: 31–55.

Makoni, Sinfree, and Alistair Pennycook. 2007. *Disinventing and reconstituting languages*. Clevedon: Multilingual Matters.

Martin-Jones, Marilyn, Adrian Blackledge and Angela Creese. Eds. 2012. *The Routledge handbook of multilingualism*. Abingdon: Routledge.

May, Stephen. 2011. *Language and minority rights: ethnicity, nationalism and the politics of language*. Routledge: New York.

Maylor, Uvanney et al. 2010. *Impact of supplementary schools on pupils' attainment*. London: Department of Children, Schools and Families.

Meddegamma, Indu V. 2013. The enactment of status and power in the linguistic practices of three multilingual, Malayali families in the UK. Unpublished PhD thesis, University of Leeds.

Miller, Wick R. 1971. The death of a language or serendipity among the Shoshoni. *Anthropological Linguistics* 13.3: 114–120.

Milroy, Lesley. 1987. *Language and social networks*. Oxford: Blackwell.

Milroy, Lesley, and Matthew Gordon. 2003. *Sociolinguistics: methods and interpretation*. Oxford: Blackwell.

Milroy, Lesley, Wei Li and Suzanne Moffatt. 1991. Discourse patterns and fieldwork strategies in urban settings: some methodological problems for researchers of bilingual communities. *Journal of Multilingual and Multicultural Development* 12.4: 287–300.

Moelleken, Wolfgang M. 1983. Language maintenance and language shift in Pennsylvania German: a comparative investigation. *Monatshefte* 75.2: 172–186.

Monheit, Doris. 1975. The role of the German ethnic school in maintaining the German language in Melbourne. Unpublished BA (Hons.) thesis, Monash University.

Mowbray, Alistair. 2012. *Cases, materials and commentary on the European convention on human rights*. Oxford: Oxford University Press.

Nelde, Peter, Miquel Strubell and Glyn Williams. 1996. *Euromosaic: the production and reproduction of the minority language groups of the EU*. Luxembourg: Publications Offices.

Nettle, Daniel, and Suzanne Romaine. 2000. *Vanishing voices: the extinction of the world's languages*. Oxford: Oxford University Press.

Nicholas, Joe. 1988. British language diversity surveys (1977–1987): a critical examination. *Language and Education* 2: 15–33.

Ogulnick, Karen. 1999. Introspection as a method of raising critical language awareness. *Journal of Humanities, Education and Development* 37: 145–159.

Okita, Toshie. 2002. *Invisible work: bilingualism, language choice and childrearing in intermarried families*. Amsterdam: John Benjamins.

Omoniyi, Tope, and Joshua Fishman. Eds. 2006. *Explorations in the sociology of language and religion*. Amsterdam: John Benjamins.

Orman, Jon. 2008. *Language policy and nation-building in post-apartheid South Africa*. Dordrecht: Springer.

Ortega, Lourdes. Ed. 2011. *Second language acquisition*. 6 volumes. London: Routledge.

Otsui, Emi, and Alistair Pennycook. 2010. Metrolingualism: fixity, fluidity and language in flux. *International Journal of Multilingualism* 7.3: 240–254.

Overberg, Henk. 1981. Dutch in Victoria, 1947–80: community and ideology. *Journal of Intercultural Studies* 2.1: 17–36.

Ozolins, Uldis. 1993. *The politics of language in Australia*. Cambridge: Cambridge University Press.

Park, Seon Ho. 2001. A sociolinguistic and social psychological study of Korean communities in New Zealand: language maintenance and second language learning. Unpublished PhD dissertation, Victoria University of Wellington.

Pauwels, Anne. 1980. The effect of mixed marriages on language shift in the Dutch community in Australia. Unpublished Master's thesis, Monash University.

   1983. Limburgs and Swabian in Australia. Unpublished PhD dissertation, Monash University.

   1985. The role of mixed marriages in language shift in the Dutch community. In M. Clyne (ed.), *Australia: meeting place of languages*. Canberra: Department of Linguistics, Research School of Pacific Studies, Australian National University, 39–55.

   1986. *Immigrant dialects and language maintenance in Australia*. Dordrecht: Foris Publications.

   1994. Applying linguistic insights in intercultural communication to professional training programs: an Australian case study. *Multilingua* 13.1–2: 195–212.

   1995. Linguistic practices and language maintenance among bilingual women and men in Australia. *Nordlyd* 23: 21–50.

1997. The role of gender in immigrant language maintenance in Australia. In W. Wölck and A. De Houwer (eds.), *Recent studies in contact linguistics*. Bonn: Dümmler Verlag, 276–286.

2005. Maintaining the community language in Australia: challenges and roles for families. *International Journal of Bilingual Education and Bilingualism* 8: 124–31.

2011. Risking or boosting masculinity? Men's language choices in multilingual settings. *Applied Linguistics Review* 2: 147–168.

2013. Dutch as a minority language in Australia: from birthplace to cyberspace. In F. Hinskens and J. Taeldeman (eds.), *Language and space: Dutch*. Berlin: Mouton de Gruyter, 858–878.

2014. Rethinking the learning of languages in the context of globalization and hyperlingualism. In Dagmar Abendroth-Timmer and Eva Henning (eds.), *Plurilingualism and multiliteracies: international research on identity construction in language education*. Frankfurt: Peter Lang. 41–56.

Ed. 1988. *The future of ethnic languages in Australia*. International Journal of the Sociology of Language 72. Berlin: Mouton de Gruyter.

Pavlenko, Aneta. 2007. Autobiographic narratives as data in applied linguistics. *Applied Linguistics* 28.2: 163–188.

Pavlenko, Aneta, Adrian Blackledge, Ingrid Piller and Maria Teutsch-Dwyer. Eds. 2001. *Multilingualism, second language learning, and gender*. Berlin: Mouton de Gruyter.

Peyton, Joyce K., Donald Ranard and Scott McGinnis. Eds. 2001. *Heritage languages in America: preserving a national resource*. Washington, DC: CAL.

Phillipson, Robert, and Tove Skutnabb-Kangas. 1995. Linguistic rights and wrongs. *Applied Linguistics* 16.4: 483–504.

1999. Linguicide. In B. Spolsky (ed.), *Concise encyclopedia of educational linguistics*. Oxford: Pergamon, 48–49.

Piller, Ingrid. 2002. *Bilingual couples talk: the discursive construction of hybridity*. Amsterdam: John Benjamins.

Poplack, Shana. 1979. Function and process in a variable phonology. Unpublished PhD dissertation, University of Pennsylvania.

Porsché, Donald. 1983. *Die Zweisprachigkeit während des primären Spracherwerbs* [Bilingualism during the primary language acquisition process]. Tübingen: Gunter Narr.

Potowski, Kim, and Jason Rothman. Eds. 2011. *Bilingual youth*. Amsterdam: John Benjamins.

Pupavac, Vanessa. 2012. *Language rights: from free speech to linguistic governance*. London: Palgrave Macmillan.

Ramanathan, Vaidehi. 2013. *Language policies and (dis)citizenship: rights, access and pedagogies*. Clevedon: Multilingual Matters.

Rampton, Ben. 1995. *Crossing: language and ethnicity among adolescents*. London: St Jerome Publishing/Routledge.

2006. *Language in late modernity: interaction in an urban school.* Cambridge: Cambridge University Press.

Reynolds, Henry. 1995. *Fate of a free people.* Melbourne: Penguin.

Rietveld, Toni, and Roeland van Hout. 1993. *Statistical techniques in the study of language and language behaviour.* Berlin: Mouton de Gruyter.

Riggins, Stephen Harold. Ed. 1992. *Ethnic minority media: an international perspective.* London: Sage.

Robinson, Patricia A. 1989. French mother tongue transmission in mixed mother tongue families. *The Canadian Journal of Sociology /Cahiers Canadiens de Sociologie* 14.3: 317–334.

Romaine, Suzanne. 1983. Collecting and interpreting self-reported language data of linguistic minorities by means of 'language diaries'. *MALS Journal* 9: 1–10.

1995. *Bilingualism*, second edition. Oxford: Blackwell.

Ed. 1990. *Language in Australia.* Cambridge: Cambridge University Press.

Ronjat, Jules. 1913. *Le développement du langage observé chez un enfant bilingue* [The development of language observed in a bilingual child]. Paris: Librairie Ancienne H. Champion.

Rosowsky, Andrey. 2008. *Heavenly readings: liturgical literacy in a multilingual context.* Clevedon: Multilingual Matters.

Rubino, Antonia. 1993. From trilingualism to monolingualism: a case study in language shift in a Sicilian-Australian family. Unpublished PhD dissertation, University of Sydney.

2006. Linguistic practices and language attitudes of second-generation Italo-Australians. *International Journal of the Sociology of Language* 180: 71–88.

2007. Immigrant minorities: Australia. In M. Hellinger and A. Pauwels (eds.), *Handbook of language and communication: diversity and change.* Volume 9 (Handbooks of Applied Linguistics). Berlin: Mouton de Gruyter, 87–122.

2014. *Trilingual talk in Sicilian-Australian families.* Basingstoke: Palgrave Macmillan.

Ryan, Camille. 2013. Language use in the United States. www.census.gov/prod/2013pubs/acs-22.pdf, accessed 17 June 2015.

Ryang, Sonia. 2008. *Writing selves in diaspora. Ethnography of autobiographies of Korean women in Japan and the United States.* Plymouth: Lexington Books.

Santana, John. 1999. *Americanization; A Dominican immigrant's autobiographic study of cultural and linguistic learning.* Unpublished doctoral dissertation, New York University.

Saunders, George. 1982. *Bilingual children: guidance for the family.* Clevedon: Multilingual Matters.

1988. *Bilingual children: from birth to teens.* Clevedon: Multilingual Matters.

Schirmunski, Viktor M. 1928a. *Die deutschen Kolonien in der Ukraine. Geschichte, Mundarten, Volkslied, Volkskunde* [The German colonies in the

Ukraine. History, dialects, folksong and ethnic studies]. Moscow: Zentral Völkerverlag.

1928b. Die schwäbischen Mundarten in Transkaukasien und Südukraine [The Swabian dialects in the Transcaucasus and South Ukraine]. *Teuthonista* 5.1: 38–60.

Schmid, Monika. 2011. *Language attrition*. Cambridge: Cambridge University Press.

Sheller, Mimi, and John Urry. 2006. The new mobilities paradigm. *Environent and Planning A* 38.2: 207–226.

Sheyholislami, Jaffer. 2011. *Kurdish identity, discourse, and new media*. New York: Palgrave Macmillan.

Shohamy, Elana. 2006. *Language policy: hidden agendas and new approaches*. Abingdon: Routledge.

Shohamy, Elana, and Durk Gorter. Eds. 2009. *Linguistic landscape: expanding the scenery*. New York: Routledge.

Sillitoe, K. 1987. *Developing questions on ethnicity and related topics for the Census*. Washington, DC: Office of Population Censuses and Surveys.

Skutnabb-Kangas, Tove. 2000. *Linguistic genocide in education – or world wide diversity and human rights*. Mahwah, NJ: Lawrence Erlbaum.

2012. Linguistic human rights. In L. M. Solan and P. M. Tiersma (eds.), *The Oxford handbook of language and the law*. Oxford: Oxford University Press, 235–247.

Skutnabb-Kangas, Tove, Robert Phillipson and Mart Rannut. 1995. *Linguistic human rights*. Berlin: Walter de Gruyter.

Smolicz, Jerzy J. 1980. Language as a core value of culture. *Journal of Applied Linguistics* 11.1: 1–13.

1981. Core values and cultural identity. *Ethnic and Racial Studies* 4: 78–90.

1991. Language core values in a multicultural setting: an Australian experience. *International Review of Education* 37.1: 33–52

Smolicz, Jerzy J., and Margaret Secombe. 1985. Community languages, core values and cultural maintenance; the Australian experience with special reference to Greek, Latvian and Polish groups. In Michael Clyne (ed.), *Australia: meeting place of languages*. Canberra: Department of Linguistics, Research School of Pacific Studies, Australian National University, 11–38.

1989. Types of language activation in an ethnically plural society. In U. Ammon (ed.), *Status and function of languages and language varieties*. Berlin and New York: de Gruyter, 478–511.

Smolicz, Jerzy J., Margaret Secombe and Dorothy Hudson. 2001. Family collectivism and minority languages as core values among ethnic groups in Australia. *Journal of Multilingual and Multicultural Development* 22.2: 152–172.

Solé, Yvette. 1978. Sociocultural and sociopsychological factors in differential language retentiveness by sex. *International Journal of the Sociology of Language* 17: 29–44.

Spolsky, Bernard. 2003. Religion as a site of language contact. *Annual Review of Applied Linguistics* 23: 81–94.

2004. *Language policy.* Cambridge: Cambridge University Press.

2010. Ferguson and Fishman: sociolinguistics and the sociology of language. In R. Wodak, B. Johnstone and P. Kerswill (eds.), *The Sage handbook of sociolinguistics.* London: Sage, 11–23.

St Amant, Kirk, and Sigrid Kelsey. Eds. 2012. *Computer-mediated communication across cultures: International interactions in online environments.* Hershey, PA: IGI Global.

Starks, Donna, and Jeong Lee. 2010. Rethinking methodology: what language diaries can offer to the study of code choice. *Language Awareness* 19.4: 233–248.

Starks, Donna, and Seon H. Youn. 1998. Language maintenance in the Auckland Korean community. *Many Voices* 12: 8–11.

Stevens, Gillian. 1985. Nativity, intermarriage and mother-tongue shift. *American Sociological Review* 50.1: 74–83.

1986. Sex differences in language shift in the United States. *Sociology and Social Research* 71: 31–36.

Stewart, William. 1962. An outline of linguistic typology for describing multilingualism. In F. Rice (ed.), *Study of the role of second languages in Asia, Africa and Latin America.* Washington, DC: Center for Applied Linguistics, 15–25.

1968. A sociolinguistic typology for describing national multilingualism. In J. Fishman (ed.), *Readings in the sociology of language.* The Hague: Mouton, 531–545.

Stoessel, Saskia. 2002. Investigating the role of social networks in language maintenance and shift. *International Journal of the Sociology of Language* 153: 93–131.

Taeschner, Trude. 1983. *The sun is feminine: a study on language acquisition in bilingual children.* Berlin: Springer.

Tagg, Caroline. 2015. *Exploring digital communication: language in action.* Abingdon: Routledge.

Tajfel, Henri. 1974. Social identity and intergroup behaviour. *Social Science Information* 13: 65–93.

Tonkin, Humphrey, and Timothy Reagan. Eds. 2003. *Language in the 21st century.* Amsterdam: John Benjamins.

Trifonas, Peter and Themistoklis Aravossitas. Eds. 2014. *Rethinking heritage language education.* Cambridge: Cambridge University Press.

Trudgill, Peter. 1972. Sex, covert prestige and linguistic change in the urban British English of Norwich. *Language in Society* 1.2: 179–195.

Ed. 1984. *Language in the British Isles.* Cambridge: Cambridge University Press.

Tsokalidou, Roula. 1994. Cracking the code: an insight into codeswitching and gender among second generation Greek Australians. Unpublished PhD dissertation, Monash University.

Tsunoda, Tasaku. 2005. *Language endangerment and language revitalization: an introduction.* Berlin: Mouton de Gruyter.

Tuominen, Anne. 1999. Who decides the home language: a look at multi-lingual families. *International Journal of the Sociology of Language* 140: 49–76.

Urry, John. 2000. *Sociology beyond societies*. London: Routledge.

2007. *Mobilities*. Cambridge: Polity Press.

Valdés, Guadalupe, Anthony Lozano and Rodolfo García-Moya. 1980. *Teaching Spanish to the Hispanic bilingual*. New York: Teachers' College Press.

Valdés, Guadalupe, Joshua A. Fishman, Rebecca Chávez and William Pérez. Eds. 2006. *Developing minority language resources*. Clevedon: Multilingual Matters.

Veltman, Calvin. 1983. *Language shift in the United States*. Berlin: Walter de Gruyter.

Vermeij, Lotte. 2004. 'Ya know what I'm sayin'?' The double meaning of language crossing among teenagers in the Netherlands. *International Journal of the Sociology of Language* 170: 141–168.

Webb, Victor. 2002. *Language in South Africa: the role of language in national transformation*. Amsterdam: John Benjamins.

Weber, Jean-Jacques, and Kristine Horner. 2012. *Introducing multilingualism: a social approach*. London: Routledge.

Wei, Li, and Melissa Moyer. Eds. 2008. *The Blackwell guide to research methods in bilingualism and multilingualism*. Oxford: Blackwell Publishing.

Weinreich, Max. 1931. Di problem fun tzveyshprakhikayt [The problem of bilingualism]. *YIVO Bleter* 1: 114–129.

1932. Tsveyshprakhikayt: mutershprakh un tsveyte shprakh. [Bilingualism: mother tongue and second language]. *YIVO Bleter* 1: 301–316.

Weinreich, Uriel. 1953. *Languages in contact*. New York: Linguistic Circle of New York.

Wiley, Terrence. 2005a. Discontinuities in heritage and community language education: challenges for educational language policies. *International Journal of Bilingual Education and Bilingualism* 8.2–3: 222–229.

2005b. *Literacy and language diversity in the United States*, second edition. Washington, DC: Center for Applied Linguistics.

Wiley, Terrence, Jin Sook Lee and Russell W. Rumberger. Eds. 2009. *The education of language minority immigrant children in the United States*. Clevedon: Multilingual Matters.

Wiley, Terrence, Joyce Kreeft Peyton, Donna Christian, Sarah Catharine K. Moore and Na Liu. Eds. 2014. *Handbook of heritage, community, and American native languages in the United States: research, policy, and educational practice*. New York and Washington, DC: Routledge and CAL.

Willemyns, Roland. 2013. *Dutch: biography of a language*. Oxford: Oxford University Press.

Williams, Frederick. 1974. The identification of linguistic attitudes. *International Journal of the Sociology of Language* 3: 21–32.

Winter, Joanne, and Anne Pauwels. 2006. The discourses of language maintenance in friendship practices among children of German, Greek and Vietnamese migrants. *International Journal of the Sociology of Language* 18: 123–139.

Woods, Anya. 2004. *Medium or message: language and faith in ethnic churches.* Clevedon: Multilingual Matters.

Wright, Wayne, Sovicheth Boun and Ofelia García. Eds. 2015. *The handbook of bilingual and multilingual education.* Oxford: Wiley Blackwell.

Wurm, Stephen. 2002. Strategies for language maintenance and revival. In D. Bradley and M. Bradley (eds.), *Language endangerment and language maintenance: an active approach.* New York: Routledge, 11–23.

Yamamoto, Masayo. 2005. What makes who choose what language to whom? Language use in Japanese-Filipino interlingual families. *International Journal of Bilingual Education and Bilingualism* 8.6: 588–606.

Zentella, Ana. 1997. *Growing up bilingual.* Oxford: Blackwell.

Index